Would Jesus Really Do That?

Making the Best Choices

Paul Borthwick and Stan Campbell

Tongue Untwisters

Darrell Pearson and Mark Oestreicher

Gotta Have It?

Darrell Pearson and Jane Vogel

NEXGEN®

Building the New Generation of Believers

An Imprint of Cook Communications Ministries
Colorado Springs, Colorado

Would Jesus Really Do That?

© 2003 Cook Communications Ministries

Unless otherwise noted, Scripture quotations are from the Holy Bible, New International Version (NIV), © 1973, 1978, 1984 by International Bible Society. Used by permission of Zondervan Publishing House.

Published by Cook Communications Ministries
4050 Lee Vance View
Colorado Springs, CO 80918
www.cookministries.com

Editorial Manager: Doug Schmidt
Product Developer: Karen Pickering
Series Creator: John Duckworth
Series Editor: Randy Southern
Cover Design: Granite Design
Interior Design: Becky Hawley Design, Inc.

Unit 1: Making the Best Choices
© 2003 Cook Communications Ministries
Editor: Randy Southern
Writers: Paul Borthwick and Stan Campbell
Option Writers: Stan Campbell, Nelson E. Copeland, Jr., and Sue Reck
Inside Illustrator: John Hayes

Unit 2: Tongue Untwisters
© 2003 Cook Communications Ministries
Editor: Randy Southern
Writers: Darrell Pearson and Mark Oestreicher
Option Writers: Stan Campbell, John Duckworth, Sue Reck, and Randy Southern
Inside Illustrator: Joe Weissmann

Unit 3: Gotta Have It?
© 2003 Cook Communications Ministries
Editor: Randy Southern
Writers: Darrell Pearson and Jane Vogel
Option Writers: Jane Vogel, Nelson E. Copeland, Jr., and Ellen Larson
Inside Illustrator: John Hayes

Printed in the U.S.A.

Contents

Unit Three: Gotta Have It?

How to Customize Your Curriculum

We know your time is valuable. That's why we've made **Custom Curriculum** as easy as possible. Follow the three steps outlined below to create custom lessons that will meet the needs of *your* group. Let's get started!

Read the basic lesson plan.

Every session in this book has four to six steps designed to meet five goals. It's important to understand these five goals as you choose the options for your group.

Getting Together

The goal for Getting Together is to break the ice. It may involve a fun way to introduce the lesson.

Getting Thirsty

The goal for Getting Thirsty is to earn students' interest before you dive into the Bible. Why should students care about your topic? Why should they care what the Bible has to say about it? This will motivate your students to dig deeper.

Getting the Word

The goal for Getting the Word is to find out what God has to say about the topic they care about. By exploring and discussing carefully-selected passages, you'll help students find out how God's Word applies to their lives.

Getting the Point

The goal for Getting the Point is to make the leap from ideals and principles to real-world situations students are likely to face. It may involve practicing biblical principles with case studies or roleplays.

Getting Personal

The goal for Getting Personal is to help each group member respond to the lesson with a specific action. What should group members do as a result of this session? This step will help each person find a specific "next step" response that works for him or her.

2 Consider your options.

Every **Custom Curriculum** session gives you 14 different types of options. How do you choose? First, take a look at the list of option categories below. Then spend some time thinking and praying about your group. How do your students learn best? What kind of goals have you set for your group? Put a check mark by the options that you're most interested in.

 Extra Action—for groups that like physical challenges and learn better when they're moving, interacting, and experiencing the lesson.

 Media—to spice up your meeting with video, music, or other popular media.

 Heard It All Before—for fresh approaches that get past the defenses of students who are jaded by years in church.

 Little Bible Background—to use when most of your students are strangers to the Bible or haven't yet made a Christian commitment.

 Extra Fun—for longer, more "festive" youth meetings where additional emphasis is put on having fun.

 Fellowship and Worship—for building deeper relationships or enabling students to praise God together.

 Mostly Girls—to address girls' concerns and to substitute activities girls might prefer.

 Mostly Guys—to address guys' concerns and to substitute activities guys might prefer.

 Small Group—for adapting activities that might be tough with groups of fewer than eight students.

 Large Group—to alter steps for groups of more than 20 students.

 Urban—for fitting sessions to urban facilities and multiethnic (especially African-American) concerns.

 Short Meeting Time—tips for condensing the meeting. The standard meeting is designed to last 45 to 60 minutes. These include options to cut, replace, or trim time off the standard steps.

 Combined Junior High/High School—to use when you're mixing age levels but an activity or case study would be too "young" or "old" for part of the group.

 Sixth Grade—appearing only in junior high/middle school volumes, this option helps you change steps that sixth graders might find hard to understand or relate to.

 Extra Challenge—appearing only in high school volumes, this option lets you crank up the voltage for students who are ready for more Scripture or more demanding personal application.

Customize your curriculum!

Here's a simple three-step plan to customize each session for your group:

1. Choose your options.

As you read the basic session plan, you'll see icons in the margin. Each icon represents a different type of option. When you see an icon, it means that type of option is offered for that step. The five pages of options are found after the Repro Resource student pages for each session. Turn to the option page noted by the icon and you'll see that option explained.

Let's say you have a small group, mostly guys who get bored if they don't keep moving. You'll want to keep an eye out for three kinds of options: Small Group, Mostly Guys, and Extra Action. As you read the basic session, you might spot icons that tell you there are Small Group options for Step 1 and Step 3—maybe a different way to play a game so that you don't need big teams, and a way to cover several Bible passages when just a few kids are looking them up. Then you see icons telling you that there are Mostly Guys options for Step 2 and Step 4—perhaps a substitute activity that doesn't require too much self-disclosure, and a case study guys will relate to. Finally you see icons indicating Extra Action options for Step 2 and Step 3—maybe an active way to get kids' opinions instead of handing out a survey, and a way to act out some verses instead of just looking them up.

2. Use the checklist.

Once you've picked your options, keep track of them with the simple checklist at the end of the option section (just before the start of the next session plan). This little form gives you a place to write down the materials you'll need too—since they depend on the options you've chosen.

3. Get your stuff together.

Gather your materials; photocopy any Repro Resources (reproducible student sheets) you've decided to use. And...you're ready!

Unit One: Making the Best Choices

Living in a Multiple-Choice Society

by Paul Borthwick

Junior highers of today make up what's been called the "multiple choice" generation. We are working with young people who are deluged with choices—from the mundane (dozens of cereal brands and potato chip varieties) to the extraordinarily profound (sexual preferences and moral convictions). Never before has a generation had so many alternatives from which to choose. Lifestyle options, elective classes, and 140 channel possibilities with just the touch of a remote all point to the myriad of selections facing today's junior higher.

Whether we're talking to young people about which videos to watch, whose value system to live by, or whose peer group to identify with, our goal is to help kids make the best possible decisions for their well-being—*from God's perspective.*

In the late nineteenth century, Charles Sheldon wrote a novel entitled *In His Steps.* Sheldon's goal was to translate the Christian life to people living in that era. In the book, he depicts the choices that citizens, business people, a newspaper editor, church leaders, and others would need to make in a non-Christian world. Throughout the book, he presents various challenges to the characters, forcing them to ask this basic question: "What would Jesus do in this situation?"

In the sessions that follow, your goal is similar to Sheldon's. Your challenge is to get your "characters"—your junior highers—to look at the real-life options they face and ask, "What would Jesus do?"

Foundations for Effectiveness

As you and your group study the tough questions in the sessions that follow, you should keep in mind two important suggestions.

First, *respect the intensity of your junior highers' feelings.* It's vitally important to remember that the issues you'll be studying are very profound in the lives of some of your junior highers. The starting point in leading these sessions is to take the issues and their impact on junior highers' lives seriously. Be empathetic.

One seventh grader came to ask me about cheating in school. Her questions made me wonder if she were just looking for me to justify her desire to get ahead by copying the work of others. I gave her a few glib answers and reminded her that cheating had no place in the life of a Christian. I thought I had settled the issue, but then she broke into tears.

"What's the matter?" I asked.

"Well, I don't know what to do," she said. "I believe that I shouldn't cheat, but my parents are putting so much pressure on me to get good grades that I'll either cheat and compromise my Christian faith or I won't cheat, and I'll get poor grades and disappoint my parents."

Her tears rebuked me. I realized that I had treated her lightly while she was dealing with a very tough decision.

The issues that follow carries varying levels of intensity in the lives of your kids. Some live daily with overly strict parents or an obnoxious older brother. Others feel that their social lives will suffer if they refuse to conform to the sexual standards of their peers. Some feel hostile toward the inconsistency at church. Others feel alone without friends.

Listen to your students as these issues are discussed. Young people will usually react most strongly to the issues that affect them most intensely. The sessions that follow will help you to discern which issues affect which kids most seriously.

On the opposite extreme, *look out for cluelessness!* In contrast to the young person who is intensely involved in a spiritual dilemma is the young person who never wrestles with questions of how the Christian faith applies to tough choices in daily life.

Three junior high guys told me on Sunday morning that they had refused to go to see an "R" rated movie with their peers on Friday night. I was proud of their choice so I asked them how they had come to this decision. I asked optimistically, "Did you explain to your friends that your commitment as a Christian prevented you from going to the movie?"

They looked at me blankly. "Heck no," replied one of the guys. "We told them that our parents would kill us if we went. The Christian thing never entered our minds."

These young men illustrate the way that a number of young people (and perhaps adults as well) live. To them, Christian faith relates to Sunday, to Bible study, and maybe to serving the needy—but it has no connection to the moral, ethical, and lifestyle choices of daily living.

The sessions that follow are designed to help kids in the "clueless" camp to connect their faith with their daily choices. Our tough task is to cause them to think, to remind them that following Jesus should affect their relationships at home, their pursuit of success or popularity at school, and their decision whether or not to drink alcohol.

As You Lead

The easiest way to address the tough choices facing kids is to tell kids what they should think and do. But our goal is more significant and long-term. We want to teach kids *how* to think, *how* to integrate their faith, and *how* to apply Christian discipleship to daily issues. If we can teach kids how to think, we'll give them skills that they can apply to other choices they'll be making throughout their lives.

The goal in all of the studies that follow is to teach decision-making skills from a biblical perspective. Rather than telling kids the opinions that we think they should have or the choices that we think they should make, our goal is to teach them how to examine Scripture (especially the life and teachings of Jesus) so that they make their own decisions based on personal, internalized convictions.

Here are some suggestions as to how you can go about this:

- *Think principles!* In the first century, Jesus did not need to decide about MTV, nor did He need to deal with cheating in school. As leaders, we need to be careful not to put words in Jesus' mouth. Instead of looking for definitive instructions on each issue, ask, "What principles apply to this decision?"

- *Develop your hooks.* Every teacher knows the value of a "hook." A hook might be a story, an illustration, a question, or a statement designed to get students' attention. Fashion some effective questions (perhaps with the help of a few junior high leadership students) that will stir some discussion on the topics. Try not to ask "leading" questions, the kind that discourage kids from offering an honest response. Instead of asking, "You don't think Jesus would go to an "R" rated movie, do you?" you might ask, "In light of what we know about Jesus, do you think He would go to an "R" rated movie? Why or why not?"

• *Be slow to speak.* Try not to reveal your personal feelings during a discussion, either by reacting negatively to far-out ideas or by speaking up too soon to relieve the silence. Allow kids to think, to wrestle, to debate the topics. During a youth group discussion on the Christian perspective on drinking alcohol, a young person raised a question about John 2, in which Jesus made wine at the wedding banquet. The youth leader jumped on the student and rebuked his insights as being naive and biblically unfounded. The youth leader's hasty response turned off the group members. Rather than wrestling with the issue, the kids began to think that the youth leader was embarrassed by Jesus' action and was "covering" for Him. Perhaps it would have been better to allow the discussion to proceed and encourage group members to decide for themselves— based on the entire life of Jesus.

The Bottom Line

In tackling the tough questions that follow, our goal is to produce group members who understand that the Christian life involves discernment, moderation, and wisdom.

Discernment involves kids understanding for themselves how to choose between good and evil. Hebrews 5:14 informs us that discernment comes to those who "by constant use have trained themselves to distinguish good from evil." Therefore, youth ministry should include "training" sessions in which kids can wrestle with "What would Jesus do?" questions so that they're able to discern the best choices to make.

Moderation involves understanding that even though some things may not be directly destructive, they still might not be the best course of action. We want to develop Christian young people who can say with Paul, "'Everything is permissible for me'—but not everything is beneficial. 'Everything is permissible for me'—but I will not be mastered by anything" (1 Cor. 6:12).

In our complicated world, one of the best things we can do for young people is to teach them to ask God for wisdom according to James 1:5. We serve the best interests of students by teaching them to look to God for insight to make the best possible choices in the midst of hundreds of options. May God richly bless you as you help your kids answer the question "What would Jesus do?"

Paul Borthwick is minister of missions at Grace Chapel in Lexington, Massachusetts. A former youth pastor and frequent speaker to youth workers, he is author of several books including Organizing Your Youth Ministry *and* Feeding Your Forgotten Soul: Spiritual Growth for Youth Workers *(Zondervan).*

The images on these two pages are designed to help you promote this course within your church and community. Feel free to photocopy anything here and adapt it to fit your publicity needs. The stuff on this page could be used as a flier that you send or hand out to kids— or as a bulletin insert. The stuff on the next page could be used to add visual interest to newsletters, calendars, bulletin boards, or other promotions. Be creative and have fun!

What If...

What if Jesus went to your school?
What if He hung around with your friends?
What if He had to live with your family?
What if He attended your church?
These are some of the questions we'll be exploring in a new course called *What Would Jesus Do?* By looking at Christ's example, you can get some valuable tips for living your own life!

Who:

When:

Where:

Questions? Call:

Unit One: Making the Best Choices

Bored? Looking for something exciting in your life?

It's party time!

Bring a friend.

What Would Jesus Do . . . for Fun?

YOUR GOALS FOR THIS SESSION:

Choose one or more

☐ To help kids see that if they aren't careful, many of their fun activities can become temptations.

☐ To help kids understand that genuine fun is generated from a positive attitude and should not depend on other personalities or external circumstances.

☐ To help kids evaluate the amount of fun they have in various areas of their lives and attempt to have more genuine fun wherever they are.

☐ Other:_____
_____

Your Bible Base:

Matthew 4:1-11
Luke 7:36-50
Colossians 3:17

STEP 1

A Really Good Day

(Needed: Paper, pencils)

OPTIONS

EXTRA ACTION

LARGE GROUP

LITTLE BIBLE BACKGROUND

FELLOWSHIP & WORSHIP

EXTRA FUN

URBAN

JR.HIGH HIGH SCHOOL COMBINED

SIXTH GRADE

Hand out paper and pencils as kids arrive. Ask them to write down what they would consider to be an almost perfect day. Their descriptions should be as detailed as possible. For example, ask:

What would be your schedule, from morning to night? Where would you go? Who would you be with? What season would it be? What temperature would it be? What music would you be listening to?

Explain that you're not looking for descriptions of wild and imaginative fantasy days in which kids have breakfast on the surf in Hawaii and then fly to Rio for lunch. Rather, you're looking for descriptions of things that group members have actually experienced or would at least have a shot at doing someday.

When kids are finished, collect their written descriptions. Read a few at random and let group members guess who wrote each one. In most cases, kids are likely to describe positive and innocent activities. In this context, few people are likely to include things such as drinking, sexual activity, or similar behaviors. Yet many young people—including Christian young people—get involved in such things, supposedly with the goal of having "fun." Point out that we can plan "perfect" days that don't include drinking, drugs, sex, or other potential pitfalls. Keep this in mind as you continue the session.

A Partying of the Ways

(Needed: Copies of Repro Resource 1)

Hand out copies of "Party Time!" (Repro Resource 1). Assign the roles to various group members. (All group members without individual parts can join the "Party Animals" chant.) Read the skit as a group.

Afterward, ask: **Would you go to this party? Why or why not?**

Have you ever had an opportunity to go to a party similar to this one? Did you go? If so, what was it like? Did you enjoy yourself?

How do you feel when you're with a group of people who suddenly begin to have "fun" by doing things you aren't really comfortable doing?

Do you think Jesus would go to the party described in the skit? Why or why not?

What do you think Jesus did for fun?

Encourage several group members to respond to each of these questions. Many of your young people might be surprised to learn that Jesus attended parties where alcohol and prostitutes were present. In fact, His first recorded miracle is providing wine for a wedding where the supply had run out (John 2:1-11). It may be hard for some people to picture Jesus in such a setting, since they know He lived a sinless life. They need to see the importance of learning how He could be exposed to booze and hookers, yet never get drunk nor commit a sexual sin.

Well-meaning Bible teachers may have painted an incomplete picture of Jesus for students. In emphasizing how He never approved of sin, some teachers may have given the impression that He disapproved of sinners as well. So make sure your group members are aware that crowds flocked around Jesus wherever He went. He hugged small children, even when His disciples tried to shoo them away. He touched lepers. He tried to open people's minds and free them from the restricted thinking of their religious leaders. All in all, Jesus certainly must have been a fun person to be around. Sure, He came to earth on a serious and solemn mission, but His mission didn't cause His personal relationships with people to be dull or gloomy.

Invitations and Temptations

(Needed: Bibles)

Explain: **Since Jesus was able to spend time at parties and around sinful people, yet remain sinless Himself, He must have had a different perspective than many of us have. Let's try to see what His "secret" might have been.**

Have kids form two groups. Instruct Group #1 to read and discuss Matthew 4:1-11, which describes Jesus' temptations in the desert. Instruct Group #2 to read and discuss Luke 7:36-50, the account of Jesus at a Pharisee's dinner party. Each group should prepare to report on its assignment, either verbally or by acting out the story. Explain that after the groups report, you'll try to find a balance for having fun without crossing the line into sinful activity.

The members of Group #1 should discover that Jesus' life certainly involved a lot more than going to parties. One of the first things He did as He prepared to begin His public ministry was go into the desert and face severe temptations. He fasted 40 days and nights, and was (not surprisingly) very hungry. Satan's first temptation was something to the effect of "I dare you to turn these stones into bread." And while there was nothing wrong with Jesus getting something to eat, He never used His power to make Himself more comfortable. Satan's second temptation was for Jesus to plunge from the top of a tall building, which would have manipulated God into saving Him. Jesus declined again, refusing to call attention to Himself simply because He might be able to do so. And finally, Satan tried to play "Let's Make a Deal" by offering Jesus kingdoms and possessions. But Jesus knew what was really important in life and told Satan to get lost. His experience of hunger and temptation was certainly not a pleasant experience, yet it brought Him closer to God, His father. Going to a few parties during this 40-day period might have been a lot more fun, but Jesus realized that this was the time to do something necessary and beneficial—for Himself and others.

The members of Group #2 will see another side of Jesus' life as they describe His behavior at a dinner party thrown by a Pharisee named Simon. It was supposed to be a quiet dinner with the Pharisee, a few of his friends, and Jesus. But it was crashed by a prostitute who came up behind Jesus and started to cry. She used her tears to wash His feet and her hair to dry them. Then she kissed His feet and anointed them with perfume. As this was going on, Simon was becoming more skeptical about Jesus, assuming that He didn't know this was a "woman of ill repute." But Jesus knew all about the woman, and He knew Simon's thoughts as well. He told a parable to try to teach the guests a lesson, He forgave the woman's sins and astounded the people at the party.

After both groups have reported, say: **Jesus' temptations were all very much like "dares" from Satan—to use His power selfishly, to call attention to Himself, and to sacrifice His relationship with God in order to pick up a few material possessions. What are some dares people your age may receive today?** If no one mentions it, point out that introductions to drinking, sex, drugs, and other harmful behaviors often come through dares. Explain that sometimes it requires more strength and courage to decline the dare than to go through with it. The temptation Jesus faced from Satan is sort of a form of peer pressure—much as we might face from our own peers.

Jesus' temptations came at a vulnerable time—after He had left home to begin His ministry and before He assembled His disciples. What potential temptations might you face as you become more independent of your parents? (Opportunities for drinking and sex become more available. Also, priorities to get ahead "at any cost" and other detrimental attitudes may develop during this time if people don't seek and obey God's will.)

In which of the previous stories do you think Jesus had more fun: fasting in the wilderness or attending the Pharisee's party? Let a few kids offer their opinions. You might want to suggest that He was equally content since He was following God's will in both cases. We may have come to perceive church as boring and parties as fun, but neither case is necessarily true. The rest of the session will try to show that fun is determined more by the attitude we choose than by a particular set of circumstances.

Which do you think was more important for Jesus: spending time alone with God or spending time with people? (Both are important. Either one without the other leads to a life that gets out of balance.)

Why do you think Jesus was able to act so kindly toward the prostitute at the party? (Perhaps because He had first spent a lot of time with God and had learned to deal with temptation. He didn't go to parties to "let His hair down." Rather, He was consistent in His character and His faith, whether alone with God His Father or in a crowd of people.)

Do you think it's possible for *us* to be as balanced as Jesus—to go to parties and have a genuine love and concern for other people, yet not get caught up in the sins that others might be participating in? (Certainly it is possible, but only if we are as committed to obeying God as Jesus was.) It needs to be pointed out that Jesus was a legal adult. For your junior highers, drinking and related activities are not only bad [sinful] habits, they are illegal as well.

Pushing Fun to the Limits

Explain that some pursuits of "fun" are obviously wrong. When young people turn to alcohol, drugs, sexual activity, and such, the immediate sensations may indeed seem thrilling. But the satisfaction provided by such things quickly begins to diminish. Only too late do most people discover the "fun" is in the blatant defiance of what is expected of them, not so much in the activities themselves. A hangover, a sexually transmitted disease, an unwanted baby, or an addiction will quickly bring fun to an end. It is much better to seek other alternatives for fun and entertainment. Yet *anything* that is repeated too frequently can lose its allure. A hot fudge sundae can be a fun treat. But if all a person eats is hot fudge sundaes, they soon cease to be so satisfying.

The following is a list of things young people do for fun. Read the activities one at a time and let group members rate each one from 1 (least) to 10 (most) in regard to how much fun it is. Have kids respond by holding up an appropriate number of fingers to show their ratings.

- **Bungee jumping**
- **Video or computer games**
- **MTV**
- **G-rated movies**
- **PG-rated movies**
- **R-rated movies**
- **Softball**
- **Volleyball**
- **Football**
- **Miniature golf**
- **Bowling**
- **Youth group**
- **Church**
- **School**
- **Homework**
- **Going to the mall**
- **Bible study**
- **Prayer**
- **Waterskiing**
- **Swimming**
- **Going to an amusement park**
- **Listening to music**
- **Going on a date**

Add activities to the list that you know some of your kids like to do. Also let group members offer suggestions of things they really enjoy that weren't included on the list.

Then ask: **Of all these fun things, do you think any of them could ever become a temptation that might cause you to sin? If so, in what ways?** Discussion might begin with things that are associated with these activities. For example, movies can expose kids to illicit sex, violence, profanity, and other nonbiblical behaviors. But at a different level, many of these things can become addictive in the sense of taking time that could be better spent doing something more constructive. We tend to recognize this problem more in things such as video or computer games, watching TV, and so forth. Yet some people go to the lake to water-ski every weekend during the summer—even on Sunday mornings when they could be in church. Many sports, especially organized sports in school, can prevent kids from attending youth group, retreats, or other beneficial activities. It's always easier to choose to do something "fun" than something we know we *should* do, such as a church function. (Again, this is where one's personal attitude comes into the picture.)

How can we participate in all of these good, fun activities, yet keep from letting them become temptations for us? (We need to follow Jesus' example. Fun activities remain fun as long as we don't neglect our relationship with God. When we make spiritual development our highest priority, fun usually takes care of itself.) Point out that even though Jesus was usually swarmed by people who wanted His healing, His company, or some other favor, He still made time to be alone with God. Sometimes it had to be "very early in the morning, while it was still dark" (Mark 1:35), but it remained a priority for Him. Consequently, He could go to parties and talk with people without losing sight of who He was or what was most important in His life. He could associate with sinners, yet keep Himself detached from sin. We need to learn to do the same.

Make Your Own Fun Wherever You Go

(Needed: Bibles, copies of Repro Resource 2, pencils)

So far the emphasis has been on *what* is fun and what isn't. Before the session ends, you need to cover some of the *whos* and *wheres*.

Ask: **Do you know people who, whenever you are with them, always seem to find something fun for the two of you to do?**

Do you have some favorite places that, whenever you go there, you almost always have a lot of fun?

In contrast, are there people or places that seem to drain the fun right out of you?

Hand out copies of "A Measure of Fun" (Repro Resource 2) and pencils. Kids will be asked to evaluate how much fun they have at various places (math class, church, etc.). They will also be asked to set some goals for how they can make their least fun places more of a joy than usual. After most of your group members have completed the sheet, discuss their responses and goals.

Then summarize: **Many times the main reason we don't have fun someplace is because we choose not to have fun. We tell ourselves, *I have to go to church—or school, or wherever—this morning. What a waste. I could be doing so many other fun things instead.* But what if we changed our attitude a bit and, before going, told ourselves, *All right! I get to go to church—or school, or wherever—this morning. I'm going to be the most fun person there. In fact, I'm going to be so much fun that it's going to rub off on everyone else.* If you had that attitude, how might it make a big difference?**

Close with a challenge for group members not to take your word for it, but to try this approach this week and see for themselves. To help them remember how important a good attitude is, have someone read Colossians 3:17: "And whatever you do, whether in word or deed, do it all in the name of the Lord Jesus, giving thanks to God the Father through him." If time permits, have your group members memorize this verse. Explain that thankful people are fun people. As we learn to appreciate the good things around us (wherever we are), we learn to maintain a higher level of joy (fun) no matter what else happens.

NOTES

PARTY TIME!

PARTY ANIMALS *(running around the room, chanting)*: Par-*tee*! Par-*tee*! Par-*tee*!

PAT: Hey, Chris! Are you going to Joe's party tomorrow night?

CHRIS: Are you kidding?! From what I hear, the whole school is going to be there—at least everyone who was invited.

PAT: And several who weren't.

PARTY ANIMALS *(still running around)*: Par-*tee*! Par-*tee*! Par-*tee*!

(STEVE and GINNY enter.)

STEVE: Hi, guys! Are you guys going to Joe's party?

PAT AND CHRIS: For sure!

GINNY: This should be great! I hear his parents are out of town—for three weeks!

STEVE: And I hear they have an *excellent* liquor cabinet.

GINNY: Who needs it? Practically everyone is bringing a six-pack—or a bottle of *something*.

CHRIS: And I hear Joe is inviting a lot of girls who are . . . let's just say, *very friendly*—if you know what I mean. They're all going to be there!

GINNY: And Joe's guy friends aren't too shabby either! Some of them are really rich.

PARTY ANIMALS *(still running around)*: Par-*tee*! Par-*tee*! Par-*tee*!

PAT: There go some of them now—fine specimens of humanity, they are.

CHRIS: Wow! A party with all of our friends.

GINNY: All of the cool people from school, tons of food—

PAT: Free-flowing beer and who knows what else—

STEVE: And plenty of "easy" girls! Who could possibly pass this one up?

CHRIS: You said it. There's only one word for this big event.

EVERYONE: Par-*tee*! Par-*tee*! Par-*tee*!

A Measure of Fun

Gas gauges on cars come in pretty handy. They let you know at any point how much fuel you have on hand, so you can stock up again before you run completely out. Wouldn't it be good to have gauges to help us measure fun? If we aren't careful, we can be at a place that *should* be a lot of fun, yet suddenly discover that we're running dangerously low—or may be completely out. So think of each of the following places and "take a reading" of your fun level in each one. Draw the needle in the appropriate place to show how full of fun you are (or how close you are to empty). Then, for any of these areas in which you aren't at least three-quarters full, think of some ways that *you* can take the initiative and create more fun on a regular basis.

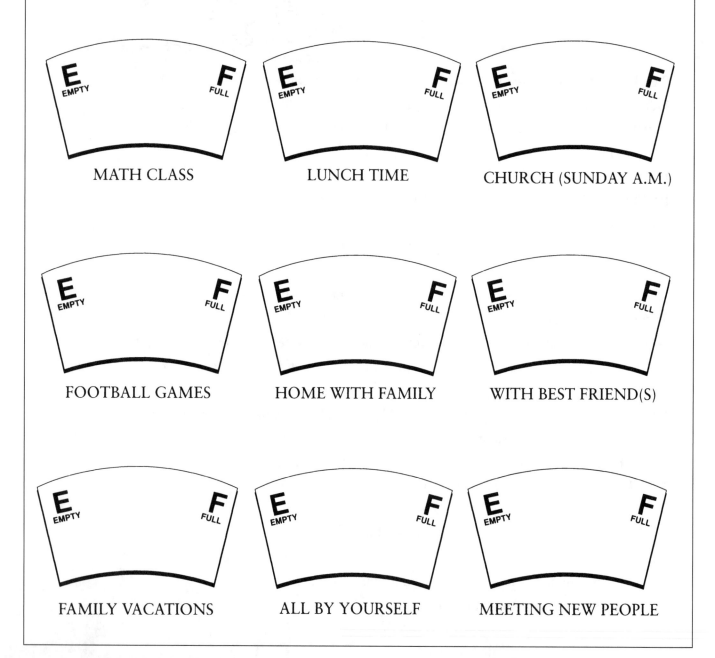

MATH CLASS

LUNCH TIME

CHURCH (SUNDAY A.M.)

FOOTBALL GAMES

HOME WITH FAMILY

WITH BEST FRIEND(S)

FAMILY VACATIONS

ALL BY YOURSELF

MEETING NEW PEOPLE

STEP 1

To begin the session, have each group member think of one of his or her favorite activities. However, the person should not mention what that activity is. Ask your group members to form a large circle, facing inward. Then, at your signal, have them simultaneously begin to pantomime the activities they have in mind. (Each person should act out only one activity.) Continue this for about a minute, while each person looks around the circle and tries to identify what everyone else is doing. After your signal to stop, let group members try to guess what each person was pantomiming. Then begin the session as written.

STEP 4

As you're discussing how "innocent" activities can turn into temptations, have kids form groups. Instruct each group to create a skit to demonstrate how innocent activities can become dangerous. Point out that while group members' initial tendency may be to use the activities listed in the session and think in terms of their own age-group, they need not do so. For example, a skit might involve a four-year-old girl asking Dad (who is not paying much attention to her) for permission to play with his chain saw. Group members should see that while there is nothing wrong with a chain saw, there are certain commonsense principles that should govern its use. The same should be true of watching television, playing videos, involvement in sports, or anything else you've discussed.

STEP 3

One advantage of a small group is that you can cover more material together and still hold everyone's attention. So rather than dividing your already small group in half to cover the two Bible stories, do them both as a single group. Both of these stories can be read as narratives by assigning various group members the quoted statements (Jesus, Satan, Simon, etc.) and designating someone else as narrator to read all of the non-quoted passages. This method will help bring the Bible characters to life— and will also help readers pay attention (so they'll be ready with their parts).

STEP 5

At the end of this session on fun, plan to do something new and different—either at your next meeting or sometime during the week. A small group should have less trouble planning something on short notice because there are fewer schedules to consider. One popular activity is a progressive dinner. Pack everyone into a car or van and make a stop at each person's house before the evening is over. Plan to have appetizers at the first house, salad at the second house, soup at the third house, followed by the main course, dessert, after-dinner hot cider, and so forth. Small groups need different and exciting outings as much as larger ones, but sometimes the small numbers don't seem "worth the effort." If a spirit of excitement can be generated among the few who are there, usually others will eventually be invited to attend, and the group will begin to grow.

STEP 1

Rather than having kids write descriptions of an ideal day and then guessing who wrote what, set up a "Temptation Table." Prior to the session, display several of your kids' favorite foods on a table where everyone is certain to see them. The foods should include things like cookies or candies (things that can be "sampled" without being noticed) rather than cakes or pies. Put a sign on the table that reads "Do Not Touch." As kids arrive, adult leaders should be nowhere in sight. Also prearrange for one group member to be a tempter. He or she should stand near the table and make comments about how delicious the food looks. If no one succumbs to initial temptations, the tempter might nibble on some of the treats and see if anyone follows suit. When the adult leaders finally show up, they should have a number of even better treats as rewards for anyone who withstood the Temptation Table. Afterward, point out that while sweets can be fun treats under the right circumstances, they can also serve as temptations for us. Like other fun things, we need to prevent them from becoming temptations for us.

STEP 5

It can be overwhelming to try to ensure that a large group is having fun on a regular basis—so let kids share the responsibility. At the end of the session, have kids form groups. Designate each group as a "fun team." Explain that the fun teams will plan fun events for future sessions on a rotating basis. These should be simple one- or two-minute events (games, jokes, riddles, skits, etc.). The only requirements are that they be clean and fun. Encourage the fun teams to be creative. Some might demonstrate "Stupid Human Tricks" (strange talents), put together a jug band, or whatever. The weirder (and "funner"), the better. Let the teams begin to brainstorm ideas during this session. Then assign the first "rotation" of dates when teams are expected to provide the fun.

STEP 2

As part of your discussion after reading the skit on Repro Resource 1, ask: **What would you say was the most surprising thing Jesus ever did?** Let each person respond. If your group members know the Bible well, they should provide a number of answers (walk on water, turn water to wine, rise from the dead, bring a major storm to a dead stop, etc.). Ask: **How do you think these surprising things affected the thinking of people around Jesus?** Point out that Jesus frequently "broke the mold" of traditional thinking. Among other things, this tendency probably created an atmosphere of fun. While everything probably was not "ha ha" humorous, there is something thrilling about not knowing what might happen next. Explain that when we tend to get in a rut, we may need to draw closer to God and see what unexpected things He might have in store for us.

STEP 3

After the Bible study groups have read and discussed their assigned stories, begin a debate. One group should defend the position that Jesus was most committed to personal spiritual integrity. The other group should argue that Jesus placed more emphasis on people and relationships (fun). Groups may draw on the Scripture passages they read as well as any others that might help make their points. Since many junior highers won't be familiar with traditional debate procedure, you might want to provide opportunities for rebuttal and/or ask questions for clarification. It should become clear through the debate (with a little additional comment from you) that Jesus placed great importance on both personal spiritual commitment *and* other people and their needs. We should do the same. People and fun are important, but not at the expense of our own individual growth.

STEP 1

Before moving on to Step 2, pass around something sticky or wet (a popcorn ball, a wet paper towel, a fish from the grocery store, etc.). Make sure everyone handles the object at least once. Then ask: **Even though you "passed on" this object when you came into contact with it, were you affected in any way?** Kids should see that even though they may have tried to remain "unaffected," they still retained a residual effect from the object (a smell that rubbed off, a bit of moisture, or whatever). Point out that they need to be careful about even *approaching* certain activities—whether or not they actually get involved—because they may be more influenced by such things than they think. Kids may be learning that certain activities are right and others are wrong, but they still need help developing a sense of spiritual discernment to determine when they may be in more danger than they can see.

STEP 3

Because so many young people have an incomplete picture of who Jesus is, spend some time helping your kids fill in the gaps. One way to do this is to have them think of three to five people they most admire. Then have them determine exactly what it is about each of those people that captures their respect. It could be that Dad provides unconditional love. A teacher might go out of her way to help the student learn. An uncle might be a role model in a specific job the kid has an interest in. After listing all of the qualities of their human role models, have group members consider whether or not Jesus fits those same criteria. In most cases, you should be able to think of an instance from Jesus' life that reflects any good or admirable quality. Help your group members see that whatever they are looking to emulate, Jesus stands as the best possible example.

STEP 1

To help increase the level of fellowship in your group, ask one of your group members a few days before the session to read and prepare a brief report on some good resource materials that promote fun in relation to Christianity. The best way to locate such resources is to wander around a local Christian bookstore until you find something that looks promising. One example is Tony Campolo's book, *The Kingdom of God Is a Party* (Word). You might assign someone to read and report on Chapter 6: "Turning Church into a Party." Your volunteer can pass along interesting anecdotes as well as challenges laid out by the author. Many resources also provide good, fun activities to try as well. Look until you find something that's right for your group. Then choose the right person to present the material, someone who can make something happen to liven up your group.

STEP 5

At the end of the session, have your group members brainstorm things they can do to help make their *worship* more fun. There are times to be serious and meditative, certainly, but there are also times to "cut loose" in their praise and worship of God. If this can be done at a congregational level, challenge them to do so. Some of their livelier songs and a few skits or short plays can bring a lot of life to a church service. But if your kids don't have such an opportunity, have them plan a fun worship service among themselves. Make sure all of the elements of worship are included: music, Bible study, fellowship, and so forth. However, each of these things should be conducted in an innovative and enjoyable way. Remember to keep your focus on God. We worship not to have fun, but to glorify Him. But fun can be a by-product of worship.

MOSTLY GIRLS

STEP 2

In a group of mostly girls, you may need to make some adjustments to the skit on Repro Resource 1. To start with, you may want to change the character named "Steve" to "Jill." You may also want to change "Joe's party" to "Kristy's party." Instead of having your actors talk about the "very friendly" or "easy" girls who will be at the party, have them discuss the "study guys" who will be there.

STEP 4

Have your girls brainstorm a list of the "fun-tations" (fun activities that could turn into temptations) that could become a problem for them. Write group members' suggestions on the board as they are named. After you've got several ideas listed, have your girls narrow the choices to create a "top 10 list." Then, as a group, talk about specific things your girls can do to help keep fun activities fun, without letting them become temptations.

MOSTLY GUYS

STEP 3

After you discuss Jesus' temptations, have each of your guys describe "The Dumbest Dare I Ever Took." At some point in their lives, most junior high guys have taken some pretty stupid dares (eating certain foods, taking physical risks, etc.). Try to get some stories started. Once a couple of guys speak up, others should begin to recall similar incidents. Focus on the *consequences* of their actions. Point out through their stories that while we sometimes "get by with" certain actions that aren't so smart, we should become more careful as we get older. The dares (temptations) become more dangerous. A dare to split a six-pack with a friend might be accepted if the perceived consequences only include getting caught by parents or perhaps the police. But few young people ever suspect that other risks include a lifetime of addiction or the possibility of harming someone while in a drunken state. Also discuss how anyone who continues to be motivated by dares is always at the mercy of others. By the time a kid is in junior high, he needs to realize that it takes more strength and sense to turn down certain dares than to feel compelled to "prove his manhood" by taking needless risks.

STEP 4

After addressing needless risks in Step 3, plan an *acceptable* risky endeavor in this step. As you discuss things your guys consider fun, listen for things they might like to try. Then actually plan to do one or more of those things as a group. Most guys would look forward to the adventure of canoeing, rafting, mountain climbing, fishing, camping, or similar activities. It's easy to *ask* them not to get involved in certain activities. It's more work (but also more effective) to provide adventurous activities that are OK for them to do. Yet if your guys are given sufficient challenges in "safe" settings, they will probably be far less likely to try to manufacture excitement on their own by means of potentially dangerous and undesirable activities.

EXTRA FUN

STEP 1

Begin the session with a "celebrity" version of the opening activity. Have each person choose a celebrity (real or fictional) and write down at least three activities that would make up an "almost perfect" day for that person. The rest of the group members will then try to guess the celebrity based on the list of activities. For instance, someone might come up with these three activities: "(1) Take Betty out for some Bronto Burgers. (2) Work on the car while my son holds it up. (3) Beat Fred in three straight games of bowling." The group members would probably guess that the celebrity being described is Barney Rubble (of *The Flintstones*).

STEP 4

Your kids are probably familiar with the Beach Boys' song, "Fun, Fun, Fun." As you discuss how certain things can start out as fun but then lose their allure or become addictive, ask: **What are some things that ruin fun activities for you?** Don't have kids answer aloud, but have everyone think of an answer. Then mention the Beach Boys song and remind everyone that the original complaint was "We'll have fun, fun, fun till her daddy takes the T-Bird away." That's what brought *their* fun to an end. Sing the lines a couple of times so everyone can see how the tune goes. Then explain that, as a group, you're going to keep singing, "We'll have fun, fun, fun till . . ." and then you'll point to someone to finish the line (singing or speaking) with his or her specific answer. Keep singing and pointing to people until everyone has had a chance to respond. Then ask: **Do you want to have fun all of the time? Do you think we should have fun all of the time? Is it necessarily a bad thing when fun comes to an end?** Kids should see that anything that happens all of the time ceases to be fun. Truly fun events may be those things that occur at repeated, but limited, intervals. They are things that can be looked forward to and then recalled with fondness.

STEP 3

Provide group members with a variety of magazines and newspapers. Instruct group members to find a number of ads that portray potentially harmful activities (such as drinking or smoking) as fun activities. Then ask everyone to look for "opposites" to these proposed fun benefits. For example, a photo of a gorgeous model seductively holding a cigarette can be countered with an article or obituary notice referring to lung cancer, the effects of secondary smoke, etc. An enticing ad for alcohol might be contrasted with a photo of a drunk person lying in an alley. Media are used effectively to promote certain products that can have disastrous effects. If possible, use those same media to show the other side of such "fun" products or activities.

STEP 4

A frequently overlooked form of media is T-shirts; yet most people wear T-shirts that promote the products and/or activities they think are fun (concerts, beer, sex, sports, etc.). If possible, take your group members to a mall or other public place to let them see how many different T-shirt "billboards" they can find. Have them list all of the products, activities, or places they find mentioned on other people's T-shirts. If a field trip is out of the question, have kids think of T-shirts they own or have seen recently that captured their attention. Most kids should be able to name several from memory. Then ask: **When people look at you, do you suppose they ever think that you must find church and/or youth group to be a fun place? Do you think they can see any excitement about being a Christian simply from watching your life? Why or why not?** As group members notice the T-shirts other people wear with pride that promote footwear, vacation spots, or whatever, challenge them to promote their faith—not just with catchy slogans on their clothing, but with their very lives.

STEP 2

Combine Steps 1 and 2 with the following activity. Write several dates on the board. These dates should span history and include the future—5000 B.C., 4 B.C., A.D. 800, 1492, 1984, 2000, 2431, etc. Have kids form groups. Assign each group one of the dates on the board. Instruct the members of each group to explain (or act out) what kids their age probably did (or will do) for fun in their assigned year. For instance, kids in 5000 B.C. might have wrestled baby dinosaurs. Kids in A.D. 2431 might cruise around in their own spaceship. After a few minutes, have each group share what it came up with. Afterward, ask: **What do you think Jesus did for fun?** Encourage several responses. Then move on to Step 3.

STEP 5

Rather than having kids take time to fill out Repro Resource 2, you can cover the material in a speedier way. Ask for two volunteers from the group. Explain that you're going to name a place or situation. When you do, your two volunteers must start suggesting ways to make that place or situation more fun. The first volunteer will have five seconds to make a suggestion; then the second volunteer will have five seconds to make another suggestion. The two will continue until one of them can't think of a new suggestion (within the time limit). Declare the other person the winner and award him or her a prize. Then ask for two more volunteers to play the next round. Play as many rounds as you have time for, using the places and situations on Repro Resource 2.

STEP 1

After your group members describe their "almost perfect day," have them describe a typical *night* in their life. How do your city kids spend the hours between 8:00 p.m. and 6:00 a.m.? Do they hang out with friends, getting into trouble? Or do they use that time for homework and rest? Make the point that what a person does during the nighttime hours greatly affects what he or she can accomplish during the daytime. In other words, an "almost perfect day" requires a well-spent night. Get a feel for how much sleep (on average) your group members get every night. For fun, you might want to use the following "grading scale":

- 1-2 hours—You're a dead head.
- 3-4 hours—You're a yawning fool.
- 5-6 hours—You're an afternoon dozer.
- 7-8 hours—You're a quality sleeper.
- 9-10 hours—You're sleeping your life away!

[NOTE: This grading scale is based on the assumption that 7-8 hours of sleep per night is ideal. Of course, some people require less sleep than that; others require more. You may want to adjust the scale to better reflect your group members' sleeping habits.]

STEP 5

After discussing the scenarios on Repro Resource 2, ask your group to brainstorm some ways to have fun in the following situations:

• Because of heavy gang violence in your neighborhood, you have to stay inside your house or apartment after school and during the weekend.

• Your local basketball court and community center are being torn down to make way for a new office building.

• You find out you have to take summer school.

STEP 1

To begin the session, ask: **What things did you think were really fun a year or two ago that you don't particularly enjoy today?** Let your junior highers respond first, and then your high schoolers. What your group members might discover is that an activity can mean a lot to them for a while, but over time, the excitement of that activity can fade— or even disappear. Some of the responses of your high schoolers may surprise your junior highers. The younger kids may just be discovering the joy of certain things that the older ones have already "burned out" on. If so, make the point that throughout life, certain things are going to be fun for a time. But if they're not enjoyed in moderation, they may become nothing more than occasional pastimes or mere memories.

STEP 2

It may be difficult for your junior highers to agree with high schoolers (who may be more mature and sophisticated) on activities they both consider to be fun. But after going through the skit and discussing the questions in Step 2, have your group members create a list of "elements of a great party." Agree ahead of time that nothing goes on the list unless a majority of both junior highers and high schoolers agree to it. Then after you compile the list, plan the party! Divide the responsibilities so that all of the elements will be included. Someone can volunteer to get the "right" music. Others can sign up to arrange favorite kinds of foods. If a special location is needed (such as a gymnasium or swimming pool), have someone agree to make some calls and line up a place. It's one thing to teach about what constitutes fun. The important thing is that you model it and show that some things can be equally enjoyed by any age-group.

STEP 1

Rather than having group members write out what a perfect day would be like for them, provide some paper and an assortment of markers, crayons, paints, and other art supplies. Ask group members to *draw* a perfect day and then be prepared to describe it to the rest of the group. Give the kids a few minutes to work. When everyone is finished, have group members explain what they've drawn and describe the emotions, activities, and so forth that they couldn't express artistically.

STEP 5

As you wrap up the session, ask: **How do you think your definition of fun will change by the time you're in high school? What things will you think are fun then that you aren't able to do today?** One of the major goals of many young kids is driving, although sixth graders still have several years to wait and may not even be thinking seriously about it at this time. Sometimes you'll get some interesting answers by asking young people to speculate about the future. Their answers are likely to alert you to what the older people in their lives consider to be fun activities. Assure group members that they'll be able to do more "adult" things soon enough. Then encourage them to look for new and exciting things they can do as sixth graders. Later in life they may be surprised to remember exactly how much fun those things were (even if such things don't seem so special right now).

DATE USED:

Approx. Time

STEP 1: *A Really Good Day* _____
- ❑ Extra Action
- ❑ Large Group
- ❑ Little Bible Background
- ❑ Fellowship & Worship
- ❑ Extra Fun
- ❑ Urban
- ❑ Combined Jr. High/High School
- ❑ Sixth Grade

Things needed:

STEP 2: *A Partying of the Ways* _____
- ❑ Heard It All Before
- ❑ Mostly Girls
- ❑ Short Meeting Time
- ❑ Combined Jr. High/High School

Things needed:

STEP 3: *Invitations and Temptations* _____
- ❑ Small Group
- ❑ Heard It All Before
- ❑ Little Bible Background
- ❑ Mostly Guys
- ❑ Media

Things needed:

STEP 4: *Pushing Fun to the Limits* _____
- ❑ Extra Action
- ❑ Mostly Girls
- ❑ Mostly Guys
- ❑ Extra Fun
- ❑ Media

Things needed:

STEP 5: *Make Your Own Fun Wherever You Go* _____
- ❑ Small Group
- ❑ Large Group
- ❑ Fellowship & Worship
- ❑ Short Meeting Time
- ❑ Urban
- ❑ Sixth Grade

Things needed:

What Would Jesus Do . . . at My School?

YOUR GOALS FOR THIS SESSION:

Choose one or more

☐ To help kids imagine what Jesus might have been like as a junior high student in a school similar to theirs.

☐ To help kids understand that they should begin now to demonstrate their faith—at school as well as at church.

☐ To help kids see that a get-ahead-at-any-cost mentality will prevent spiritual growth, and to challenge them to set goals to become more servant-minded.

☐ Other:_____

Your Bible Base:

Matthew 20:20-28
Luke 2:41-52

STEP 1

Whatever It Takes

O P T I O N S

SMALL GROUP

MOSTLY GIRLS

EXTRA FUN

JR. HIGH HIGH SCHOOL COMBINED

SIXTH GRADE

To begin the session, have group members form teams. Instruct each team to plan a skit. In the skit, one person should have a goal that he or she is desperate to accomplish. Other group members may portray teachers, parents, other adults, fellow students, etc. The skits should show the extreme lengths that kids go to in order to do something they feel driven to do. Explain that the skits need not reflect what your specific group members would necessarily do (since they are so good and pure), but rather what lengths *other* desperate junior highers might go to. Some of the skits might include the following scenarios:

- Someone is desperate to make an A in a class that he or she has never made better than a C in. (Options might include recruiting study partners, finding a tutor, copying homework, cheating on tests, changing the teacher's grade book, attempted bribery, etc.)
- Someone wants to break into a snooty clique at school. (He or she might pester members, buy gifts for key people, ditch existing friends, act in a manner completely opposite to his or her true personality, etc.)
- A football player who sits on the bench all of the time wants to get into a game. (He could follow the coach around, try to trip and injure one of the other players, do exercises continually on the sideline to get noticed, trade jerseys with another player to get on the field, etc.)
- Someone wants to get rid of a nerdy friend who threatens to damage his or her reputation. The two people have been friends, but the person wants to move up the social ladder at school and feels he or she can't do it and retain this particular friendship. (He or she might confront the friend with some fancy excuses to couch the blow, followed by subtle or not-so-subtle hints. When all else fails, the person will probably have to come right out with the truth. But any and all other options kids think of should be encouraged.)
- Someone likes another person very much and wants to be asked out; but the other person has shown no interest. (Options might include the old "I'll have one of my friends talk to one of his or her friends" routine, the direct approach, stalking the other person around the halls and neighborhoods, etc.)

After the skits have been performed, ask: **Do any of these things remind you of things you've done in the past?**

Why do you think we sometimes become so desperate to impress certain people or achieve certain goals—especially at school?

What's the most embarrassing thing you've ever done to try to accomplish a goal similar to the ones we've acted out? What were the results of your actions? Get responses from several of your group members for each question.

STEP
2

A New Kid in Town

Ask a volunteer to stand in front of the rest of the group. Say: **This person has just moved to this area and will be going to your school. He (or she) knows nothing about the school, the teachers, the traditions, or anything else. What advice would you give him (or her) to help him (or her) fit in as quickly as possible?**

Let each person offer a nugget of advice. If group members have trouble coming up with ideas, you might want to have them identify who the "lousy" teachers are at school (and how to deal with them), which groups and organizations all the "cool" people belong to (and which ones are for the "losers"), what he or she needs to know about avoiding trouble with bullies, where to sit in the cafeteria, and so forth.

Try to make group members comfortable enough to be completely honest. Then, after no one has any further helpful hints, say: **Oh, by the way, this person's name is Jesus. He has some big plans when He grows up, but first He has to get through junior high and high school.**

Would any of your group members be a bit embarrassed or uncomfortable to have told a young Jesus some of the things they did? Explain that sometimes we have one set of standards that we discuss and display at church, but those things never quite make it to the hallways at school. It's very difficult to live out what we say we believe in a pressure-packed situation like school. Yet it is important that we begin to do so, or at least make a good attempt.

OPTIONS

HEARD IT ALL BEFORE

LITTLE BIBLE BACKGROUND

FELLOWSHIP & WORSHIP

MOSTLY GIRLS

MEDIA

SHORT MEETING TIME

URBAN

Cause for Concern?

(Needed: Copies of Repro Resource 3, pencils)

Have group members continue thinking about how Jesus might fit in as a student at their school(s) as you hand out copies of "Checkin' Out the School Scene" (Repro Resource 3) and pencils. Group members will be asked to estimate Jesus' level of comfort in a number of different situations He might experience on an average school day. They will then compare that degree of comfort in each category with their own comfort level.

Group members may discover that they have learned to take for granted or to dismiss certain activities that *should* be cause for concern. If so, try to let them struggle with these discoveries on their own. Resist any inclination to suggest what they should think about peers who choose to cheat, manipulate, and so forth. It is important that young people learn to monitor *their own* actions and attitudes. As they do, they will then become better able to deal with *others* who may not agree with them. Later in the session, group members will have the opportunity to think more about their attitudes and set some goals for themselves.

After everyone has completed the sheet, ask: **Do you think Jesus would like school? Why or why not?**

What do you think He would like most? What would He like least?

How do you think Jesus would dress for school?

Who would be His closest friends? Which groups would He belong to?

What would be in His locker? How might His locker be decorated?

It may be difficult for group members to envision Jesus as a junior high student. We know very little about His childhood, yet your group members need to be reminded that at one time He was indeed a young teen. And only by trying to see how He might have fit in at school can your kids see how *they* ought to try to fit in and what changes they might need to make in their attitudes or behavior.

STEP 4

Rabbi's Pet?

(Needed: Bibles, copies of Repro Resource 4, pencils)

Ask: **If you could ditch your parents for three days—let's say they have to go off on a trip while you stay home—and you could do anything you wanted without getting caught, what might you do?** Let group members speculate about their actions. Some might attempt wild kinds of things. Most would probably not try anything too ambitious.

What do you think Jesus might do under the same conditions? Get a few responses.

Explain to your group members that we do have one good look at Jesus as a young teen, and that single peek suggests an answer to the previous question. Have someone read Luke 2:41-52. Then explain that the synagogue at this time was not simply a place to worship once a week. It was also a center of teaching and learning—a place of schooling in addition to worship. Knowledgeable visitors would frequently be invited to teach, and attenders had the opportunity to learn from a number of people.

Ask: **What do you find most unusual about this story?** Get a few responses.

Do you think Jesus was too young to be hobnobbing with the religious teachers? (In this culture, age 13 was the accepted time for males to begin to be accepted as adults. So at age 12, it was not so unusual for them to be preparing for their "official" acceptance into society.)

If you suddenly dropped into the teachers' lounge at school and began a deep discussion about the things you were being taught, who in the group do you think would be most surprised? Why?

Why do you think Jesus stayed in Jerusalem—in school—instead of going with His parents? Do you think He was wrong in staying? Why?

Do you think Jesus was a young show-off with a "know-it-all" attitude? Explain. (It doesn't appear so. We read that He was "listening to them and asking them questions" [vs. 46].)

On a scale of 1 to 10—with 10 being the highest—how well would you say you listen during most of your classes?

O P T I O N S

HEARD IT ALL BEFORE

FELLOWSHIP & WORSHIP

MOSTLY GUYS

SHORT MEETING TIME

JR.HIGH HIGH SCHOOL COMBINED

How frequently do you take enough interest to ask questions about the things you've heard?

Do you think Jesus knew things without having to study, or did He need to learn just like everyone else? (Verse 52 tells us He "grew in wisdom," so it appears that—though He was divine—He learned in much the same way that other young teens of His time learned.)

Do you think there's a difference in the kind of learning Jesus was doing in the synagogue and the kind of learning you do in school? If so, what is it? If no one mentions it, point out that in church settings we tend to place a higher value on spiritual learning than on, say, geometry. Yet if we truly believe that all truth is God's truth, *everything* we learn can help make us better Christians. Perhaps if we looked harder to find reflections of God at school—in the unchanging logic of geometry, the fascinating workings of the body in biology, the annals of history, and so forth—classes would be less of a drudgery for many people.

Hand out copies of "Jesus and Me" (Repro Resource 4). Whereas Repro Resource 3 had kids compare their responses to Jesus' expected response in a number of school-related settings, this one asks them to focus more on spiritual areas. Have them compare their own commitment toward spiritual learning to that of Jesus when He was approximately their age. The sheet should follow up your group discussion with some personal considerations. When everyone finishes, let volunteers share some of the observations they made about themselves.

Don't Know Much about Servanthood

(Needed: Bibles, paper, pencils)

Ask: **When you think about an average day at school, what three adjectives come to mind?** Encourage honest responses.

What words would you use to describe your *attitude* toward school? Some kids may truly enjoy the learning aspects of school. Others may focus primarily on the social opportunities. A few group members may have little interest in anything school has to offer.

If getting ahead at school were more important than anything else to you—if you wanted to make straight A's, be accepted by all of the cool people, and get involved in all of the extracurricular activities you enjoy—what would you need to do differently than you're doing now? Let kids respond.

Should this be a goal for us—to get ahead no matter what?

After some discussion, explain: **Jesus' disciples had similar concerns about which one was the greatest** (Luke 22:24), **and—as you're about to see—one of their mothers even got involved in trying to convince Jesus to let her sons be His number one and number two students. Jesus had to "referee" to keep His disciples from getting too far off track. It wasn't that He didn't want them to excel. But He wanted to make it clear that there were things more important than straight A's, awards, and other public recognition.**

Have someone read Matthew 20:20-28. Then say: **These verses are usually used in reference to spiritual growth. How might they apply to your life *at school*?**

After some discussion, hand out paper and pencils. Ask group members to make two columns on the paper. As they think about Jesus' command to be servants, they should list in the first column, "Things I need to *start* doing in order to be a better servant at school." The second column should contain a list of "Things I need to *stop* doing in order to be a better servant at school." After giving group members some time to make their lists, let volunteers share their responses.

Then ask: **What are some ways you could be a "servant" or a "slave" to other people at school? Of these things that you've listed, which ones might you actually be willing to try? Which ones do you feel are simply asking too much of you?**

Think back to some of the skits at the beginning of this session. In the context of these verses, how do you think Jesus would feel about your cheating on tests in order to get into a better college? How about breaking off relationships merely to move up the social ladder? Get several responses.

Why should we be willing to serve other people at school when they don't care for us or even acknowledge that we exist? (Some things we ought to do because we know they're right actions and not necessarily because we're getting anything out of them. As Christians, we can do our best to be better friends to each other without getting caught in the get-ahead-at-any-cost mentality.)

As you close, challenge your group members with a mental assignment for the next time they return to school. Ask them to go through as much of the day as possible attempting to see everything as if Jesus

OPTIONS

EXTRA ACTION

SMALL GROUP

LARGE GROUP

LITTLE BIBLE BACKGROUND

EXTRA FUN

were observing it. They should try to become more aware of over-heard conversations, rest room graffiti, social and ethnic divisions, and so forth. In addition, they should see *themselves* from a different perspective. Their comments, relationships, behavior toward authority, and everything else should be examined. It's fairly common to speak of Jesus being with us all the time and knowing all about us, but it can be quite an eye-opening experience to imagine Him actually walking school halls and getting a firsthand view of what's going on.

Checkin' Out the
School Scene

Suppose Jesus is your age, and you are assigned to show Him around your school. Naturally, you would come across a number of sights or activities that might seem strange to Him. You may be used to them, but as He sees them for the first time, He might not be as comfortable with them as you've become. So for each activity that is listed, rate how you think Jesus would feel after witnessing it. Use a scale of 1 to 10 (in which 1 indicates "No discomfort at all with this activity" and 10 indicates "Extreme discomfort with this activity"). Then rate how *you* would feel normally upon seeing the same thing— without Jesus around.

	JESUS	ME
People are copying each other's homework. They have good excuses for not doing it on their own.		
People are cheating on tests to make better grades.		
At lunch, certain people aren't welcome at your table.		
The language in the locker room is a little rough.		
People are making fun of teachers behind their backs.		
Some kids are taking steroids to do better in their sports.		
A bully frequently picks on smaller and weaker students.		
Kids are sleeping in classes when they know they won't get caught.		
You attend a football game and sit in the middle of the student crowd.		
You attend a pep rally.		
You attend a party where a few kids are drinking.		
Some students are "kissing up" to others in order to be accepted.		
A couple is doing some fairly heavy making out in the hallway.		
You read the "poetry" on the bathroom walls.		
You go home after school and watch your favorite video.		

JESUS AND ME

The life of Christ has probably been examined more closely than anyone else's—and for good reason. We have much to learn from the example of Jesus, who was God in human form. Yet even as a twelve year old, Jesus was very impressive and shows us what is possible for young teens to achieve.

In each of the cases below, Jesus' response is given. It's up to you to describe (honestly) what you would do in each instance.

THE TRUST FACTOR

Apparently, Jesus' parents trusted Him to take care of Himself—even when they were away from home in a different city.

When my parents leave me alone to do whatever I want, what usually happens is . . .

FREE TIME

When Jesus was alone in the big city and able to do anything He wanted to do, He chose to spend almost all of His time in the temple (shall we say the local church?).

During summer vacation when I have the opportunity to devote a lot more time to church and personal spiritual growth, I . . .

SPIRITUAL CURIOSITY

Jesus not only spent time in the temple, He also listened attentively and asked questions while He was there.

When I'm in church, my attitude toward learning can best be described as . . .

CONTINUED LEARNING

By the time Jesus was twelve, He was already devoted to continued intellectual growth as well as ongoing spiritual commitment.

When I look ahead at all of the years of school I still have (and even beyond that), and when I think about how much I don't know about God and the Bible, I feel . . .

NOTES

STEP 3

You can convert Repro Resource 3 into a more active exercise by assigning parts and letting kids act out several of the situations, rather than simply having them fill out the sheet. One person can play the role of the young Jesus and another can play the role of the person showing Him around school. The pair should literally walk around the room, where other group members are playing the roles of students who are doing things like copying homework, harassing others, snubbing people at the lunch table, and so forth. At each confrontation, "freeze" the action and let group members determine how uncomfortable they think they might be if they were with Jesus at that particular moment in real life. Then move on to the next setting.

STEP 5

After the discussion about serving other people at school, have kids form groups. Instruct each group to write and choreograph a few servanthood cheers—catchy and enthusiastic challenges that will help kids remember that they need to put other people first. (For example: "We're number two! We're number two! We serve you, so we're number two!") Give the groups a few minutes to practice their arm motions and choreography before they present their cheers to everyone else. Many group members will probably be familiar with actual cheers they can imitate, but even those who don't should be able to come up with some good ones anyway.

STEP 1

Rather than opening the session with the skits as written (which would require having the same people perform a number of them), begin instead with a complete-the-sentence activity. Begin a number of sentences (one at a time) and then have each group member complete them. The sentences should be school-related, and might include the following:

• **The hardest thing about school is . . .**

• **I feel most alone at school when . . .**

• **The thing everyone seems to be good at in school except me is . . .**

• **If I could change one thing about school, it would be . . .**

• **When it comes to grades, I think . . .**

STEP 5

Have your group members make "servanthood commitments" to each other. Distribute paper and pencils. Instruct kids to create three vertical columns across the top of the sheet: "Name," "Act of Service," and "Date/Time." Under the "Name" column, have them list the names of all the other group members. Then challenge each person to commit to performing an act of service for everyone else in the group. The acts of service should be done sometime during the following week—not immediately, or the tendency will be to do small things to "get it over with." (This activity should require some serious thought.) When group members complete an act of service, they should record it in the second column as well as listing the date and time in the third column. Explain that some of the best acts of service are things that are done anonymously, such as sending "Secret Pal" cards or gifts, doing a dreaded chore for someone when he or she isn't looking, etc. Follow up next week to see if everyone has fulfilled his or her commitments.

STEP 3

Follow up the "Jesus comes to your school" concept by taking an "official poll." Ask a number of questions and then determine the percentage of people who respond with a yes, no, or "undecided." Here are some questions you might use:

• **Would you walk up to and welcome a Jewish stranger on his first day at your school?**
• **If a new kid seemed to be lost, would you volunteer to help?**
• **Would you make jokes about a stranger to your "regular" friends?**
• **Would you be jealous of a new kid who seemed to be smarter and/or nicer than you were?**

Encourage your group members to be honest about how they would respond to a *normal* stranger. Obviously, if they knew the person was Jesus, they would be more likely to treat Him kindly. But the challenge is to learn to treat everyone kindly.

STEP 5

Learning to be a servant to others (especially at school) is a difficult thing to do—partially because young people may not tend to think about Christian living when they get into the "rhythm" of an average day at school. To help group members remember the importance of carrying their faith into their school hallways, create something as a group that kids can wear on a specified day or week. You might want to come up with a T-shirt design, make buttons, cut cloth swatches or ribbons, or use any number of other methods. But if you have a large group, and everyone agrees to wear something symbolic to help him or her remember to be a servant in school, kids won't have the excuse of "spiritual amnesia." In addition, as kids at school question why so many others are wearing the same symbol, your group members can explain that it's to help remind them to invite new people to your youth group or Sunday school (which certainly qualifies as helping to "serve" people).

STEP 2

Sometimes it helps to address a "heard it all before" mentality by making some rapid about-turns in your teaching. So after your group members get into the Jesus-as-fellow-student concept, suddenly shift the discussion. Say: **Suppose Jesus were one of your *teachers*. Do you think that would be a good thing or a bad thing? Why?** Let group members respond. If you wish, have kids act out a scene in which Jesus is trying to teach a class of rowdy students. Try to help group members see that in reality, Jesus serves both as our friend and our teacher. We need to learn to relate to Him on both levels and, based on His example, learn to relate better to other people as well.

STEP 4

If your kids are occasionally difficult to teach due to a know-it-all attitude, spend some time immediately after reading Luke 2:41-52 in a discussion of Jesus' attitude as described in this passage. Ask: **What attitude should we have toward parents and teachers—even if we might know more than they do?** (We should be submissive and obedient.) **Why do you think Jesus was submissive to His parents, even though they didn't understand Him?** (If children don't submit to parents, there is little, if any, order within a family. Besides, a child's submission usually reduces conflict within the family and gives parents the opportunity to change their minds and apologize if they are wrong.) **If you were to follow Jesus' example at school, what are some things you might need to do differently?** (Be less argumentative when disagreeing with a teacher? Be patient in asking questions? Learn without being so self-assured that you already know it all?) Point out that if anyone had the right to claim, "I've heard it all before," it was Jesus, who left heaven to come to earth. But if even *He* didn't give His teachers a hard time (at least, not when He was twelve), then neither should anyone else.

STEP 2

For people unfamiliar with the Bible, the concept of Jesus as a junior higher may be hard to grasp. They may be dealing with artistic portrayals filed away in their minds—pictures of a rather weak-looking adult who doesn't look very happy. It may be difficult for them to think of Jesus as a happy and active teenager. So spend a little time helping your kids make that mental shift. Say: **Think of the things you've done at school and at school-related functions during the past week. Which of those things do you think Jesus would really have enjoyed? Which do you think He might have avoided? Why?** Keep asking questions to try to show that Jesus was fully human. He felt many of the identical emotions and feelings that we have every day. Only by relating to His human experiences can we fully appreciate His divine function in our ultimate forgiveness and salvation.

STEP 5

When you get to the end of the session, don't downplay the importance of applying what has been learned. Just because your kids may not know much about the Bible doesn't mean they can't put into practice what they *do* know. So focus on the importance of servanthood with a skit. Simulate a restaurant setting in which three or four people are seated. Another person should approach and say, "Hello. My name is _____. I'll be your server this evening. What can I do for you?" The seated kids should answer honestly by listing needs they have. The server may or may not be able to help, but should try to do whatever he or she can do to accommodate the requests. Afterward, discuss how service need not be a negative or inconvenient concept. Willing servants learn to genuinely enjoy what they do for other people. After several of your group members have had the opportunity to "practice" on each other, challenge them to become more servant-minded toward other people at school.

STEP 2

At the end of Step 2, after challenging group members to live out their faith at school, continue the discussion by having kids analyze some of their friendships. Ask: **What do friends do that bring them closer together? What are the qualities and characteristics that you look for in a friend? Which of these attributes do you feel are most important?** Group members should come up with a list of elements of friendship that includes qualities such as good communication, shared interests, time spent together, forgiveness, patience, and so forth. After they do, go back through the list and discuss how each of these characteristics might apply to a relationship with Jesus. Can a relationship with Him grow stronger if we don't spend time, share what's on our minds, ask for help when we need it, and so forth? If group members can begin to perceive Jesus as a close friend rather than a remote force of the universe, their fellowship with each other will become stronger and their worship of Him will be more heartfelt and effective.

STEP 4

When Jesus was in the temple with the religious leaders, He was not only "listening to them," but He also had the opportunity for "asking them questions." Many young people have little, if any, opportunity to converse with church leaders one on one. If this is true for your group members, plan to have your pastor sit in on this session. Or you may want to plan a separate session in which group members can ask the pastor anything. Most young people are likely to have questions in mind—if not of their own, perhaps of some of the things they are asked by non-Christian kids at school. If they are slow getting started with their own questions, begin with a few of your own ("Where did the Bible come from and how do we know it's the Word of God?" "What do you tell someone who asks you what we believe at our church?").

STEP 1

For your group of mostly girls, you might want to add the following scenario to the skit choices at the beginning of the session:

• Someone is the only girl in the entire junior high school who doesn't wear makeup. Her parents have said she must wait until she's in high school. (She might keep makeup hidden and put it on when she gets to school, openly defy her parents and wear it anyway, try to sneak it past her parents, etc.)

STEP 2

If there are no guys in your group, you might want to ask a male from your church to make a guest appearance to portray Jesus. If possible, you could use a guy from another Sunday school class or someone your group members don't know at all. If you can't find a male recruit, ask one of your girls to portray Jesus. Give her some "male" props (such as a baseball cap) to use during the activity. No matter who you use for the roleplay, make sure you suggest to the group that this new student is a bit "different." Afterward, you can talk about how group members' advice would or wouldn't differ according to whether they thought the new person was a "loser" or not.

STEP 3

In the discussion about what Jesus might have been like, encourage your guys to speculate on the "toughness" of Jesus. Ask: **If Jesus were your age and going to your school, do you think He would get beat up a lot? Would He try out for baseball, football, soccer, or other sports? If so, what position(s) would He play? Would He enjoy roughhousing with the guys? If we were to hold an arm-wrestling competition among ourselves, where do you think He would place?** Explain that Jesus was never a weakling as an adult, and there is no reason to believe He might have been as a child. Though some guys have a tendency to think of Christian living as somehow unmanly, Jesus was perhaps the strongest person who ever lived when we consider His willingness to die on the cross for our sins.

STEP 4

Point out that Jesus was consistent in His behavior. He didn't seem to have one standard when His parents and teachers were around, and an entirely different one when they were absent. Can your guys make the same claim? Have a couple of group members create a number of skits in which someone walks up to his best friend and asks, "What did you do at the party this weekend?" The friend might admit that he checked out the girls, listened to some new rock CDs that were sexually suggestive, maybe had a drink or two, etc. After the conversation between friends, have someone playing your pastor walk up to the guy and ask exactly the same question. See how the person's answer varies. Other questions for additional skits might include the following: "How was your date with Jane the other night?" "What kind of trouble have you gotten into this week?" "Have you seen the latest *Sports Illustrated* swimsuit edition?"

STEP 1

Begin the session by playing Seat Shuffle. Have everyone sit in chairs in a circle (facing inward)—except for one person, who stands in the center. There should be one empty chair in the circle. The goal of the center person is to sit down. But as he or she approaches the empty seat, other group members should shift to that seat to try to prevent the person from sitting. This, of course, opens other seats. So the center person continues to try to fit in somewhere. When he or she finally lunges into an empty seat, the person to his or her right goes to the center. The game can demonstrate how difficult it is to "break in" to certain groups at school or elsewhere. Explain that even though it may be difficult to make honor clubs, sports teams, or other worthwhile groups, it is usually worth the effort. Even if we don't eventually make it, the struggle to get there can be beneficial.

STEP 5

You can make the application exercise more fun by adding a number of comic possibilities. For example, you might hand out index cards and pencils and ask kids to list the following:

(1) A word to describe their cafeteria food

(2) A nickname they might give their least liked teacher

(3) A word to describe the smell of their locker

(4) Something specific they plan to do this week to be better servants of others at school

Collect the cards and see how well group members can guess who wrote what. Pay special attention to the intended acts of service, but have fun with the rest.

MEDIA

STEP 2

If Jesus actually showed up at your group members' school(s), what kind of attention might it generate? Have kids form small groups. Instruct the members of each group to work together to write headlines and lead sentences for the school newspaper's coverage of Jesus' visit. As time permits, they can also work on the rest of the article. But their primary focus should be to craft a headline that will capture people's attention, followed by a lead sentence that would provide information and generate excitement about Jesus' unexpected appearance at school. Give the groups a few minutes to work. When everyone is finished, have each group share what it came up with.

STEP 3

Another thing kids would need to think about if Jesus were going to their school (as a fellow junior higher) would be what to write in His yearbook. Once a year, no medium is more important to young people than the yearbook. Ask: **How many times do you think Jesus' picture would be in the yearbook? What clubs would He belong to? In the candid shots, what do you think He would be doing?** After the discussion, pass around pieces of paper. Have each group member write down (1) what he or she would write in Jesus' yearbook, and (2) what he or she thinks Jesus might write (in return) at the end of a year spent together. Read group members' comments and see if they're beginning to get a sense of what Jesus might have been like as a junior higher.

SHORT MEETING TIME

STEP 2

Combine Steps 1 and 2 with the following activity. Explain that there's a kid who is hurriedly getting ready for his first day of junior high. He could really use some advice about what to do, what not to do, whom to hang out with, which teachers to avoid, etc. Unfortunately, he doesn't have time to stand around and talk; he has to catch the bus. So each of your group members should write this person a brief note that he can read on the bus, giving him some advice to alleviate the pressure of the first day of school. After a few minutes, ask volunteers to read their notes. Then announce that the new kid is Jesus. See if any kids would change their advice, knowing now who they're advising. Then move on to Step 3.

STEP 4

Skip Step 4; use the passage in Step 5 (Matthew 20:20-28) for your Bible study. To help kids understand what it means to be a "servant" at school, name some everyday school situations and let kids tell you what a servant's response would be. Here are some situations you could use:

• **One of your friends asks you to help him study for an upcoming history test. Usually when you study with this person, you spend so much time answering his questions that you don't get to study for yourself. The history test is two days away. If you help your friend study, you may not have enough time to prepare for the test yourself.**

• **Inga, the new transfer student from Sweden, asks you to sit with her at lunch. You're uncomfortable around Inga because you have a hard time understanding her when she speaks. You try to get some of your other friends to accompany you, but they refuse. They tease you about how boring your lunch with Inga is going to be and make plans to sit at a nearby table to make faces at you behind Inga's back.**

URBAN

STEP 2

For many urban kids who live in tough neighborhoods, simply getting to and from school is difficult. Add this fact to the "new kid" scenario. Ask your group members what advice they would give the new kid about getting to and from school safely. Some group members may suggest that the new kid get involved in extracurricular activities to avoid being out on the streets right after school. Others might suggest taking a bus or cab to school, if possible. Still others may suggest joining a gang for "protection." After you reveal that the new kid is Jesus, see how many of your group members would change their advice.

STEP 3

Bring in a wide array of clothing styles that one might find at a typical urban junior high school. (If such clothes aren't hanging in your closet, you may want to ask your group members to bring them in.) Place these clothes at the front of the room. Have kids form groups. Assign each group a particular "clique" or social group found in most urban junior high schools—jocks, computer geeks, burnouts, future "yuppies" or "buppies," etc. Instruct each group to come to the front of the room one at a time to choose the clothes that a person would have to wear to fit into its assigned social group. Afterward, discuss the importance of having the "right" clothes when it comes to fitting in at school.

STEP 1

When you form teams and assign skit topics, make sure you have at least one team of junior highers and one team of high schoolers. Instruct the teams to plan a skit in which a person's goal is to impress members of the other team. For example, the junior high team should act out the things a junior higher would do to try to capture the high schoolers' attention and admiration. The high school group, on the other hand, should try to come up with things they think junior highers would respond to. From the actions included in the skits, you should see how your kids perceive each other. After the skits have been performed, ask: **Which of the things illustrated by the other team did you find most effective? Which things wouldn't have worked on you at all? Do you find yourself ever trying to impress people who are older or younger than you? Why?**

STEP 4

After you read the story of Jesus in the temple, discuss what impact this twelve year old might have had on the "older and wiser" religious leaders. We know that the people in the temple were "amazed at His understanding and His answers," but we don't know exactly what they were thinking. Speculate about this. Have one of your youngest guys represent Jesus. Place him in the center of the room. Have everyone else suppose that he has just finished explaining to them exactly how the message of the minor prophets is relevant to young people today. Point out that besides his vast spiritual knowledge, the person is absolutely normal. Have other kids express what they would be thinking if this actually happened. Then discuss how the crowd of religious teachers must have felt as they witnessed such wisdom from a twelve year old. Challenge kids not to be intimidated by older people if they have something to say. They should contribute their own God-given wisdom in appropriate ways, regardless of the setting.

STEP 1

Begin the session very formally, as if it were a school classroom. (Or you might want to create an excuse to be absent and have another adult "fill in" for you. Your replacement should be very "proper" in demeanor and presentation of material.) Watch the responses of group members. How do they respond to a setting that is very much like school? Is it with dread? Rebellion? Enjoyment? Follow up with a verbal discussion of how they were feeling. Ask: **What things do we do in this group that you enjoy more than school? What are some things you do at school that might make this group more fun? What are the best emotions you feel at school? What are the worst?** It shouldn't take long to discover a lot about your group members' attitude toward school before going on with the rest of the session.

STEP 3

Repro Resource 3 may not apply as well to sixth graders as it does to older kids. Rather than make copies of the sheet and hand it out, you might want to pick and choose the activities on the sheet you want your kids to deal with (and add other situations of your own). One of the simplest ways to have group members respond is to read each statement and have everyone simultaneously hold up a number of fingers between 1 and 10 to indicate his or her level of comfort in that particular instance. Encourage people at either extreme of the scale to explain why they feel so strongly. It won't take long to go through the sheet with this method, and you can still cover much of the same material without dealing with things you don't feel group members are yet ready for.

DATE USED:

Approx. Time

STEP 1: *Whatever It Takes* _____
- ❏ Small Group
- ❏ Mostly Girls
- ❏ Extra Fun
- ❏ Combined Jr. High/High School
- ❏ Sixth Grade
Things needed:

STEP 2: *A New Kid in Town* _____
- ❏ Heard It All Before
- ❏ Little Bible Background
- ❏ Fellowship & Worship
- ❏ Mostly Girls
- ❏ Media
- ❏ Short Meeting Time
- ❏ Urban
Things needed:

STEP 3: *Cause for Concern?* _____
- ❏ Extra Action
- ❏ Large Group
- ❏ Mostly Guys
- ❏ Media
- ❏ Urban
- ❏ Sixth Grade
Things needed:

STEP 4: *Rabbi's Pet?* _____
- ❏ Heard It All Before
- ❏ Fellowship & Worship
- ❏ Mostly Guys
- ❏ Short Meeting Time
- ❏ Combined Jr. High/High School
Things needed:

STEP 5: *Don't Know Much About Servanthood* _____
- ❏ Extra Action
- ❏ Small Group
- ❏ Large Group
- ❏ Little Bible Background
- ❏ Extra Fun
Things needed:

What Would Jesus Do . . . in My Church?

YOUR GOALS FOR THIS SESSION:
Choose one or more

☐ To help kids see that much of their behavior at church may not reflect the intended goals of worship or of building a sense of community.

☐ To help kids understand that they are indeed valuable members of the body of Christ and should assume more ownership of what takes place during the church service.

☐ To help kids learn to tolerate the parts of the church service they find boring or nonproductive and to help them establish a stronger one-on-one relationship with Jesus as they do.

☐ Other:_____
_____

Your Bible Base:

Matthew 6:1-18
Luke 4:14-30
John 2:12-16

Praying Attention

(Needed: Copies of Repro Resource 5, pencils)

OPTIONS

Call for volunteers, one pair at a time. Each pair should conduct a "conversation" in which each person talks only about one of his or her concerns while neglecting to listen to the other person. For example, one person might talk about Friday night's game while the other talks about problems with her parents. The participants should take turns speaking, as in a conversation, yet not give any indication of hearing or responding to the other. See how long your volunteers can go without acknowledging what each other is saying. To add a twist to the activity, you might instruct the members of one pair to converse without using the word *I*. Then you might have the members of another pair use the word *I* in every sentence they speak.

Afterward, explain that these conversations model some of our attempts at worship and prayer. Sometimes we pour out everything we want Jesus to do for us, and He tries to answer; but because we haven't trained ourselves to listen, we can't hear Him. We just keep talking. Other times we may focus entirely on ourselves, or go to the other extreme and become so detached from the act of worship that we'd do just as well not to be there.

Hand out copies of "No-Point Bulletin" (Repro Resource 5) and pencils. Challenge group members to be honest as they describe what they *actually* do during certain segments of a worship service.

When everyone is finished, ask: **Do you find your mind wandering during church services pretty often, or only every once in a while?**

Why do you think it's sometimes so difficult to stay focused on what's going on in the church service?

On a scale of 1 to 10—with 10 being the worst—how bad do you think it is to sit through a church worship service without really paying attention to what's going on? Why?
Get several responses to each of these questions.

STEP 2

The Problem with Church

If group members seem tentative or reluctant to come right out and say that sometimes the church worship service just isn't exciting enough to hold their attention, have them respond to the following agree/disagree statements. Designate one wall as "Totally agree" and the opposite wall as "Totally disagree." Then read one statement at a time and let group members stand at the appropriate place in the room to show to what extent they agree with it. Here are some suggestions to get you started:

- **If people don't get something out of the church service, it indicates a spiritual problem on their part.**
- **People should leave every worship service feeling spiritually challenged, fulfilled, and excited.**
- **To be absolutely truthful, I find church boring much of the time.**
- **I would probably get more out of worship if I went off by myself and worshiped God on my own.**
- **Our church service is mostly for older people, not for people my age.**
- **The sermons are usually too long and formal.**
- **The music couldn't be any better.**
- **If I were in charge of the worship service, things would be a lot different.**

Some young people may be surprised to discover that not every older person is completely happy with the structure and format of corporate worship. You might want to be honest about any changes *you* would like to see, or describe alternative types of activities you've witnessed in other churches.

Then ask: **When people don't like the format of a church service, is their best option to leave and find another church? Explain.** If no one mentions it, suggest that finding another church might be the final answer, but it shouldn't be the first one. People need to express their opinions courteously to the appropriate leaders in the church—the pastor, board members, and so forth.

What can you do if you would like to see things done differently? It is fairly common to hear young people complain about how boring church is, but we may need to pay more attention to their comments. Such remarks show that they are involved and desire to see things change for the better. Help kids discover what steps they could take to suggest changes in your specific church. Might they volunteer to lead a service and teach some livelier songs to the congregation? Could representatives attend a board meeting or congregational meeting to express the feelings of the young people?

STEP 3

Rebel with a Cause

(Needed: Bibles)

OPTIONS

Ask: **If Jesus walked into our church and sat through the worship service one day, do you think He would want to see any changes made in the format? If so, what? Or do you think His primary concern would be in the responses and attitudes of the people in the congregation?** The first response of your young people might be that Jesus would note their lack of attention and want them to stop whining about the tempo of the songs and the length of the sermon. More than likely, they assume you're going to tell them to improve their attitudes. And while that might be a good idea, it is also important for them to see that even Jesus didn't always fit in during established, formal worship services.

Before you get into the actual Bible study in Step 4, have volunteers look up and read Luke 4:14-30 and John 2:12-16. Explain (somewhat tongue in cheek): **Since we look to Jesus as a model for how to live in almost every area of life, we should surely find good help for how to act in response to religious teaching and church life. These days we worship Jesus, but let's see what kind of worshiper Jesus was.**

Have your first volunteer read Luke 4:14-30. In this passage, group members should discover that

- Jesus took an active part in the worship services He attended, teaching in many places.
- Jesus was a good teacher. ("Everyone praised him" [vs. 15].)
- When He got to His hometown of Nazareth, He was not perceived so much as "Jesus, the great teacher," but rather "Jesus, Joe's kid."
- Jesus spoke the absolute truth even when He knew it might irritate His listeners. He didn't simply tell people what they wanted to hear.
- His "friends and neighbors" became so irate with Him that they tried to toss Him off a cliff.

Have your second volunteer read John 2:12-16. In this passage, group members should discover that

- Jesus worshiped not only on the sabbath, but also took part in special religious celebrations like the Passover.
- When He saw things He didn't like, He took action to do something about them.
- In extreme circumstances, His actions were immediate and severe.
- His anger was not due to His personal dissatisfaction with the worship, but rather that God's house was being treated with extreme disrespect.

Ask: **Are these our two best options for improving the church service: to speak our minds and risk death at the hands of fellow congregation members, or to pick up a whip and physically change the things we don't like? If not, what can we learn from these two examples of Jesus?** Point out that in both cases, Jesus displayed a desire for change. In one case, He was extremely vulnerable; in the other, He was extremely bold. It would appear that there is no single correct way to respond to the things we are dissatisfied with in our worship services. Our behavior should depend largely on the good or bad things that are taking place. We also need to remember that Jesus was a knowledgeable teacher who knew for sure what was right and wrong. Most young people are still in the learning stages. So they may not be justified in taking the exact same action that Jesus displayed.

Ask: **If you are powerless to change things you don't like or don't agree with in the worship service, what can you do?** Get a few responses.

STEP
4

It's a Secret

(Needed: Bibles)

Have kids form three groups. Assign each group a short section of Matthew 6 to read and discuss:

Group #1—Matthew 6:1-4
Group #2—Matthew 6:5-15
Group #3—Matthew 6:16-18

Explain that this portion of Scripture is part of Jesus' famous Sermon on the Mount. In this section He is dealing with right and wrong ways to

O P T I O N S

LARGE GROUP

LITTLE BIBLE BACKGROUND

FELLOWSHIP & WORSHIP

MOSTLY GIRLS

JR. HIGH HIGH SCHOOL COMBINED

worship. Ask each group to explain and/or demonstrate a right way and a wrong way to worship God, based on its assigned passage.

Group #1 should discuss the issue of giving. The wrong way to give to the needy is to make a big deal about it. Jesus describes trumpets being blown to announce giving by hypocritical men. Today some churches have other means of honoring major donors to the church. But Jesus says these people have their reward. God Himself rewards giving done in secret.

Group #2 will discuss the topic of prayer. Some people seem to enjoy praying "for show." Jesus tells us to pray on our own to God the Father. He also tells us that the quantity of our words is not nearly as important as the quality of what we're saying. Prayer should also be accompanied by action. As we ask God to forgive the things we've done wrong, we need to forgive people who've done things to offend us.

Group #3 has the shortest, but most challenging, of the passages. Since fasting is not a widespread church discipline these days, you might want to have group members think in terms of "suffering for the Lord." Sometimes people make a big deal about the sacrifices they make to be a good Christian. The principles concerning fasting can apply in such cases. If we're truly doing these things for God, we shouldn't complain or try to get other Christians to give us a pity party. Rather, we should show how much we're enjoying ourselves as we devote ourselves more completely to Him.

Say: **It's unrealistic to expect everything in a public worship service to conform exactly to the way we want it. Probably no church you attend will do everything to perfectly suit your mood every single Sunday. Much of what we get out of any church service has to do with what we put into it. And in extreme cases, you may find that the church is way off track and that you need to go somewhere else.** (Most congregations frown on young teens storming down the aisles with whips. These days we have many more options than worshipers during Jesus' time.)

But one thing Jesus tells us in the Sermon on the Mount is that *the secret to worship is secret worship.* **We shouldn't expect to have all of our needs met in a public church service. The church is comprised of many different kinds of people and personalities. It should be clear that not** *every-one* **will be completely satisfied with what goes on for one hour on Sunday morning. So Jesus tells us that our needs will be attended to during our regular personal times with God. If Jesus Himself didn't fit into a traditional worship service, we can expect to find ourselves feeling out of place from time to time. But Jesus didn't walk away and give up, and we shouldn't either. We should follow His example and try to make improvements where we can, all the while keeping our personal relationship with Him strong.**

Consultant Results

(Needed: Copies of Repro Resource 6, pencils)

Explain that sometimes churches spend large amounts of money to bring in consultants who will sit through several worship services and make recommendations for changes that will improve the quality of the worship. Designate your group members to be a consultant group and give them the same assignment. Hand out copies of "Any Ideas?" (Repro Resource 6), which will provide them with some things they need to consider in their evaluations. As time permits, try to tailor the sheet for your own worship service. Brainstorm specific goals to add to those already on the sheet. Each church is different, and the more specific you can be as to what group members should look for, the more they should get out of this exercise.

You might also want to have group members predict what they will discover during the church service, and later compare their expectations with what they actually discover. It's not unusual to focus so much on the few things we dislike about church that we miss out on all of the good things that take place. When young people take a fresh and objective look at the worship service, the church frequently looks like a much more promising place than they had originally thought.

Emphasize that group members should make evaluations based not on personal preferences, but on whether or not Jesus would be pleased with what's going on. The focus of a worship service should be Christ. When this is true, the good feelings of the participants usually become an automatic by-product.

Close with a challenge for your group members to work on any lax personal worship habits they might have developed. Encourage them to eliminate any signs of hypocrisy or other sinful attitudes from their own lives—and not to be so critical of others. Finally, offer praise in a closing prayer, asking Jesus to provide the insight to allow all group members (and leaders) to keep Him preeminent in their personal and corporate spiritual lives.

No-Point Bulletin

Believe it or not, a lot of thought goes into the structure of most church services. The pastor chooses the sermon topic and delivers it with much concern for the message. Hymns and other musical choices are made by someone—deliberately and with a lot of care. Offerings, prayers, and other aspects of the worship service are all planned to have a desired effect on the worshiper. So how do you think all of those planners feel when people come to church and talk or sleep through the whole service?

Below is a bulletin from an average Sunday at First Typical Church. You see what is planned, and the *intent* of each activity. But be honest in describing what you *really* do during each of these activities. Your list might include daydreaming, concentrating on what's being said, gum chewing, homework, note passing, and so forth.

PRELUDE (Instrumental music to prepare people's hearts and minds for worship)

DOXOLOGY (Singing "Praise God from whom all blessings flow . . ." helps us take our minds off of ourselves and focus our thoughts, together, on God.)

HYMNS (Sung to express joy and praise to God)

SPECIAL MUSIC/TESTIMONY (An opportunity for individuals to share spiritual blessings with the entire congregation)

OFFERING (The privilege of giving back to God a portion of what He has provided for us)

PASTORAL PRAYER (The pastor takes the needs of the congregation to the Lord in prayer and asks God for His blessing on the service.)

SERMON (The pastor helps make God's Word more relevant to us.)

CLOSING SONG (A final opportunity to send everyone away joyful and praising God)

BENEDICTION (A request for God's ongoing blessing on His people during the next week)

NOTES

Any Ideas?

   Let's suppose you've never attended your church before in your life, and you're going for the first time. In addition, let's say that someone is paying you to evaluate the worship service and make recommendations for things that might need to be changed and made better.

   Your first assignment is to sit through a church worship service, paying close attention to everything that goes on. As you do, assign a rating to each of the following categories by placing an X in the appropriate box (E = Excellent; G = Good; F = Fair; N = Needs improvement). Then, for everything that isn't already "Excellent," make some recommendations for how you think it can be improved. Remember, you must witness a church service from a fresh and unbiased point of view before your results will be considered valid.

	E	G	F	N	RECOMMENDATIONS
OVERALL ENVIRONMENT *THE BUILDING ITSELF* (Does everything look clean? Are the seats comfortable? Is the lighting good?)					
PERSONAL ATMOSPHERE (Are you greeted as you enter the door? Do the people seem friendly?)					
THE WORSHIP SERVICE *MUSIC* (Does the music set the proper mood for worship? Is it varied or pretty much the same style and tempo?)					
SERMON (Is the Word of God presented clearly? Did you learn anything you can apply this week?)					
FELLOWSHIP (Do you feel like part of a larger "body"? Is there an opportunity for you to contribute anything?)					
MISCELLANEOUS ASPECTS (Does the sequence of worship activities make sense? Did the service go smoothly?)					
OTHER CONSIDERATIONS In the space below, list other things you want to consider for your specific church; then rate them as you did the items above.					

NOTES

STEP 1

Begin the session with some kind of keep-away game (perhaps "Monkey in the Middle"), in which one person stands between two other people and tries to intercept a ball they are passing back and forth. If he or she successfully intercepts the ball, the person who threw it goes to the middle. Since the goal of the game is to prevent one person from receiving something sent from another, it can demonstrate the fact that sometimes we may be responsible for keeping other people from receiving a message or benefit from God. As you go through the rest of the session, focus on how we can help others worship more effectively rather than standing in their way.

STEP 2

As you begin to discuss problems with the church, take your group members to the sanctuary. When someone has a comment to make about some problem in the church or a suggested improvement, have him or her go to the appropriate place in the sanctuary and express his or her opinion. For example, if the person wants to say, "I think the preaching is too boring," he or she should go to the pulpit to make the statement. At that point, other group members should cheer or applaud at a level that will indicate their agreement with the statement. Give everyone who wishes to do so the opportunity to stand in an appropriate spot and state opinions about the church worship service as others reply with various levels of noise. Group members' comments will probably cover many of the agree/disagree statements listed in Step 2. If not, you can initiate a discussion on the points they neglect to mention.

STEP 2

Sometimes a young person's perceptions about church are strong, but not necessarily accurate. He or she may feel out of place or vastly outnumbered by "old" people. To see how accurate your kids' perceptions are, it might be interesting to estimate the average age of the people who go to your church. Have kids call out the names of everyone they can think of who attends your church. Write the names on the board as kids supply them. When you have a fairly sizable list of names, go back through them and try to estimate each person's age. Then add up the ages and divide that total by the number of names on the list to get your average. In many cases, when you consider the youngsters as well as the adults, the average age of churchgoers may not be nearly as high as your kids think. If you can help kids realize that they aren't so far from the median age of churchgoers, they may be willing to get more involved and feel that they're part of the church now, rather than waiting to "grow up" and participate at some future point.

STEP 5

Create a scenario in which a new disease of epidemic proportions has wiped out the entire world except for the people in your room. (Perhaps church potluck food was the only antidote to the disease.) Now that your kids are the future of the world, ask them how they plan to keep the church going. Would this be an important priority for them? What changes would they make as they set up *their* new church? Who will be responsible for making sure they continue to read and study the Bible? Who will lead the singing? Is anyone willing to take on the teaching and praying responsibilities? After some discussion, have kids consider that some day such responsibilities may indeed be theirs. The sooner they get involved and become more serious about contributing their talents and gifts to the church, the better prepared they will be when the opportunity eventually arises.

STEP 4

When you get ready to discuss the importance of individual worship, be aware that sometimes the tendency of members of a large group is to let participation in the group replace devotion to a more structured church service and/or personal spiritual growth. You might want to check to see if this is true of your group members. Explain that you will read a number of statements. Group members should stand if they agree and sit if they disagree. Some of your statements might include the following:
- **I think it's OK to miss church occasionally as long as I keep coming to this group.** (Answers may depend on what group members define as "occasionally.")
- **I think going to church is more important than coming to this group.**
- **I think spending time alone with God every day is more important than coming to this group once a week.**
- **I spend time alone with God every day.**

Use other statements you know will capture the attention of your specific group of young people.

STEP 5

As a follow-up to the discussion on the pros and cons of your own particular church service, you might want to set up groups to visit other churches in your area. First, have group members use Repro Resource 6 to evaluate your own church service. But then arrange to have them do the same thing in other churches. Many times young people have questions about what other denominations believe or how they worship. By forming groups to visit other churches and report back to the large group, kids will be able to answer a lot of their questions as well as get a better perspective on and appreciation for your church's own style of worship.

HEARD IT ALL BEFORE

STEP 2

Prior to the meeting, collect bulletins from a number of different churches in your area. Also bring a recent bulletin from your own church. Based only on the bulletins, have your kids rate the churches in order of best to worst. See where your own church fits in their estimation. Discuss what led kids to establish the ratings they chose. Then challenge some of their assumptions. For example, a church with a lot of youth activities scheduled for the week might have ranked high. If so, ask: **Would you be willing to spend 12** (or however many) **hours every week participating in these activities as well as Sunday worship, Bible study, and so forth? What if this church had so many people the leaders didn't even know your name?** Try to help kids see that they may tend to contrast the best points of other churches with the weaknesses of your church. If your kids are prone to jumping to conclusions before thinking a matter all the way through, this exercise might help them see that the carpeting isn't always greener in churches on the other side of town. Their own church has many good points and much to offer them.

STEP 3

After allowing kids to voice complaints about church in Step 2 and then considering what Jesus might think of your church in Step 3, try to make sure everyone has expressed his or her strongest dissatisfaction. Then have someone read I Corinthians 12:12, 26, 27. Have kids think in terms of the church as the body of Christ. Ask: **How do you think Jesus must feel when we complain about what He has called His "body"?** Point out that when we think of "church" as a building or a place to spend an hour on Sunday mornings, it's easy to find things to criticize. But if we shift our thinking to see it more as the body of Christ—of which each person is a valuable part—we may not be quite so quick to complain.

LITTLE BIBLE BACKGROUND

STEP 3

If your kids have little Bible background, you'll need to be careful as you cover the story of Jesus driving the salespeople out of the temple. Most kids should be able to understand why Jesus would be so angry—as long as you're careful to explain it and allow them to ask questions. Try to create a modern-day equivalent of the problem caused by the moneylenders. Say: **Suppose that you're in church this Sunday and the pastor is trying to explain an important passage to the congregation. Everyone is eager to hear what he has to say. Suddenly, people start walking up and down the aisles shouting, "T-shirts! Get your Pastor Smith T-shirts right here! Show your support. Only $18.95." Others are selling hot dogs and soft drinks "to help you keep up your strength and your attention level." Even though they might give valid reasons for selling their merchandise, do you think these people should be allowed to continue?** Let kids respond.

STEP 4

Kids with little Bible background are likely to need help both with understanding the reasons why personal daily devotions are important and how to get started. Be prepared to provide them with some help. You may be able to find good devotional books at a Christian bookstore. If not, have kids read through one of the Gospels. Break down the book into several short readings that can be studied a day at a time. The advantage of having kids focus on the same passages during their devotional time is that they can discuss what they're learning when they get together as a group. They can also ask questions, knowing that their confusion may be shared by others. Be careful to start slow and simple, and not to intimidate kids by challenging them to do too much. Once they get in the habit, they should begin to find their own pace for individual study.

FELLOWSHIP & WORSHIP

STEP 2

To increase the quality of your group members' corporate worship, you might want to plan a "pre-worship worship service" for Sunday morning. Arrange to meet together as a group just prior to the morning worship service. (Five or ten minutes should be plenty.) During this time when young people are so often running around, catching up on gossip, staking out the "best" seats in the back of the church, and so forth, have them instead focus on the upcoming worship service. Give group members the opportunity to volunteer to lead one-minute devotionals, pray, lead a praise chorus, or otherwise help everyone prepare to worship God more effectively during the following hour. If your kids become more expectant about getting something out of a worship service, the experience is much more likely to be beneficial for them.

STEP 4

A group devoted to improving worship may want to spend more time than most on the basics in Matthew 6. Rather than simply mentioning the activities in order to identify needs for personal devotion, group members should also evaluate how well they are doing in the areas of (1) giving, (2) prayer, and (3) fasting. They should set goals in each of these areas that need improvement. While as junior highers they may not have great quantities of money, and doing without food for long periods of time is not healthy for them, they should still be able to come up with some ideas that will make their personal times of worship more fulfilling. And when worship becomes more satisfying on a personal level, it should also be more uplifting in group settings as well.

MOSTLY GIRLS

MOSTLY GUYS

EXTRA FUN

STEP 1

After your girls have completed their "conversations," ask: **How did you feel when you were talking and you could tell the other person wasn't listening at all?** (Degraded, hurt, unvalued.) **How did it feel to see people not responding to each other?** (Frustrating.) **Have you ever been in a conversation like the ones we just heard? If so, how did you feel?** Use this discussion to introduce the topic of prayer.

STEP 4

As a group, brainstorm a list of specific things your group members can do to keep their personal relationships with Christ strong. Ideas might include having a personal praise time using favorite Christian music, starting a Bible study before or after school, keeping a consistent prayer time, etc. Be prepared to give personal examples that may help your girls think of other creative ways to worship God on their own that they may not have considered.

STEP 2

Guys who are actively involved in sports are probably familiar with awards ceremonies. Many junior highers have sat through such events that honor older athletes. Ask: **What if the church gave awards for achievement? What do you think some of the awards should be? Who in our church—or group—do you think might deserve to be recognized?** Group members should see that truly admirable qualities are things like humility, servanthood, and forgiveness. The whole concept of publicly awarding people for being humble may seem silly. Yet that is exactly the reason we need to be more alert to selfless acts by other people. They *aren't* getting awards for such qualities—at least, not while they're here on earth—so the least we can do is express appreciation for what others do for us and thank them every time we see them doing something selfless.

STEP 3

The idea of Jesus as a religious "rebel" may be new to your guys (who may be rebels in a different sense). Ask: **Is it really OK to stand up against traditions when those traditions are not good ones? Is it always right to do so, or would you say there are guidelines we should follow? What are some of those guidelines?** Many junior high guys tend to think of church and Christian things as "goody-goody." To help combat this tendency, you might want to ask your pastor or a male church board member to speak to the group about his own "normal" childhood. It may help your guys to discover that the pastor once borrowed a car to go joyriding, dated a lot of girls in college, used to work as a bookie, or whatever. It will also give the speaker an opportunity to explain how he went from being a "normal" guy to a leader of the church. Try to help kids see that much rebellion is destructive, yet there comes a time to rebel against a harmful, sinful lifestyle and dare to find something better.

STEP 2

Have group members compete in a "hymn sword drill." Give each participant a hymnal. Explain that you will call out a hymn and a verse number. The first person to stand and read the first line of the verse you asked for wins the round. Play as many rounds as you have time for. Afterward, lead in to a discussion of the things your kids dislike about your church's worship service.

STEP 5

Even if your group members don't have an opportunity (or the inclination) to lead a worship service and invigorate it with new and different ideas, they can still make church a more fun place to be. Have them think of an area of the church that they could decorate. Then get permission for them to do so. For example, they might paint a Sunday school room a brighter color. They might make posters or hang streamers. Or they might plan to bring snacks for the entire church one week. While the fun of this exercise seems to be directed toward other people, your group members should discover the sheer joy of working together in a spirit of servanthood. Few will be disappointed with the experience.

STEP 1

Perhaps your church's worship service seems too slow-paced for members of the MTV generation. So have your group members imagine that they're the people who put together MTV shows. They should think in terms of how to make the elements of worship more relevant and interesting for young people. What would be the setting? How many people would be involved in each worship service? How could they keep things from dragging? How will they ensure that the focus remains on worshiping Jesus and not merely on being entertained? Have kids struggle with all of these issues. Also challenge them to use as many different media as they can without hindering the flow of the events. When they finish, you might even want to carry out their ideas—if not for the entire congregation, at least among yourselves. While not every worship service needs to be (or ought to be) fast-paced, an occasional "peppy" one would probably be appreciated by everyone.

STEP 5

It might help your group members' efforts to act as a consultant group in your church if you videotape the worship service. If this is not done on a regular basis, have someone set up a video camera in an unobtrusive spot to capture the worship service on tape. Later, as group members comment on the things they noted on Repro Resource 6, you'll have the opportunity to locate their specific observations on the videotape and discuss them as a group. Another advantage of a videotape record is that it provides the chance to see exactly how much content of the worship service was overlooked the first time. Kids will probably find significant pieces of information or procedure they missed the first time.

STEP 2

Combine Steps 1 and 2 with the following activity. Have kids form groups. Instruct each group to plan an "ideal" Sunday worship service. In planning this service, group members should take into account as many factors as possible. For instance, what time would the service begin? How long would it last? What kinds of hymns or choruses would the congregation sing? Who would perform the special music? What topics would be covered in the pastor's sermon? How long would the sermon last? After a few minutes, have each group share and explain its ideal service. Then lead in to a discussion on what changes *Jesus* might make in your church's worship service.

STEP 5

Rather than handing out copies of Repro Resource 6 and trying to tailor the sheet to fit your church, ask kids to "rate" various areas of your church and its worship service. You might have them rate each area on a scale of 1 to 10 (with ten being the highest) by holding up the appropriate number of fingers to indicate their rating. Go through the list on Repro Resource 6, pausing after each category to allow a couple of group members to explain their rating. Then as you wrap up the session, challenge kids to focus on their *personal* worship habits.

STEP 2

If you find that your kids are reluctant or unable to identify specific weaknesses in their church, try offering them a biblical "measuring stick." Distribute paper and pencils. As a group, read Psalms 122, 133, and 150. After each psalm is read, have kids grade their church on a scale of 1 to 10 (with 10 being the highest) as to how well it practices the principles of that psalm. Group members should come up with three number grades (one for each psalm). When they've done that, they should add up the three numbers to get a "final grade" for the church. Use the following scale as a discussion starter regarding your kids' scores:

- 26-30—The church is riding high!
- 21-25—The church is cruising along nicely.
- 16-20—The church's engine is starting to sputter.
- 11-15—The church is just coasting.
- 0-10—The church's engine is dead!

STEP 5

As you wrap up the session, focus on the church's responsibility to its surrounding community. Ask: **On a scale of 1 to 10—with 10 being the highest— how much involvement do the churches in your area have in your community? Explain. How much involvement *should* churches have in their communities? Why? What would you like to see *your* church do for the people in your community?** You might want to use these questions in conjunction with the "church consultant" activity.

STEP 4

After you discuss the importance of personal worship, hand out graph paper and pencils. Ask group members to create "spiritual growth graphs." At intervals across the bottom of the page, on a horizontal line, they should write their ages, beginning with age six or so and continuing to their present age. The vertical portion of the graph will indicate degrees of spiritual commitment, with the age line as zero and the top of the page as a maximum level. Ask group members to think back as far as they can remember and create a graph to show periods of spiritual growth, times when they drifted away from God, and so forth. Assure them that most people will have a number of peaks and valleys. Theoretically, we should grow regularly throughout our lives, but most of us face spurts of growth—frequently after a very low period. Obviously your high schoolers will have a few more years to work with than the junior highers. Use this opportunity to see if they are getting closer to God during that time or farther away from Him. Point out that high school usually forces young people to go one direction or the other. Challenge your kids to continue to seek God's wisdom and power no matter what they face.

STEP 5

If personal devotions are to become a priority for your group members, many of your kids may need to be accountable to someone. You aren't likely to have enough time to monitor the daily devotions of all group members, so let them hold *each other* accountable. Pair kids together for regular devotions. Challenge them to maintain their personal devotionals every day (or almost every day), but also to get together with their assigned partner at least once a week. Try to team less mature people with those who can help them out (perhaps pairing high schoolers with junior highers). Check in a week or so to see how things are working out.

STEP 1

Replace the opening activity with an informal quiz. It's sometimes difficult to tell how much sixth graders know about certain basic spiritual truths, so try to get a feel for your group members' level of understanding before you try to lead this session. You might ask them to define terms such as *prayer, church, body of Christ, fellowship,* etc. Or you might have them try to draw such things using Pictionary rules. Whatever you think your group members would enjoy, watch and listen to see how complete their definitions and perceptions are about such things. If your kids don't have a good grasp of the basics, try to spend some time during the session explaining the concepts more thoroughly. If group members already have a good working knowledge of these spiritual concepts, you can move ahead with the session and build on what they know.

STEP 5

When you instruct group members to act as church consultants, be aware that many of your sixth graders may sit with their parents in church. Encourage them to sit together as a group as they take on the responsibility of evaluating the church service. It will help for them to compare observations, point out things to each other that might otherwise be missed, and begin to interact with each other on a positive level rather than simply talking or goofing off during the worship service. Sitting together should also begin to help them feel more "adult"—more like members of an important group instead of mere kids.

DATE USED:

Approx. Time

STEP 1: *Praying Attention* _____
- ❏ Extra Action
- ❏ Mostly Girls
- ❏ Media
- ❏ Sixth Grade
Things needed:

STEP 2: *The Problem with Church* _____
- ❏ Extra Action
- ❏ Small Group
- ❏ Heard It All Before
- ❏ Fellowship & Worship
- ❏ Mostly Guys
- ❏ Extra Fun
- ❏ Short Meeting Time
- ❏ Urban
Things needed:

STEP 3: *Rebel with a Cause* _____
- ❏ Heard It All Before
- ❏ Little Bible Background
- ❏ Mostly Guys
Things needed:

STEP 4: *It's a Secret* _____
- ❏ Large Group
- ❏ Little Bible Background
- ❏ Fellowship & Worship
- ❏ Mostly Girls
- ❏ Combined Jr. High/High School
Things needed:

STEP 5: *Consultant Results* _____
- ❏ Small Group
- ❏ Large Group
- ❏ Extra Fun
- ❏ Media
- ❏ Short Meeting Time
- ❏ Urban
- ❏ Combined Jr. High/High School
- ❏ Sixth Grade
Things needed:

4 What Would Jesus Do... with a Family Like Mine?

YOUR GOALS FOR THIS SESSION:

Choose one or more

☐ To help kids see that the problems they face in their families are probably shared by many other group members as well.

☐ To help kids understand that peace in the family is as much up to them as it is to their parents and siblings.

☐ To help kids create a specific plan to minimize problems and become happier within their families.

☐ Other:_____

_____

Your Bible Base:

Matthew 13:53-58
John 7:1-13; 19:25-27

The World's Best Family Member

(Needed: Copies of Repro Resource 7, pencils, tray of assorted items, prizes [optional])

Before kids arrive, place a tray of assorted items in the center of the meeting room. These can be any kind of items—just clean out the nearest closet, lost-and-found box, or odds-and-ends drawer. As kids arrive, ask them to familiarize themselves with the items. Then, as you begin the session, have each person select an item that represents his or her family in some way. Ask the person to explain his or her choice to the rest of the group. (For example, "My family is like this old Rubik's Cube, because once it gets out of whack it's almost impossible to get it together again." Or "The members of my family are like this pair of sunglasses because we are rarely completely open with each other. We seem to hide what we really feel.")

Explain: **Most families have problems—especially those that have junior high kids in them. But with a little effort from everyone involved, those problems can be worked out and differences can be settled.**

Of course, some kids are better than others, so we're going to have a "Best Family Member" contest. The first part of the contest will consist of an evaluation. Hand out copies of "The Best-Family-Member-in-the-World Contest" (Repro Resource 7) and pencils. **In the second part of the contest, the top-scoring people will undergo an interview process.**

Once group members complete the sheet, have them score their evaluations by adding together all of their points. (The maximum score is 200.) Call the three people who rated themselves highest to the front of the room. These will be your finalists. Let other group members ask them questions that will determine if they are truly the model children they have determined themselves to be. Group members should be allowed to challenge the answers of the finalists if they know differently. Or they might choose to ask how the finalists would react to certain situations. (For example, "Suppose your parents left you alone with specific instructions to wait for a very important phone call and a warning not to leave the house for any reason. If you then happened to see a $100 bill blowing across your yard, would you go out to get it?")

After sufficiently quizzing your finalists, let group members vote for who should win by using the old "volume of applause" method. If you wish, award your winner a prize for being your group's "Best Family Member" (or perhaps for being the "Group Member with the Answers Most Like the Ones the Leader Wanted to Hear").

God's Gift to Siblings

Have kids form two groups. Ask each group to put together a skit. Explain that you want both groups to consider what it must have been like for Jesus to have been a "typical" junior higher. Their skits should speculate on what life at home might have been like for Jesus as a young teen. You might preface the skits with this quote from *Halley's Bible Handbook:* "Of [Jesus'] childhood the Bible says little. . . . Jesus was the eldest of a family of [at least] seven children. . . . How we wish we had a glimpse of his home life—how the Son of God as a growing boy bore himself under the daily round of irritations usual in such a situation."

The first group should perform a skit to show Jesus at home, being "bossed around" by His parents. (Group members may want to drop in some of their favorite "hated" phrases that parents seem to use so often.) Knowing that it is God's will for children to obey and honor their parents, how would He have responded to being bossed around? (One possible result of this skit is to show that parents aren't sadistic. If a child does all he or she is asked to do, parents will usually be very pleased and accommodating.)

The second group should place the young Jesus in a more contemporary setting. Have the group members suppose that their parents have agreed to sponsor a transfer student from Israel. The student turns out to be the young Jesus. How would your group members relate to living in the same home with Him? What situations might cause some potential conflict or stress?

As the groups perform their skits, make a list of questions that are raised as to what behaviors Jesus might or might not display. As soon as the skits are over, divide the room into four quarters, designated as (1) Yes, definitely; (2) Probably; (3) Probably not; and (4) Definitely not. Read the questions one at a time. Group members should respond by standing in the appropriate quadrant of the room.

As necessary, use the following questions to supplement the ones you come up with.

OPTIONS

HEARD IT ALL BEFORE

LITTLE BIBLE BACKGROUND

FELLOWSHIP & WORSHIP

MOSTLY GIRLS

MOSTLY GUYS

JR. HIGH / HIGH SCHOOL COMBINED

- **Would Jesus ever question a command His parents gave Him?**
- **Would Jesus kiss His parents good-night?**
- **Would Jesus tell on His brothers and sisters when they misbehaved?**
- **Would Jesus ever yell at His brothers and sisters?**
- **Would Jesus ever have to be asked more than once to do something He said He would do?**
- **Would Jesus ever run away from home?**
- **Would Jesus try to grow up to be what His parents wanted Him to be—a doctor, a lawyer, etc.?**
- **Would Jesus ever tell anyone to hate his or her parents?**

This last query is a trick question. In fact, Jesus is quoted in Luke 14:26 as saying, "If anyone comes to me and does not hate his father and mother, his wife and children, his brothers and sisters—yes, even his own life—he cannot be my disciple." The next-to-last question should also provoke some thought. Junior highers are in the process of learning to think and reason for themselves, though most are still expected to do what their parents say. But if Jesus had not sought out His heavenly Father's will for His life, He may have lived a long and safe (and unnoticed) life as a carpenter like His earthly stepfather.

Explain: **Certainly we are to *love* and *obey* our parents according to the teachings of Scripture—and of Jesus. Yet at some point we must make our own decisions in life, particularly in regard to issues such as faith, salvation, and spiritual growth. If, as adults, we discover we cannot follow both the wishes of our parents and the commands of God, we may need to make some hard decisions to put the wishes of Jesus before even the wishes of our parents. Jesus is not telling us to *literally* hate our parents and siblings, yet we are not to allow even these people who are closest to us to interfere with our personal dedication to the Gospel.**

If you have completed Session 2 in this book, review the passage in Luke 2 that describes Jesus' extra days in the temple in Jerusalem after His parents had started home. Say: **When Jesus' parents came to get Him, they couldn't understand why their twelve-year-old boy had done what He did. And even though He could have been arrogant or argumentative, Scripture tells us "He went down to Nazareth with them and was obedient to them." When we think—or even are sure—that we know better than our parents, it is usually right to be obedient to them anyway. When we're older we can determine whether or not to do something other than what they advise.** You may want to mention that certainly exceptions should be made if a child is in an abusive or dangerous environment.

STEP
3

Our Brother Who Art Here among Us

(Needed: Bibles, paper, pencils)

OPTIONS

SMALL GROUP

LARGE GROUP

EXTRA FUN

Now that you've speculated on what it might be like for Jesus to interact with a human family, explain that we *are* able to know a little bit about what it was like for Him as a young adult.

Say: **God instituted the family structure, yet it sometimes falls far short of His intentions. Even Jesus' family had its problems. In fact, His family members had the extra burden of trying to cope with a "celebrity" who was followed by crowds, hated by religious leaders, and capable of wondrous and amazing miracles. How do you think Jesus' brothers and sisters felt when He began His public ministry and became so popular? Were they jealous? Doubtful? Confused? Angry?**

Have kids form three groups. Distribute paper and pencils and assign the following passages for the groups to read and report on:

Group #1—John 7:1-13
Group #2—John 19:25-27
Group #3—Matthew 13:53-58

In addition to explaining the facts of the story, each group should make a list of "principles for understanding and/or improving your family," based on the passage. You might want to suggest that it stands to reason that if Jesus Himself had family problems, we should expect them as well.

Group #1 (John 7:1-13) should see that Jesus' brothers had a problem with sibling rivalry. They seemed to be trying to get rid of Him. Even though they didn't believe in Him, they were trying to convince Him to "go public." Perhaps they thought if He became a famous person they wouldn't have to deal with Him anymore. Maybe they thought He would only embarrass Himself. Or were they aware that the Jewish leaders wanted to take His life? Whatever their motives, Jesus had to live with the problems that resulted.

Here are a few family principles that might come from this passage:

- Being good is not an absolute guarantee for getting along with family members. Families contain a number of imperfect people. No matter how pure one person is, problems can arise from others.
- Be yourself, not who someone else wants you to be.
- Evaluate the advice you receive from other family members.
- Find a way to put up with the problems you face. (For Jesus it meant sending His brothers off on their own while He kept to Himself.)

Group #2 (John 19:25-27) will discover that even when Jesus was dying on the cross, He was concerned about His mother's well-being. (It is generally assumed that His stepfather, Joseph, was no longer living at this time.) Even though Jesus had gotten in trouble with the law, had been accused of terrible things by the religious leaders, and was hanging on a cross as a public spectacle of humiliation, He wanted to do what He could for His mother.

Here are a few family principles that might come from this passage:
- No matter how old you get, don't lose your basic commitment to your parents. (Therefore, we should do what we can not to weaken or sever the relationship during our teen years.)
- When a parent-child relationship is good, you can expect that no matter how grim your circumstances get, your parents will be there for you. (And if the situation is reversed, you will be there for them.)
- Even though parents may not understand or agree with everything you do, they may still love you unconditionally.

Group #3 (Matt. 13:53-58) will deal more with the issue of family reputation. After becoming a public figure and amazing people throughout the area with His teachings, Jesus returned to His hometown. But when He got there, the townspeople couldn't appreciate Him for who He had become. They recited the names of His other family members as if to suggest, "Since the rest of His family are 'nobodies,' what makes Him think He's so special?" The family's reputation can have an effect on its individuals.

Here are a few family principles that might come from this passage:
- Sometimes we have to rise above, or perhaps struggle to live up to, the reputations of our families.
- People who put down you or your family a lot aren't necessarily right.
- People may judge our families as a group, but God will reward us as individuals. (So we can be supportive of our families, yet shouldn't let them hold us back if we sense that God has bigger plans for us than they do.)

These suggested principles are simply starting points. Your group members may come up with answers that are completely different, but even more meaningful to them.

STEP 4

The Good, the Bad, and the Family

OPTIONS

Of course, the whole reason we need to create principles to understand and get along better in our families is that families aren't perfect. Yet each person may tend to feel that the problems in his or her family are abnormal. The assumption may be that other families are like the Cleavers while one's own nuclear unit is more like the Addams Family. So spend a few minutes having everyone share his or her concerns and complaints by completing this sentence: "The worst thing about my family is . . ." Be sure group members think in terms of brothers and sisters (and even extended family) as well as parents. They may discover they share more complaints than they would have expected and will begin to empathize more with each other.

Then, when everyone has had a say, explain that it's easy to focus on what is wrong with families. So go around again and have each person complete this sentence: "The *best* thing about my family is . . ."

Help kids see that all families have their good *and* bad points. No family is perfect, nor is any family likely to be so completely terrible that it's worth giving up on. Explain that no matter what problems someone may be facing in his or her family, he or she can usually do *something* to begin to remedy the problem—even if no one else in the family seems willing to do so.

STEP 5

Today's Special: Complaints

(Needed: Cut-apart copies of Repro Resource 8, chalkboard and chalk or newsprint and marker)

Point out that when we face problems in our families, there are many options we can choose. The tendency may be to wait for parents to take action, but in many cases young people can play an active role in resolving family conflict. So have group members think of the "worst

O P T I O N S

SMALL GROUP

HEARD IT ALL BEFORE

FELLOWSHIP & WORSHIP

MOSTLY GIRLS

JR.HIGH HIGH SCHOOL COMBINED

SIXTH GRADE

things" they listed in Step 4 and then brainstorm ways that *they* might be able to make those situations better.

After compiling a list on the board, point out that even when your group members can't take an active role in making a bad situation better, they can take a *passive* one. On your list on the board you might want to include such options as being patient, not talking back even when parents might be wrong (and waiting for a better time to discuss the problem), and so forth. Explain that many times the things we *don't* do will improve a situation more than the things we actually try to do.

With this in mind, point out that the one thing that almost *never* works is complaining. Yet many times that is the most common course of action for young people. Summarize: **It's natural to complain when we don't like something or when we feel we're being treated unfairly. Yet if we don't set some limits on how much we complain, we tend to do it all of the time. Then our parents and other family members stop listening to what we have to say, even when we are trying to be helpful.**

Hand out "Complaint Coupons" (Repro Resource 8). (These should have been copied and cut apart prior to the session.) Explain that each time group members complain to a parent or family member this week, they should give up one of their coupons. Most parents understand that a certain amount of complaining is to be expected. But when the coupons run out, group members are no longer entitled to complain. Also explain that simply because they complain about something doesn't mean that the parent or family member must do what the young person wants. The coupon simply entitles him or her to strongly disagree. Determine as a group how many coupons each person should receive for the week. Also send home the parental explanation sheet that is included on Repro Resource 8 so the parents will understand how this activity should work. Then, at your next meeting, see if anyone has any coupons left (and how many people used theirs up on the first day).

Point out that you're not attempting to have group members deny what they are feeling. Emotions are natural and healthy. Yet there are usually constructive steps to take within our families when things don't go our way. Complaining is too negative and too easy. We need to work a bit harder to have the kind of families that pull together during hard times and are there for us when we need them.

Close with a prayer, specifically to give thanks for the families of your group members and to ask for the wisdom and perseverance to live at peace with family members as much of the time as possible.

The Best-Family-Member-in-the-World Contest

For each of the following statements, rate yourself as to how well you do (on average). A "1" means "Not at all" and a "10" means "All of the time." (For any statements that don't apply to you, give yourself a "5.")

I have a good attitude toward my mother and/or father.	1 2 3 4 5 6 7 8 9 10
I have a good attitude toward my sisters and/or brothers.	1 2 3 4 5 6 7 8 9 10
I add a lot of personality to my family.	1 2 3 4 5 6 7 8 9 10
I genuinely love and care for all of my family members.	1 2 3 4 5 6 7 8 9 10
When I don't get my own way, I am mature about it.	1 2 3 4 5 6 7 8 9 10
I am a peacemaker in my home.	1 2 3 4 5 6 7 8 9 10
I submit to the wishes of my parents.	1 2 3 4 5 6 7 8 9 10
I voluntarily act as a servant in my home.	1 2 3 4 5 6 7 8 9 10
I keep my room clean to please my parents.	1 2 3 4 5 6 7 8 9 10
I do whatever chores my parents ask, the first time they ask.	1 2 3 4 5 6 7 8 9 10
I am honest with my parents about how I feel.	1 2 3 4 5 6 7 8 9 10
I act the same when my parents aren't around as I do when they are.	1 2 3 4 5 6 7 8 9 10
I express content for whatever allowance my parents offer.	1 2 3 4 5 6 7 8 9 10
I am an excellent role model for my brothers and/or sisters.	1 2 3 4 5 6 7 8 9 10
No matter what happens, I refrain from whining.	1 2 3 4 5 6 7 8 9 10
I do all of my homework without my parents having to ask.	1 2 3 4 5 6 7 8 9 10
I get up in the morning the first time my parents wake me.	1 2 3 4 5 6 7 8 9 10
My thoughts toward my parents are pure.	1 2 3 4 5 6 7 8 9 10
I limit my time with things like TV, video games, and sports so I can develop better family relationships.	1 2 3 4 5 6 7 8 9 10
I tell family members most every day that I love them.	1 2 3 4 5 6 7 8 9 10

COMPLAINT COUPONS

EXPLANATION TO PARENTS

Dear Parents: We would appreciate your help with an experiment. The members of our group have been challenged to keep their complaining at home to a minimum. Toward this end, they have been issued a number of Complaint Coupons. Each time they whine or complain about something you don't feel is justified, request a coupon from them. When they run out, they should be expected to stop complaining. If possible, try to help them "ration" their coupons throughout the next week. We appreciate your support.

COMPLAINT COUPON

This coupon entitles the bearer to one complaint of his or her choice.

COMPLAINT COUPON

This coupon entitles the bearer to five complaints of his or her choice.

COMPLAINT COUPON
TWO-FOR-ONE SPECIAL

This coupon entitles the bearer to any two of the following activities:
Griping
Whining
Complaining
Moaning
Acting as if the world is about to come to an end

STEP 1

Rather than using existing objects to represent families in some way or another, hand out modeling clay and let group members create their own objects, shapes, or whatever. For example, you could start by having them create something to symbolize their families. Then they could form something to represent their *usual* feelings toward their families, their *current* attitude toward family members, the thing that holds their family together, something that interferes with family togetherness, and so forth. Most young people are good at creating symbols to represent feelings, attitudes, and other intangible concepts, so don't be reluctant to let them try.

STEP 4

Rather than merely having group members name the best and worst things about their families, use charades to do the same thing. One at a time, let group members act out what they consider to be the worst thing about their families. Then have them act out what they consider to be the best thing about their families. Keep the activity moving quickly, or it can drag out. If you keep up the pace, it probably won't take long for others to guess what each person is acting out.

STEP 3

Rather than having kids form small groups to cover all three passages, focus solely on John 7:1-13. Work on it as a group and then discuss it thoroughly, searching for practical application as you do. Ask: **Do you think Jesus fit in with His family? Why or why not? Do you ever feel left out of something the rest of your family likes to do? What can you learn from Jesus to help you deal with conflict or differences of opinion within the family? What else can you learn about family matters from this passage?** With a small group, make the most of the opportunity to interact with one another and offer support.

STEP 5

As part of the application of the material in this session, challenge kids to see fellow group members as a "family" of sorts. Ask: **How are we like a family? What are some things we can do to grow closer together? In what ways might this group be even better than your flesh-and-blood family?** In many cases, young people are able to be more open about problems and concerns with their peers in a safe environment rather than at home where they may feel they're being "grilled" by their parents. Try to do whatever you can to develop the feeling of family, perhaps even to the point of planning some meals together, sharing responsibilities and advice, and so forth.

STEP 1

Begin the meeting in an extremely small and cramped area. You may want to remove all chairs and have group members sit on the floor, with no room to stretch or get comfortable. See how far you can get in the session before kids start to complain or get on one another's nerves. At that point, move to a larger and more comfortable area to discuss how sometimes family problems can result from similar conditions of "not enough space" within the confines of one's house. Suggest that when we sense others are "cramping our style," we can choose to retreat and carve out some space for ourselves, rather than making life needlessly miserable for everyone else.

STEP 3

One advantage of a large group is being able to capitalize on the numerous insights and opinions on any given topic or passage. So when you get ready to do the Bible study, don't limit the number of groups to three. Form as many small groups as you can. Have several of them study each of the three passages given in the session. Ask the members of each small group to look closely for *three* principles for getting along better with their families. After a few minutes, have each group share its list of principles. While you're almost certain to get a bit of duplication, it may be surprising to see how varied some of the principles are from groups who studied the same passage. What may seem very clear to one group may have been missed completely by another.

HEARD IT ALL BEFORE

LITTLE BIBLE BACKGROUND

FELLOWSHIP & WORSHIP

STEP 2

After reminding group members of Jesus' attitude when His parents found Him in the temple, point out that they can (and should) imitate His example. To help them remember this, have them create a slogan based on the story and then make buttons or posters to broadcast the slogan. For example, they might come up with "Don't Push It!" as a catchy reminder that even though they may be right in disagreeing with a friend or family member, they can choose to be submissive as well. After several group members have offered ideas for slogans, choose one as a group to use for your buttons or posters. Encourage group members to remind one another of the slogan during stressful times when someone may seem to have forgotten about it.

STEP 5

Distribute paper and pencils. Instruct group members to write a description of a typical day in their family. In their descriptions, they should include information about what time each family member gets up; what it's like trying to get ready in the morning; which family members go to work, which ones go to school, and which ones stay home; what time everyone gets home; what everyone does in the evening; what time each person goes to bed; etc. After a few minutes, collect the sheets and shuffle them. Then read each one aloud while group members try to guess whose it is. Afterward, emphasize that for better or worse, all families are unique.

STEP 1

If your group members don't know a lot about the Bible, perhaps their parents don't either. If this is true, you might want to plan a "parents night" to present the material in this session. The parents might benefit just as much as the kids from a session on family relationships. In addition, this can be a natural opportunity to help both kids and their parents get a bit more comfortable with a church setting. You have something specific to offer since the teaching is more practical than theological. Almost every parent has the desire to do a good job raising kids. If you can provide good suggestions and challenge kids and parents simultaneously, who knows what might happen in the lives of your group members?

STEP 2

Kids don't need a lot of Bible background to know what it's like to experience sibling rivalry. Start with your group members' feelings about their brothers and sisters as you work your way into the Bible study. In addition to the agree/disagree questions about Jesus in the session, use the following discussion questions: **What would it feel like to have a brother who was a lot more popular than you? If you were jealous, what are some things you might do to "get even"? What would it be like to realize that your brother could "zap" you if he wanted to? Would you be more likely to ignore him, or to see how much you could get by with?** The Bible passages don't say much about Jesus and His siblings. The more you can help your group members learn to "read between the lines," the better they should be able to remember and apply the Bible to their own lives.

STEP 2

Have someone read Matthew 12:46-50. Point out that Jesus didn't limit His definition of "family" to those who were related to Him by flesh and blood. Rather, He included "whoever does the will of my Father in heaven." Using this definition, ask group members to expand *their* "families" this week. Have each person think of at least three people with whom he or she could spend time during the next week in an attempt to develop a sense of family. Point out that so far in life, your junior highers have had little inclination or opportunity to go beyond the concept of the nuclear family. But someday many of them will be going to college, jobs in other areas, or perhaps military service. When they do, they need to know how to make new friends and create an "extended family."

STEP 5

Close the session by putting together an impromptu worship time based on the family aspect of Christian faith—one that acknowledges what it means to be a member of the "family of God." Ask group members to tell you everything they know about being part of this family. They may wish to draw from Bible verses, songs, choruses, etc. (Rom. 8:15-17 is an excellent passage that deals with spiritual adoption, the privilege of calling God "Father," the rights of being co-heirs with Christ, and much more.) Remind group members that when they face problems in their *human* families, they should always remember that they can find unconditional love, forgiveness, and acceptance as a valued member of the family of God.

MOSTLY GIRLS

MOSTLY GUYS

EXTRA FUN

STEP 2

Use the following questions to supplement your discussion of Jesus: **Does the fact that Jesus was a man make it more difficult for you to identify with Him? Why or why not? If you were Jesus' sister, what do you think you would most admire about Him? Why? Do you think it would be difficult to grow up with a brother who never did anything wrong? Explain.**

STEP 5

In addition to using their "Complaint Coupons" this week, you may also wish to have your girls keep track of the things they complain about throughout the week. Then they can look at the list to see if there's a pattern or theme to their complaints. This may help your girls identify a specific trouble spot that needs some healing and/or discussion. Make yourself available to help group members with any problems they may wish to discuss.

STEP 1

The opening activity in the session may be a bit too abstract for some guys (who usually prefer a more direct approach). Instead, simply have group members complete the following sentences:

- **My family is so weird that . . .**
- **There's nothing wrong with my family that a good _____ wouldn't fix!**
- **If I turn out to be just like my parents, I think I'll . . .**
- **I think I could do without my family, except when . . .**

Some of the answers you receive may be exaggerated or comedic, but that's OK. Most will have a root of truth that will introduce problems or matters of concern to your guys. So as you go through the session, you'll be better prepared to deal with specifics rather than abstract concepts.

STEP 2

As you talk about how Jesus would likely respond in a number of home situations, try to emphasize to your guys that real men don't always need to prove that they're more correct, stronger, or more aggressive than everyone else. Sometimes they need to prove (like Jesus did) that they can take whatever anyone else can dish out, and then walk away—especially in family conflicts in which they have little to gain by pressing a point. You might even want to plan a "Nothing Fazes Me Night" for your guys. They should agree for a specified amount of time to live at peace with all family members—to neither provoke an argument nor respond in a way that would allow someone else to start one. This may sound easy, but is likely to be more difficult than kids think. (You may also want to mention this night to some of the parents, so they can monitor group members' success.)

STEP 1

A fun thing to do while you have a tray full of items on hand is play a memory game. Make sure you have at least twenty items on the tray. Keep the tray covered until you give a signal. Then, after letting the kids study the items for thirty seconds or so, cover the tray again. Hand out paper and pencils. Then have group members list all of the things they remember seeing on the tray. See which of your group members have the best memories. Later in the session, you can refer to how often we have "short-term memory" when it comes to how we act toward other family members. We know how we're *supposed* to treat them, but frequently we just don't take the time to recall what we know and put it into practice.

STEP 3

Begin this step with some role-reversal skits. Sometimes during conflicts with parents, kids get so accustomed to using their same old arguments that they hardly know what they're saying. So have some fun by letting group members play the roles of their parents while adults play the roles of kids. (If necessary, recruit some adults from the church for this activity.) Create some scenes in which your "kids" are trying to convince their "parents" to let them buy an expensive jacket, host a major party, buy a drum set, etc. Note the responses of the "parents." Do they say no while roleplaying adults simply because that's what they would expect to hear as kids? Or will they come up with several valid considerations before deciding whether to allow their "kids" to act on their wishes? After doing these skits and then discussing the problems Jesus faced in His family, group members may be able to recognize the many factors that are involved in making decisions—both on the part of parents in response to kids' requests, and for young people trying to keep peace within a family.

MEDIA

SHORT MEETING TIME

URBAN

STEP 1

After everyone has filled out the questionnaire on Repro Resource 7 and the top-scoring people have been announced, create a "media event." Have kids form groups, and let each group "campaign" for one of the "candidates." Instruct the groups to model their efforts after political campaigns as they write slogans, make posters, put together TV "ads," and so forth. After a few minutes, let each group make its presentation. You or some other impartial adult might want to evaluate the groups' campaigns based on effectiveness of the message, creativity, honesty, and so forth.

STEP 4

Rather than simply having group members express the best and worst things about their families, set up the room to resemble a talk show (Donahue, Oprah, or one of your favorites). Explain that today's topic is "Weird Families and the Strange Junior Highers Who Belong to Them." Wander around the room, soliciting comments about families. Whenever someone shares a "best" or "worst" thing, turn to the rest of the "audience" to see if they've been through a similar experience. You, as "host," might also take on an aggressive demeanor and challenge group members' answers. ("Oh, come on! Do you expect us to believe that's the worst thing about your family? Tell us how you *really* feel!") If you have access to a video camera, have someone tape the "show" so you can refer back to group members' comments if you need to.

STEP 1

If you want to cover a lot of material quickly, one option is to conduct your own "Family Feud" survey prior to the session. Talk to a number of parents and get their opinions on questions such as the following:

• **What is the major source of conflict in families?**

• **What is your favorite family tradition?**

• **What word or phrase do parents use perhaps a bit too often in your home?**

• **What word or phrase do kids use perhaps a bit too often in your home?**

• **How many times each hour would you say the average teenager complains about something?**

• **What is the least effective form of discipline/punishment used in your home?**

After getting answers from a number of parents, compute percentages to use for points. Then, to begin the session, play the game with your group members according to "Family Feud" rules. After playing the game, make appropriate comments about each problem area discussed.

STEP 4

If you're really short on time, combine Steps 3 and 4. Instead of having kids form small groups to report on the Scripture passages, go through the passages as a group. (Be sure to emphasize the principles outlined in the session.) During the Bible study, pass around two sheets of paper. At the top of one sheet, write "The worst thing about my family is . . ."; at the top of the other sheet, write "The best thing about my family is . . ." Have group members complete these statements and then pass the sheets on. At the end of the Bible study, collect the sheets and read aloud some of your group members' comments.

STEP 1

For a more accurate reading of your group members' family lives, have kids go through Repro Resource 7 again—this time marking an "X" on the scores that they believe their *family members* would give them. It's likely that at least some of these scores will be lower than the ones group members gave themselves. When kids have finished marking the second set of answers, have them add up the scores. Then have them compare the total from their second set of answers with the total from the first set. How much lower is the second total? As a group, discuss why family members might view us differently than we view ourselves.

STEP 4

Try using a brief object lesson to illustrate the point that good and bad things can be found in almost any family. Pass around an overripe apple—one that has gone bad in many spots, but is still edible. Say: **This apple is like most people's family life: There are good and rotten areas. But with God's help, the rotten can be sliced away while the good remains.** Using a knife, cut away the rotten parts of the apple, leaving only that which is edible. Then eat the remaining part of the apple.

STEP 2

Before the session, ask a junior higher to imagine that he or she is Jesus during the next few minutes. He or she should make mental notes of things that happen during the opening exercises that might capture Jesus' attention. The person shouldn't act any differently toward others, but should simply look for exemplary actions or areas that need improvement. When you get to Step 2 and begin to discuss how Jesus might respond in certain situations, let your volunteer report on what he or she has witnessed. Explain that even though the topic of the session is family relationships, the applications are the same. If older or stronger people tend to dominate others in a group setting, they're likely to do the same thing at home.

STEP 5

When kids disagree with parental rules, there are several options they can pursue: obey, throw a tantrum, rebel, complain, etc. Another option you might want to consider as a group is negotiation. Since young people are getting older and more capable of making their own decisions, they need to learn to reason with authority figures with whom they disagree. Set up some roleplays in which junior highers play themselves and high schoolers play their parents. The situations should involve the "parents" taking a very strict stand and the "children" wanting more freedom. Have the kids practice negotiating. See if they reach a point where they can agree that if the child meets certain criteria, the parents will allow a particular privilege. If the negotiations go well between your high schoolers and junior highers, you might suggest that kids find appropriate opportunities to try negotiating at home.

STEP 4

Older kids are likely to be able to think of the worst things about their families and automatically begin to think of ways to work them out. Once they identify the problem, the solutions are sometimes fairly simple. But younger kids may need some help realizing that they might be able to take the initiative to alleviate a problem. So after each person names the worst thing about his or her family, have the rest of the group members brainstorm ideas to help the person improve the situation. Some kids may be able to share out of personal experience. Others can offer fresh ideas and impartial insight. Young people may resist the advice of parents, teachers, or other authority figures. But if the same advice comes from a peer, they may be much more willing to try it.

STEP 5

Have all of your group members take hold (using only one hand) of a dollar bill at the same time. Explain that the person who holds on longest can keep it. See what happens in the tug-of-war that ensues. It may be that the dollar bill is ripped apart. Or perhaps one person will get it at the expense of all the others. Explain that families can be similarly damaged if we decide to do what we want to do—no matter what. Sixth graders are probably still very close to their parents. Now is a good time to challenge them to remain that way. Encourage them to be pliable as they go through adolescence—to yield to their parents' wishes much of the time even as they are developing their own unique personalities. If they aren't willing to give in a little bit, the family is likely to tear apart.

DATE USED:

Approx. Time

STEP 1: *The World's Best Family Member* _____
- ❏ Extra Action
- ❏ Large Group
- ❏ Little Bible Background
- ❏ Mostly Guys
- ❏ Extra Fun
- ❏ Media
- ❏ Short Meeting Time
- ❏ Urban
Things needed:

STEP 2: *God's Gift to Siblings* _____
- ❏ Heard It All Before
- ❏ Little Bible Background
- ❏ Fellowship & Worship
- ❏ Mostly Girls
- ❏ Mostly Guys
- ❏ Combined Jr. High/High School
Things needed:

STEP 3: *Our Brother Who Art Here among Us* _____
- ❏ Small Group
- ❏ Large Group
- ❏ Extra Fun
Things needed:

STEP 4: *The Good, the Bad, and the Family* _____
- ❏ Extra Action
- ❏ Media
- ❏ Short Meeting Time
- ❏ Urban
- ❏ Sixth Grade
Things needed:

STEP 5: *Today's Special: Complaints* _____
- ❏ Small Group
- ❏ Heard It All Before
- ❏ Fellowship & Worship
- ❏ Mostly Girls
- ❏ Combined Jr. High/High School
- ❏ Sixth Grade
Things needed:

What Would Jesus Do... with Friends Like Mine?

YOUR GOALS FOR THIS SESSION:
C h o o s e   o n e   o r   m o r e

☐ To help kids see that friendships can be established with various levels of commitment, and to challenge them to pursue positive and productive relationships.

☐ To help kids understand that they can relate to Jesus as a friend.

☐ To have kids discover more about others in the group and find common bonds that will help them strengthen current friendships and begin new ones.

☐ Other:_____
_____

Your Bible Base:

Proverbs 27:17
Matthew 14:22-33;
    16:13-28; 26:69-75
Luke 5:1-11
John 15:12-17; 21:15-19

Friendship Criteria

(Needed: Copies of Repro Resource 9, pencils)

Hand out copies of "Acme Build-Your-Own-Friend Design Kit" (Repro Resource 9) and pencils as kids arrive. Instruct group members to design the "perfect" friend. When they finish, have some volunteers describe the friends they created.

Then ask: **How similar is your description to a good friend you *already* have?** It may be common for young people to describe someone they know rather than conceptualize new possibilities. Have them consider that they have already put a lot of time and energy into existing relationships, and have learned to see the best in each other while overlooking most shortcomings. These friendships may seem "perfect" only because the friends have learned to like each other "as is." Rather than *perfect*, the relationship may be better described as comfortable and familiar.

How similar is your description to yourself? A person who lists his or her own qualities as those desired from a "perfect" friend might tend to feel that those are qualities *anyone* would look for. However, such people may have trouble making friends with people who have a different set of behaviors and characteristics.

If we are aware of what people are looking for in a friend, why aren't we better friends to more people? (It's one thing to know that people want unconditional love, forgiveness, and such qualities; it's quite another to *demonstrate* such characteristics consistently.)

Would you say that your "perfect" friend is stronger or weaker than you are? In what ways? Sometimes young people choose friends who aren't as strong or pretty as they are so they don't feel threatened. Others tend to gravitate toward more dynamic personalities who can provide them with a lot of friends, adventure, or other benefits. Both of these extremes can be based on selfish concerns and may need to be avoided.

STEP 2

Dream Come True?

Have a group of volunteers perform a skit. One person (perhaps a small person, but one who can take a lot of verbal chiding) should be the Victim. A number of others should be Tormentors who subject the Victim to a lot of merciless teasing, name-calling, and so forth. Ask the Tormentors to, as much as possible, use names and insults that they actually hear at school or in their neighborhoods. The Victim can try to defend himself verbally, though the others should outnumber him in size, number, and volume—making his attempts to endure the experience rather feeble.

After a while, stop the skit and "run it ahead" to the next day. Explain: **The group of tormentors tells the victim to return tomorrow, or they'll hunt him down and do even worse things to him. Their last words are "Don't make us come looking for you, or you'll be doubly sorry!" That night the victim doesn't sleep well, but at one point he dreams that he has the incredible power to do anything he wants to anyone. When he awakes, he finds that he actually has this power! When the neighbor's yipping chihuahua won't shut up, he says, "I wish that dog's lips were glued together for ten minutes so I could get some peace and quiet." Instantly the sound changes from a high-pitched bark to a rather confused whine. A few other experiments confirm that he can do *anything* he wants: grow an extra nose—temporarily—on his sister's forehead, shrink cattle to the size of Barbie dolls, or whatever. Now, armed with his new ability, it's time for him to meet his tormentors again.**

Resume the skit as the Victim approaches the group of Tormentors. But this time, the Victim can stop the action at any point and use his power if he so desires. He can simply say "Freeze," have the action come to a stop, and then explain what he wants done to each person.

Watch closely. Will the victim retaliate against his aggressors? If so, does he inflict the entire group at once or "pick them off" one at a time? Does he go after the leader only and see if the others then back off? After giving the Victim time to act, thank the skit participants and have them rejoin the group.

Ask: **What things would others of you have done to someone who treated you this way?**

OPTIONS

HEARD IT ALL BEFORE

MOSTLY GIRLS

MOSTLY GUYS

URBAN

Do you think the victim was (or would have been) justified in using his power? Why?

What *positive* changes would you like to make in your enemies—or even your friends—that would make them more fun to be around?

Explain that when Jesus was on earth, His situation wasn't much different from that of the victim in your skit. He was called names, made fun of, and criticized in numerous ways. He also had miraculous power at His disposal. But Jesus never used His power to harm anyone, or even (ordinarily) to get Himself out of a jam. It was used to help others. Rather than dwell on the torments and chiding of His enemies, Jesus focused on the positive things He could do with His friends and those who believed in Him. We can learn a lot from His example.

A Friend in Deed

(Needed: Bibles, paper, pencils, chalkboard and chalk or newsprint and markers)

Some of the sessions in this book have been (by necessity) somewhat speculative. We have no written record of how Jesus behaved in school, at home as a young teenager, and so forth. But we can see how He treated His friends—at least as an adult. In fact, there is far too much written about Jesus' relationships to cover in one meeting. This section will narrow the focus by examining a few "snapshots" of Jesus' friendship with one person—Peter.

Have kids form four groups. Assign one of the following "snapshots" to each group:

Group #1—Luke 5:1-11
Group #2—Matthew 14:22-33
Group #3—Matthew 16:13-28
Group #4—Matthew 26:69-75; John 21:15-19

Instruct the groups to read and discuss their assigned passages, and to write down anything they think is important for us to learn about friendship from the things Jesus and Peter (Simon) did together. After the groups have covered the material and compiled their lists, discuss their findings. At this point, try to keep the discussion and applications on an interpersonal level. Even though Peter was relating to Jesus (who was God), look for things that apply to a person-to-person relationship rather than making person-to-God applications.

Group #1 will look at one of Peter's first encounters with Jesus. Among other things, the group should discover that

- Jesus chose friends not for what they could do for Him, but for what He could do for them.
- Surprising things can happen when we lend our possessions to friends (as Peter discovered when he let Jesus use his boat).
- The advice of friends is worthwhile even when we feel we may know more than they do about a particular subject. (Even though Peter was an experienced fisherman, he obeyed Jesus' instructions—and benefited by doing so.)
- Some friendships in life will be more important than others, and deserve more of our time and energy. While we certainly shouldn't exclude people who want to be our friends, some of our relationships improve our lives while others don't. We need to devote more energy to relationships that will improve our lives rather than those that tempt us to do wrong or simply waste our time.
- People are more important than possessions. (Peter "left everything" to follow Jesus.)

Group #2 will examine a pastime that Jesus and Peter shared: walking on water. Among other things, the group should discover that

- Even our closest friends need a little "space" to be to themselves (as Jesus did).
- When situations seem strange, close friends encourage us (vs. 27).
- Friends should support each other in taking healthy risks (vss. 28-29).
- The expectations we have for our close friends may be higher than for other people. (Jesus chided Peter's lack of faith [vs. 31] even though Peter was the only one of the twelve who had ventured out of the boat.)

Group #3 should discuss Peter's confession of faith to Jesus, followed almost immediately by his inability to understand Jesus' mission. Among other things, the group should discover that

- Close friends have insight into each other that others don't. (While Peter's insight in this case was clearly God-given, the principle holds true in other cases as well. Time spent together and shared intimacies allow close friends to better understand each other.)
- Friends trust each other with responsibility (vs. 18).
- Friends trust each other with secrets that other people may not be able to cope with or keep to themselves (vss. 20-21).
- True friends should be able to deal with the truth about each other—no matter how distressing that truth might be (vss. 22-23).
- As close as we are to our friends, we should make sure we're even closer to God—for our own good as well as for theirs (vs. 23).

- Friends must make sacrifices in other areas to keep the friendship strong (vss. 24-28).

Group #4 will see Peter's denial of Jesus, followed by Jesus' post-resurrection reconciliation with Peter. Among other things, the group should discover that

- Personal fear can damage or destroy relationships.
- During stressful situations (like Jesus' arrest), even little things can seem threatening. For Peter, all it took was a couple of servant girls. For us, other things seem more dangerous than usual.
- Letting down a friend, for any reason, can be emotionally traumatic for both people (Matt. 26:75).
- True friends will forgive any offense against them (John 21:15-17).
- Close friends can talk about difficult subjects, even death (John 21:18-19).

As the groups report on their findings, try to compile a master list of "Friendship Principles" on the board (using only a word or two to abbreviate each principle.) Later in the session you will refer back to specific principles.

Friends in High Places

(Needed: Bibles, Repro Resource 9, list of friendship principles from Step 3)

Explain that the passages you examined concerning the relationship between Jesus and Peter provide a rich source from which we can draw principles to develop better friendships of our own. However, someone may point out that Peter had it easy. With Jesus as his friend, Peter could always be forgiven, always feel accepted and challenged, and so forth. Some young people may feel that their friends don't quite measure up to that standard.

Have someone read John 15:12-17. Many times this passage is used because of Jesus' command to "love each other." But this time point out that Jesus makes a significant change in the "status" of people who follow Him. He continues to be their Master, but *He also becomes their friend.*

Ask: **What do you think is the most important benefit of being a friend of Jesus? What do you think is the greatest responsibility?** Get a few responses.

Instruct group members to review their completed copies of Repro Resource 9. Then ask: **What qualities were you looking for in the**

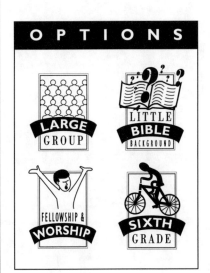

O P T I O N S

LARGE GROUP

LITTLE BIBLE BACKGROUND

FELLOWSHIP & WORSHIP

SIXTH GRADE

"perfect" friend? Other than specific physical specifications, how well does Jesus meet the descriptions you gave?

Refer again to the list of "Friendship Principles" compiled in Step 3. Ask: **Since Jesus has declared Himself to be our friend, what are some things from this list we can count on Him doing for us?**

What makes Jesus a *unique* friend? What can He do as our friend that no one else can do? It should be obvious that Jesus is the only *perfect* friend. His love is completely unconditional. His forgiveness is complete. His support and encouragement is unmatched. And with Jesus as a *best* friend, all of our other friendships grow stronger as well.

Is there anything you're looking for in a friend that Jesus *can't* provide? If young people are honest, a few may admit to occasionally looking to their friends to be "accomplices" in some activity they shouldn't be involved in. Older kids might want friends to be "drinking buddies." Younger ones may look for friends who will help them cheat on tests, copy homework, shoplift, experiment with smoking, and so forth. Many of these activities are rarely done on an individual level. Young people look for allies so they won't have to "take the rap" alone if they happen to get caught. Point out that Jesus is not that kind of "friend." A true friend will help others rise above such tendencies and do other things that will accomplish the same purposes (study with the person instead of cheating, loaning money instead of stealing, going bungee-jumping in search of adventure rather than smoking, etc.).

Have someone read Proverbs 27:17: "As iron sharpens iron, so one man sharpens another." Challenge your group members to become "sharpening" friends—people who have a positive influence of growth and self-improvement on each other.

STEP 5

Common Bond Bingo

(Needed: Copies of Repro Resource 10, pencils)

Ask: **Are there people you know whom you *shouldn't* be friendly with?** This may be a difficult question for some junior highers. As children, they were taught to avoid strangers. Yet as they near adulthood, your group members need to become a bit less reclusive and more open to new opportunities for relationships. It's easy to get within a group (clique) and not have to worry about people outside that group—especially when other people may have reputations as troublemakers, dweebs, snobs, or whatever. It's easier to write off such people for their negative characteristics rather than considering that they may have positive ones as well.

Summarize: **One reason so many people liked Jesus as a friend is that He liked them first. A person's reputation— what he or she had done in the past—didn't matter to Jesus. The important thing was what He could do for that person. And one of Jesus' best methods of making new friends was finding common bonds. With Simon Peter and Andrew, He started out by talking about fishing** (Mark 1:16-18). **With religious leaders, He used logic and knowledge to pique their interest** (John 3:1-21). **And with an unknown woman from another area—one whom most other men of His land would have avoided—He got a conversation started with the common bond of being thirsty** (John 4:1-26). **Many times the people who started out as strangers ended up as His friends and disciples.**

Explain that we can make friends with people we don't expect to be our friends if we start by finding something in common with those people. Even within your group there may be undiscovered common bonds that could help bring members closer together. Hand out copies of "Common Bond Bingo" (Repro Resource 10). See who can collect the most initials during the time you have left. And after group members get the hang of things to look for, challenge them to try the same thing with people at school—people who may seem lonely, overlooked, or otherwise in need of a friend. It's what Jesus would have done. And who knows? Just a bit of effort on the part of your group members this week might result in new (and lifelong) friendships.

NOTES

Acme Build-Your-Own-Friend Design Kit

You want friends, right? You pick and choose from all of the available options, but it seems so difficult to find someone who fits all of your criteria *perfectly*. Well, that's where we come in. We here at Acme Design-a-Friend want to help. Here is one of our sample forms for you to fill out. When you get finished, send us your specs. We'll search our vast files and deliver your new friend to you for a lifetime of friendship pleasure.

GENDER OF NEW FRIEND: o Male   o Female

DESIRED HEIGHT: _____

DESIRED WEIGHT: _____

DESIRED AGE: _____

HAIR COLOR: o Blond   o Black   o Brown   o Red   o Other: _____

HAIR STYLE: o Buzz cut   o Dreadlocks   o Beehive   o Other : _____

EYE COLOR: o Brown   o Blue   o Green   o Red   o Other: _____

APPEARANCE: o Drop-dead gorgeous   o Nice looking   o Pretty plain

OPTIONS:	YES	NO
Glasses	o	o
Contacts	o	o
Dandruff	o	o
Dimples	o	o
Freckles	o	o
Perfect suntan	o	o
"Genius" IQ	o	o

Other requests: _____

INTERESTS:
What extracurricular activities should this person be involved in?

What hobbies should this person enjoy?

SOCIAL LIFE: o Heavy dater   o Occasional dater   o Never dates

POPULARITY: o One of the cool people   o Average   o Kind of a dweeb

OTHER DESIRED "CUSTOMIZED" SPECIFICATIONS (qualities, strengths, weaknesses, etc.):

COMMON BOND BINGO

One of the secrets to making new friends and strengthening existing friendships is to find things you and other people have in common. So look for the following common bonds between you and other people in the group. When you find someone who fits a category, have him or her initial the appropriate square. However, you may use each person for only one category. The purpose is to see how many "bingos" you can get (up, down, or diagonally), so you may want to strategize a bit before letting people fill in the first category that applies.

Someone with a parent who has the same first, middle, or last name as one of your parents	Someone with the same hobby as you	Someone with the same teacher as you	Someone with the same favorite dessert as you	Someone with the same favorite sports team as you
Someone born the same month as you (regardless of age)	Someone the same height as you	Someone with the same number of brothers and sisters as you	Someone with the same favorite soft drink as you	Someone you've recently eaten a meal with
Someone you genuinely admire	Someone who shares your fondness for an unusual food or activity	**FREE SPACE**	Someone you would be willing to sing a duet with	Someone dressed in the same color as you are
Someone who knows one of your secrets	Someone whose voice sounds a little (or a lot) like yours	Someone with the same hair color as you	Someone just like you in terms of whether or not you wear braces and glasses/contacts	Someone just like you in terms of being right-handed or left-handed
Someone with the same favorite musical group as you	Someone with the same number of living grandparents as you	Someone with the same number of pets as you	Someone who enjoys your favorite board game or video game	Someone with the same hair length (or very close) as you

EXTRA ACTION

SMALL GROUP

LARGE GROUP

STEP 1

Begin the session with a drawing game (similar to Pictionary). Have kids form teams. Distribute paper and pencils to each team. Then allow one volunteer from each team to see the word he or she is to draw. At your signal, volunteers will begin to draw something to help their teammates guess the word. (Drawers may not use letters or symbols.) The first team to guess correctly wins a point. Play several rounds, using different drawers each time. The words you use for the game should represent characteristics of relationships. Some might be traits of true friendship, such as *honesty, communication, encouragement,* and *sacrifice.* Others might be symptoms of poor friendships, such as *gossip, flattery, put-downs, selfishness, jealousy,* and *conceit.* At the end of the game, have group members think back to what they've drawn and separate the qualities they want in their friendships from those they hope to avoid.

STEP 3

As each group discusses its assigned passage, have the members try to think of a similar incident in their own lives. They should then prepare a skit based on that incident. For instance, Group #1 might come up with a skit in which someone leaves one kind of lifestyle as soon as he or she makes a new friend who shows him or her a better way to live. Group #2 might come up with a skit about friends who challenge each other to greater levels of adventure and faith. Group #3 might come up with a skit about friends who see the best in each other. Group #4 might come up with a skit in which someone is forgiven for a terrible offense by a good friend. If groups need assistance, give general suggestions, but leave it up to them to come up with specifics. After each group presents its skit, the members should explain what it had to do with the Bible story they read.

STEP 3

Rather than using all four passages, focus solely on Luke 5:1-11. After reading the passage as a group, direct the discussion to the selection of Jesus' other disciples. Ask: **Why do you think Jesus limited the number of His disciples to 12? Why do you think Jesus spent more time with Peter, James, and John than He did with the other disciples? Did He like them better, or was there some other reason?** Help your kids see that Jesus seemed to know the benefits of having a small group. He could be more intimate with a circle of 12 (and even more so with a smaller group of three) than He could with huge crowds. He could train a small group to carry on after Him when He was gone. He could teach them how to relate not only to God, but to each other as well. Try to use this example to build up the members of your small group and help them become more devoted to each other.

STEP 5

The Bingo activity on Repro Resource 10 won't work as well with a small group as it will with a large one. But you can accomplish the same result in a number of other ways. One option is to pair up group members who don't know each very well (if that's possible in a small group), and then have the pairs compete to see which partners can find the most (or the most unusual) common bonds. Another option is to do the same thing *as a group.* If you have four people in the group, you must find common bonds among all four. Make a list of the common bonds you discover. Then plan some fun activities based on those common bonds.

STEP 3

Rather than having group members study the assigned passages, you might choose to have them act out some "friendship parables" instead. Explain that many of Jesus' parables were based on the needs and actions of friends. Have your kids form small groups. Assign each group one of Jesus' parables. Instruct the group to create a mini-play based on the parable. Among the parables you might use are the Friend in Need (Luke 11:5-10), the Good Samaritan (Luke 10:30-37), the Shrewd Manager (Luke 16:1-9), the Unmerciful Servant (Matthew 18:23-34), and the Moneylender (Luke 7:41-43). After each parable reenactment, have group members discuss what they think Jesus was saying in the parable. Also have them look for principles specifically related to friendship that they can find in these parables.

STEP 4

If a major goal of friendship is to "sharpen" one another (Proverbs 27:17), a large group of friends should be filled with opportunities. To help kids find out more about such opportunities, give each person a pencil and two sheets of paper. On the first sheet of paper, he or she should make a list of "Things I frequently need help with." On the other sheet, he or she should list "Things I'm pretty good at." Both lists should be specific and detailed. When everyone finishes, collect the sheets and look for matches. For example, some kids may frequently need help with math, while others are good at figuring out and explaining math problems. Sometimes kids are reluctant to share their needs with others. But if you can foster an environment of help and support in your group, many of your members may discover that much of their confusion and suffering is in vain.

STEP 1

Friendship is a fairly common topic—one that experienced youth group attenders are sure to have covered several times. To help them generate a new enthusiasm for the subject, begin the session by having kids imagine that this is the first time they're meeting. No one should know anything about anyone else. Have each person introduce himself or herself, sharing the things about his or her life that are most important. Afterward, ask: **If all you knew about anyone here is what you've just heard, who do you think you would try to make friends with first? Why?** (Some kids may be attracted to a person's sense of humor or some other characteristic. Others might pursue a common interest or hobby.) Look for surprises—people who hadn't considered themselves close friends who discover they have a lot in common. Point out that if we try to expand our circle of friends, we may discover many other people who will become just as close to us as our existing friends.

STEP 2

After the Tormentors/Victim skit, ask: **Are you more frequently a Tormentor of others or a Victim? Explain. Do you think this skit needed another character? If so, whom would you have added?** Let group members respond. If no one mentions it, point out that the skit probably could have used a person or persons to stand up for the Victim. It's good that we choose not to pick on people, but it's not enough. When we see people being tormented, we need to get involved on behalf of the victim. Sometimes "heard it all before" kids have a good grasp of the black and white sides of issues, but they are likely to need help seeing the shades of gray in between and their own need to perhaps reconsider where they're drawing personal lines of responsibility.

STEP 3

Most people have friends, but not everyone has thought about the quality of his or her friendships. Ask for three volunteers to act out the old scenario of a person trying to make a decision while a devil whispers temptations in one ear and an angel whispers good advice in the other ear. See which of the influences is more persuasive. Then, as you move into the Bible study, try to show that we need to choose our friends carefully. Point out that Jesus chose specific people to train as disciples, and those people chose to leave everything behind to follow Him. Say: **Think of all the friends you have now. Can you think of any wants or needs you have that those friendships don't fulfill?** Let kids respond. Point out the importance of having Christian friends who can help fill needs such as spiritual growth and genuine acceptance. Challenge group members to be more positive influences on the friends they currently have.

STEP 4

To people with little Bible background, the concept of Jesus being a friend may be new and incredible. Have group members list all of the specific acts of friendship they've experienced during the past week: receiving gifts, having favors done, spending time together with someone, being forgiven, etc. Then, in each case, try to help them see how Jesus fulfills that same function. Even though we don't have the opportunity to relate with Him in a tangible way, His friendship is more complete and long-lasting (eternal) than any other we could ever hope for. Try to help group members discover the value of having a friend who will never give up on them—no matter what they do.

STEP 3

After looking at the stories of Jesus' friendship with one person, Peter, have kids dwell on the *diversity* of friends Jesus had. Remind them that He was known (in an unflattering way) as "a friend of tax collectors and 'sinners'" (Matthew 11:19). Have kids name all of the people they can think of who were befriended by Jesus. The list might include His disciples (including a zealot, a tax collector, and a bunch of blue-collar workers), lepers, the woman at the well, Nicodemus (a pharisee), sick people, rich people, etc. After kids have come up with a sizable list, have them conduct a "celebration of uniqueness," in which each person thanks Jesus for his or her uniqueness. Point out that not only has God created a great diversity of people, but His Son accepts each of us equally. Then challenge kids to be more accepting of friends who are not at all like them.

STEP 4

Point out that we often look forward to going out with our friends. We plan fun stuff to do, things to talk about, etc. If Jesus is truly a friend, we should do the same thing with Him. Ask group members to write out (1) specific things Jesus has done for them that they haven't thanked Him for; (2) problems they need help with or advice for; (3) concerns about other friends or family members; (4) anything else they would normally discuss with a friend. Then ask kids to think of a specific time during the next week when they can get away from phones, TVs, and stereos long enough to spend time with Jesus. Encourage them to take a Bible along as well, because Jesus often talks to us through His written Word. Attempting to relate to Jesus as a "normal" friend may feel strange to your kids at first, but assure them it will become much more natural as they practice and get used to it.

STEP 1

Repro Resource 9 focuses primarily on outward or physical characteristics. So after your group members have completed the sheet, challenge them to make a list of internal qualities that they would like in a "perfect" friend. Then ask: **Do you know anyone who has all of these qualities? Do you think you'll ever know anyone who has the exact combination of qualities you described? Why or why not? What would it be like to have a friend like that?**

STEP 2

During the skit, make a list of the insults that are hurled at the Victim. Then, at the end of Step 2, refer back to the list. Ask: **How do you think the Victim felt when she heard these insults? How do you think you would have felt if you were the Victim?** As a group, discuss how Jesus might have responded to each insult.

STEP 2

Sometimes guys are better at losing friends than making them. So after the skit, ask each person to tell one or more "Tales of Lost Friendship." These should be true stories of why certain friendships ended. The stories should be as specific as possible. Group members should see that sometimes one person matures and outgrows a relationship. Sometimes friends move away and lose touch. Any number of valid reasons can break up a friendship. But if some of the stories include conflicts that could have been resolved, but weren't, explain that such arguments can break up relationships throughout our lives until we won't have any friends left. Challenge group members to attempt to resolve old conflicts that may still be lingering—even if they can't restore the friendship to what it was. Explain that it takes a strong person to "turn the other cheek" when offended by someone else.

STEP 5

Perhaps the hardest friendships for junior high boys to make are with junior high girls. So you might skip the "Common Bond Bingo" game. (Most guys have plenty of common interests.) Instead, have your guys brainstorm ways to strengthen their relationships with girls—as friends, not potential dating partners. (Try to keep the discussion on a very general level: **How can junior high guys get along better with junior high girls?** Otherwise, the conversation may quickly drift to who likes whom.) List suggestions on the board. Then say: **Think of three girls you know. Then think of at least one of the things we've listed that you can do to make your friendship with each girl stronger. Sometime this week try out the ideas with the girls you've chosen. Be ready to report at the next meeting and tell us what happened.** Make sure everyone agrees to do this. Agree as a group that anyone who fails to do this must do twice as much the following week.

STEP 1

Friends experience a lot of emotions during the development of their relationships. But sometimes it's difficult to express those emotions. To demonstrate this in a fun way, assign everyone in the group a different feeling or emotion. This should be done secretly—with the emotions either written on slips of paper or whispered in kids' ears. Some of the emotions might include rage, fear, love, pride, confusion, shock, disbelief, boredom, hatred, conceit, jealousy, panic, loneliness, rebellion, guilt, anxiety, and worthlessness. Have kids sit in a circle so that they can see everyone else. At your signal, simultaneously have everyone try to express his or her emotion *using facial expressions only*. Kids should try to hold their expressions so everyone else has a chance to see them. Then, one by one, let kids make their expressions while others guess what emotion the person is trying to convey.

STEP 5

If the "Common Bond Bingo" game works well with your group, continue the theme on a more personal level. Have kids sit in a circle. See how far you can get around the circle building a "bonding chain." Start with any group member and the person to his or her left. The two should find something they have in common—foods, hobbies, sports teams, likes, dislikes, etc. When they decide on something, it cannot be used again by any other pair. Then the second and third persons in the circle should try to find a common bond, and so on around the circle. This will seem very easy at first, particularly following the Bingo exercise. But establish a time limit so that pairs must think quickly. Anytime a pair is unable to find a common bond within the time limit, both must drop out. Then the bonding responsibilities are passed along to the next two people. Continue until time runs out or until you reduce the group to a single winning pair.

STEP 1

Friendship is a popular theme in the TV and film media. Have group members think of their favorite shows that demonstrate friendship. If possible, ask them to record key scenes ahead of time. If not, have them simply describe the friendship relationship and explain why it stands out for them. Then have them think of a TV or movie "pair" that represents their strongest friendship. (For example, a romantic friendship could be represented by *Antony and Cleopatra, Romeo and Juliet, Benny and Joon,* etc. A wacky friendship might be represented by *Beavis and Butthead.* If someone's best friend is a dog, an appropriate pair might be *Turner and Hooch.*) Encourage kids to be as creative as possible. To help them, you might want to have available some issues of *TV Guide* or movie review resources.

STEP 5

As an offshoot of video dating services, have your group members create a "video friendship service." Set up a video camera in a separate room. While the meeting is going on, pull out one person at a time to sit in front of the camera and give his or her name, interests, strong points, and qualifications for friendship. At the end of the session, have everyone watch the series of clips and see the wonderful variety of friendships contained within the group.

STEP 1

Rather than having everyone complete Repro Resource 9, ask two volunteers to act out a build-your-own-friend scenario. You'll need to have plenty of props and costume items available, including clothes, pillows, wigs, makeup, hair-styling gel, hairspray, eyeglasses, "instant tan" lotion, etc. Explain that one of the volunteers will play a person trying to build a "perfect" friend; the other person will play the friend he or she is trying to create. The first person will choose from Repro Resource 9 the "options" he or she wants his or her perfect friend to have. The second person will then put on the proper costume items to reflect those options. For instance, if the first person desires that his or her friend weigh 250 pounds, the second person must stuff two or three pillows under his or her shirt. If the first person desires that his or her friend have a beehive hairstyle, the second person must get to work with the styling gel and hairspray. Afterward, have your group members call out some of the things they look for in a friend.

STEP 5

Obviously, the "Common Bond Bingo" game could take a long time to complete. So instead of using it, instruct each group member to find three other people in the group with whom he or she has something in common. After a minute or two, ask volunteers to share any unusual common bonds they discovered. Then as you wrap up the session, point out that looking for common bonds is one of the first steps in making new friends.

STEP 2

As a group, brainstorm a list of ways in which a city kid might make an enemy of someone. Among other things, your kids might list the following actions: flashing gang signs, disputing a call in basketball, stealing someone else's boyfriend or girlfriend, spreading rumors about someone, etc. Then for each item on the list, brainstorm as a group three practical suggestions for turning that enemy into a friend. Encourage kids to write down the suggestions the group comes up with and use them as needed.

STEP 5

If you don't think "Common Bond Bingo" would work well with your urban group, try a game of "Be a Friend" instead. Give each person a pad of sticky notes and a pencil. After you point out that one of the reasons for Jesus' popularity was that He took the initiative in forming friendships, give your kids an opportunity to follow Jesus' example. Explain that the object of the game is to write each group member's full name (first, middle, and last)—along with something nice about that person—on a sticky note, and stick the note on the person's back. The first person to complete and stick notes on all other group members is the winner. To help ensure that kids will write sincerely nice comments about each other, you might list trite and obvious comments on the board that kids may not use. These might include comments like "You're nice," "You're funny," or "You're pretty." Requiring kids to write each other's full names will ensure that they talk to each other; creating a list of "off limits" comments will help ensure that they offer genuine compliments to each other. After the game, have kids pair up. Instruct each person to read to his or her partner the comments on the partner's back.

STEP 1

Combine your junior highers and high schoolers—literally. At the beginning of the session, use cords or lengths of yarn to connect high schoolers with junior highers (in pairs, or larger groups if necessary). Depending on your seating structure and planned activities, consider connecting wrists, ankles, or waists. Space should be provided for group members to maneuver without too much difficulty, but they should be close enough to be aware of each other's presence. Go through the skits, games, and other portions of the session with everyone "connected." At the end of the session, explain that just as it takes effort to operate when *literally* connected to someone else, it also takes effort to stay close to our friends, and to reach beyond our usual circle of acquaintances to include other people—especially those who may be older or younger than we are.

STEP 5

Since you have junior highers and high schoolers in the same group, let the members of each age-group serve as "experts" to represent the opinions of all people their age. Ask your experts to compile a list of specific things members of the other age-group need to do if they want to be friends with the experts' age-group. For example, ask your junior highers what high schoolers need to do to get along better with junior highers. You might want to have them fill in the blanks of a sentence like "If high schoolers really want to be friends with junior highers, they would stop _____ and start _____." After junior highers put together their list of what high schoolers should and shouldn't do, have the high schoolers list the things junior highers need to do to be better friends with the older age-group. Both groups may come up with some surprises about things they like and don't like.

STEP 1

Instead of using Repro Resource 9 to let individuals design perfect friends, work as a group (or groups) to do the same thing in person. Let one person from each group be the "prototype" for the perfect friend you're building. He or she should stand next to a wall as other group members write out criteria on pieces of paper, and either tape them to the wall behind the person or attach them in appropriate places on the person's clothing or body. ("A loving heart" would be attached to a shirt pocket; "Encouragement" would go near the mouth; etc.) Since you're dealing with real people, you should focus more on desired qualities and characteristics rather than physical attributes. Look for instances in which group members disagree on desired traits. Such differences of opinion are likely to be areas you need to deal with during the session that follows.

STEP 4

As you talk about having "sharpening" friends, and of how Jesus is a friend, you might want to provide a lasting reminder of how important these things are. Many sixth graders enjoy craft activities, and friendship bracelets are currently popular. You might want to provide the materials and let group members make bracelets, rings, or some other token of friendship that they could take home as a tangible reminder of the things they discuss during the meeting. If the items you make are "cool" enough, the kids are likely to wear them to school as well, which not only helps them remember why they made them, but also creates attention and curiosity about your youth group.

DATE USED:

Approx. Time

STEP 1: *Friendship Criteria* _____
- ❑ Extra Action
- ❑ Heard It All Before
- ❑ Mostly Girls
- ❑ Extra Fun
- ❑ Media
- ❑ Short Meeting Time
- ❑ Combined Jr. High/High School
- ❑ Sixth Grade

Things needed:

STEP 2: *Dream Come True?* _____
- ❑ Heard It All Before
- ❑ Mostly Girls
- ❑ Mostly Guys
- ❑ Urban

Things needed:

STEP 3: *A Friend in Deed* _____
- ❑ Extra Action
- ❑ Small Group
- ❑ Large Group
- ❑ Little Bible Background
- ❑ Fellowship & Worship

Things needed:

STEP 4: *Friends in High Places* _____
- ❑ Large Group
- ❑ Little Bible Background
- ❑ Fellowship & Worship
- ❑ Sixth Grade

Things needed:

STEP 5: *Common Bond Bingo* _____
- ❑ Small Group
- ❑ Mostly Guys
- ❑ Extra Fun
- ❑ Media
- ❑ Short Meeting Time
- ❑ Urban
- ❑ Combined Jr. High/High School

Things needed:

NOTES

NOTES

NOTES

Unit Two: Tongue Untwisters

The Power of Words

by Darrell Pearson

There are roughly 615,000 words that the Oxford English Dictionary lists as belonging to the English language. That's a lot of words. And that number doesn't include the nuances of meaning within words that give them such variety and texture. Nor does it include specialty words, such as those science puzzlers that only three people in the world use.

So why is everybody always saying the wrong thing? Aren't there enough words to choose from to find just the right thing to say?

Mouths in Action

Obviously, everyone suffers from the malady of inappropriate speech, but teenagers just might have the disease in the worst possible way. Perhaps the reason is that they have knowledge of only, say, 598,000 words—and the really *nice* ones are yet to be learned. Or maybe kids simply lack the wisdom and ability to carefully select the proper word for the correct situation. Regardless, young people are always having trouble with the things they say.

Here's where you come in. Being an adult leader with a complete working knowledge of 615,000 words, not to mention the adept social graces to use them accurately, you are in the unique situation of being able to help your group members come to grips with their lips, so to speak. Or, if you don't feel like you actually know a half million plus words, there's certainly some good news in this book, because it's chock full of practical advice for group members to learn how to better shape what comes out of their mouths.

I'll never forget when an eighth grader named Matt was chosen to come up front for a summer camp game. When a girl of the same age was chosen to assist, Matt exclaimed, "Not her! She's ugly!" I've often wondered what effect those cruel words had on this young lady who had to endure the embarrassment of 175 people staring at her to judge whether his words were true. (By the way, Matt was no physical dream-come-true.) Matt's words hurt her, and had he understood that simple fact— or cared—one young lady's view of the world that week would have been different. I'm sure that Matt never intended to hurt her. He was just speaking the truth as he saw it, though certainly not in love.

This is what teenagers do. They are constantly getting themselves into trouble with their mouths— whether it's with parents, friends, teachers, or youth leaders. They don't always like what they say, either; but they are so quick to talk before thinking that they put themselves in regrettable circumstances.

Tongue Tips

Here are a few thoughts that might help you help your group members as you work through the material in this book.

- *Stopping a group member in mid-sentence is sometimes OK.* Our tendency is to let kids talk when they've been asked a question (after all, we want to build their self-image), and generally, it's a good thing to let them do just that, even when the answer is hard to interpret or is on the wrong subject. But when it comes to kids publicly saying something that can be hurtful to others, don't hesitate to stop them or ignore them. Often they just want to see the shock value of their words, and you don't have to pander to their motivations.

  We have this problem once in a while at our *Next Exit* junior high events. We often send a microphone into the audience to get kids' thoughts on the subject at hand, and occasionally we find ourselves in the uncomfortable situation of having to deal with an inappropriate or offensive remark. We've found it best not to respond, not to make a joke out of it, but to simply ignore it or stop it and move on. (We also hang on to the microphone to retain control while the young person talks.) The audience is able to easily and comfortably adjust and move on to the next person's response. If you need to, don't hesitate to stop a young person in mid-sentence if it will prevent someone else from being offended.

- *Some offensive language is a given with some group members.* Junior high ministry in particular has never been for the squeamish or faint of heart. The leader who blows up at every offensive statement does not understand this age group. Quite often, the words that come out of kids' mouths come out with different intentions, somehow the phrase gets messed up in the delivery. Determine if the words you are hearing are intended to be hurtful, or if the person has just said something that he or she doesn't mean. Don't be too hard on the kid who is really trying.

  I once finished a brilliant (in my perspective) Sunday school lesson with an eighth-grade class. The students were spellbound (well, they were bound). When I finished, I asked if there were any questions. There was a short pause, and then a very pleasant girl raised her hand. "What time is this over?" She didn't mean to be hurtful, she just wanted to know when I was done. It never crossed her mind that I might be a little hurt after my significant effort. Try to remind yourself that part of the joy of working with junior and senior highers is their straightforward honesty.

- *Focus on the positive things you hear.* We don't reward kids often enough for the times they do say the right thing, and instead simply harp on them when they blow it. I read a phrase a few years ago in the book *The One Minute Manager* that has always helped me in this area: "Help people reach their full potential; catch them doing something right." When a junior higher strokes someone else with their words or comments positively about another's dress or behavior, notice it and tell them you were impressed. Your reinforcement of their choice of words will be remembered.

- *Model good word choice yourself.* How many times have you said something to your group members that you later regretted? ("OK, kids, today we're—*hey, shut up!!*—talking about—*I said, shut up!!!*—about choosing your words carefully . . .") Think about what you're going to say ahead of time, and show kids with your carefully chosen words how it's supposed to be done.

  It takes great patience sometimes to choose your words carefully. But you can bet that your kids will be listening closely to what you say and how you tame your own tongue. I still remember an incident when I was in high school in which a youth director responded very inappropriately to a young person. It was the beginning of the end for the leader; his credibility and our respect for him diminished remarkably after his ill-chosen words.

- *Create symbols or signs for your group that signify that it's time to be quiet or time to give someone a verbal stroke.* The sign could be a hand in front of the face, or a thumb up, or an index finger to the ear. Create one that you will use consistently and that will become a code signal for the whole group. Be willing to follow it yourself when someone shows you the sign.
- *Be aware that the verbal modeling kids get at home is often very poor.* With so many young people living in unusual family situations, frequently they reflect what they hear all of the time at home. A ninth-grade guy once told me that the best sexual advice he ever got from his stepdad was "Use it or lose it." No wonder he struggled with choosing appropriate words.
- *Teach the words of Jesus.* Make sure that you often have group members learn and read the words of Jesus. Remind them that Jesus' words were never boring, but full of wit, truth, honesty, concern, and challenge. They were also never inappropriate.

I've noticed that my closest adult friends—ones that have been long-time Christians—will often use a short phrase from Scripture in a humorous or meaningful way. They don't think about it; it just flows out of them. It comes from years of absorbing the Word. Help your kids to do just that. Teach them not to just live like Jesus, but to sound like Him as well. I don't know if Jesus knew 615,000 words in Aramaic, but I know that of the ones He did know, He chose them carefully.

Darrell Pearson is co-founder of 10 TO 20, an organization headquartered in Colorado Springs that creates high-involvement youth events for teenagers, including Next Exit, a junior high program that tours the U.S. and Canada each year.

The images on these two pages are designed to help you promote this course within your church and community. Feel free to photocopy anything here and adapt it to fit your publicity needs. The stuff on this page could be used as a flier that you send or hand out to kids— or as a bulletin insert. The stuff on the next page could be used to add visual interest to newsletters, calendars, bulletin boards, or other promotions. Be creative and have fun!

Has Your Mouth Ever Gotten You in Trouble?

Swearing, telling dirty jokes, cutting others down, gossiping, lying— these are just a few of the many ways that the tongue can cause problems. How can we control such a powerful weapon? Find out as we begin a new series called *Tongue Untwisters*.

Who:

When:

Where:

Questions? Call:

Unit Two: Tongue Untwisters

The dark side of humor.

If you can't say something nice...

The Dark Side
of Humor

YOUR GOALS FOR THIS SESSION:

Choose one or more

☐ To help kids recognize how inappropriate humor can be destructive.

☐ To help kids understand the difference between constructive humor and destructive humor.

☐ To help kids make a commitment to use constructive humor instead of destructive humor.

☐ Other:_____

_____

Your Bible Base:

Ephesians 5:4
James 3:7-10

Funny Bone

(Needed: Adult volunteer, chalkboard and chalk or newsprint and marker, prizes)

O P T I O N S

Have kids form two or three teams. If possible, try to use some natural divisions when forming the teams. For instance, you might have guys against girls. Or you might have a sixth-grade team, a seventh-grade team, and an eighth-grade team.

Instruct the members of each team to pull their chairs together. Have the teams separate themselves from each other as much as possible. Give the teams five minutes to come up with three jokes. Emphasize that the jokes *must* be clean. Announce that each joke must be told by a different representative from the team.

You'll need to find an adult volunteer to serve as an impartial judge for this activity. This person will award points for each joke on a scale of −100 to +100. Racist humor, sexual innuendoes, or any other inappropriate joke should receive negative points. Encourage your judge to be generous with the positive points. Most group members probably won't be able to tell a joke like a comedian, so any reasonably funny joke should receive over 75 points. Even dumb jokes should receive some points.

After five minutes, bring the teams together. Explain the point system and display the prizes that the teams will be competing for. Then have a representative from the first team stand up and tell his or her joke. The judge's score should be announced immediately and displayed on the board.

Be sure to encourage all of the joke-tellers—after all, many kids probably won't want to fill this role. Having group members tell the jokes will be fun for your kids, no matter how dumb the jokes are. It will also save you from attempting to tell a few jokes that will confirm the kids' suspicions about you!

After all of the representatives have told their jokes, total the points and award the prizes to the winning team.

STEP 2

The Anatomy of Funny

(Needed: VCR and videotape [optional])

Tell some kind of humorous story about your life—preferably a time when you did something really stupid or a time when something really funny happened to you. Allow group members to laugh at you. (Chances are that kids may not need much prompting to do this.)

Then ask for volunteers to share stories of times when something really funny happened to them. (Depending on the size and comfort-level of your group, you may or may not get responses to this.) Be sure to provide support and encouragement to any kids who are brave enough to share.

Afterward, ask: **What's the funniest movie you've ever seen? What made it funny?** Get several responses.

What movie tried to be funny, but was really dumb? Why wasn't it funny? Get several responses.

What's the funniest TV show on right now? Why is it funny? Get several responses.

If you have time, it would be great to show a Ren and Stimpy cartoon or some other short, off-the-wall video. Afterward, ask the kids what parts were funny and why.

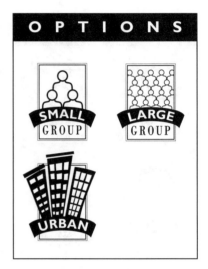

OPTIONS

SMALL GROUP

LARGE GROUP

URBAN

STEP 3

Distorted Funny

(Needed: Bibles, chalkboard and chalk or newsprint and marker, an out-of-focus picture or a pair of binoculars)

Hold up an out-of-focus picture. Ask: **What's wrong with this picture?** (It's out of focus; it's blurry.)

Is an out-of-focus picture as good as one that is clearly focused? Why not? (You can't see an out-of-focus picture as well as you can see an in-focus picture. Out-of-focus pictures bother the eyes.)

OPTIONS

EXTRA ACTION

LARGE GROUP

HEARD IT ALL BEFORE

LITTLE BIBLE BACKGROUND

MOSTLY GIRLS

MEDIA

If you can't find an out-of-focus picture, use binoculars instead. Make the binoculars as out-of-focus as possible. Then have two or three group members look through the lens and comment on what's wrong.

Afterward, say: **There are many things in our world that God made really good, but that Satan has distorted or made "out-of-focus" and turned into something bad. Can you think of some examples?** (God created music, but sometimes it gets distorted and becomes bad. God made sex, but it often gets distorted and becomes badly used. Another obvious connection is humor.)

How do you think God feels about humor? (Perhaps He enjoys some forms of humor; but He certainly frowns upon other types of humor.)

Can humor be a good thing? Explain. (Yes. Laughter can brighten a person's mood.)

Is there anything good that God didn't create? (No. All good things come from God.)

Draw a circle in the middle of your board. Write the word "good" in it. Then explain: **God wants our lives to be filled with joy. He made us to enjoy humor. Little babies can laugh long before they can talk. It's likely that there will be a lot of laughter in heaven.**

Write the word "humor" in the circle on the board. Then say: **But because Satan can't create anything on his own, he tries to distort God's good stuff—he makes things "out-of-focus."**

What are some ways that humor can get distorted and become destructive? (When it makes fun of people; when it uses sexual language that's wrong; when it tears down another race or perpetuates any kind of stereotypes.) List group members' answers on the board to the right of the circle.

Have kids form three groups. Assign each group one of the following Scripture passages: James 3:9-10; Ephesians 5:4; and James 3:7-8. Instruct each group to read its passage and discuss what the passage has to do with distorted or destructive humor.

After a few minutes, have each group share its conclusions. Use the following information to supplement your discussion of the passages.
- *James 3:9-10*—We're all made in God's likeness. When we joke about other people, not only are we hurting them, we're insulting God's craftsmanship.
- *Ephesians 5:4*—This is a clear command not to be involved in sexual humor.
- *James 3:7-8*—We can do a lot of destruction and damage to people with inappropriate joking.

Afterward, say: **Satan can really distort God's good creation of humor with this destructive stuff.** Point to the words and phrases you wrote to the right of the circle on the board. **Satan's very tricky. Just when we figure out how he's distorting**

God's truth in one direction, he'll distort it in a completely different direction. Point to the blank space to the left of the circle.

Ask: **If we're careful to avoid destructive humor, what's another way Satan could distort God's good creation of humor?** This question may be a little hard for your kids. If they can't come up with any ideas, ask: **Have you ever met a Christian who's being so careful to avoid bad humor that he or she refuses to have any fun at all?**

After you get a few responses, write "No Humor" to the left of the circle on the board. Then summarize: **God made humor. He made us to laugh. But Satan would love to distort that—to make it out-of-focus—in either direction. Satan would love you to live a boring life with no humor or joy at all. He'd also love you to involve yourself in a lot of destructive humor—listening and telling jokes and funny stories that are sexual, racial, mean, or even that mock God Himself.**

What's Good, What's Not?

(Needed: Copies of Repro Resource 1, pencils)

Hand out copies of "Humor Meter" (Repro Resource 1) and pencils. Say: **Let's see how good your judgment is. Some humor is obviously good and some humor is obviously destructive. But some humor isn't obvious at all. Draw a needle on each of the humor meters on this sheet to indicate how good or destructive you think that humor is.**

Give kids a few minutes to complete the sheet. When everyone is finished, go through the sheet one situation at a time, asking kids to share their responses for each humor meter. If you get varying results, ask kids to explain their responses. Encourage kids with strong feelings about a particular situation to debate the issue, but don't let arguments get out of hand.

STEP
5

Moving Forward

(Needed: Copies of Repro Resource 2, pencils)

Say: **Our world is full of destructive humor—and Satan makes sure that a lot of that destructive humor seems really fun to us.**

Hand out copies of "The Humor Highway" (Repro Resource 2). It would be great if you could copy this back-to-back with Repro Resource 1. Say: **Because this is such a tough area, let's think about taking one step forward on the "humor highway" this week.**

Have group members take a few minutes to privately mark where they would honestly place themselves on the Humor Highway diagram right now. Assure them that you won't be collecting these papers and that no one will see their answers.

Then say: **If you are willing to commit yourself to God to try to move one step forward on the diagram this week, draw a little arrow from where you first marked to where you'll try to be by the end of next week.** Instruct kids to sign their names next to the arrow to symbolize their commitment.

Close the session in prayer, asking God to give your group members strength to keep these commitments and to give them many opportunities to enjoy good humor the way He made it.

HUMOR METER

Draw a needle on each humor meter to indicate how good or destructive you think that type of humor is.

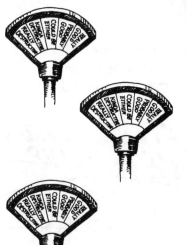

1. Your best friend tells you a dumb "knock-knock" joke.

2. A bunch of guys in a locker room are making jokes about the female anatomy.

3. A kid at your lunch table starts a joke by saying, "There was a Jew and a black guy walking down the street . . ."

4. You tell your brother that your parents want to sell him to a family overseas.

5. You and your friends are laughing about the size of your art teacher's nose.

6. A Christian kid from your youth group tells you a joke about Jesus stealing from someone.

7. A comedian on TV tells a whole series of jokes about having sex with her boyfriend.

8. You're reading the Sunday comics, and one of them about a caveman really cracks you up.

THE HUMOR HIGHWAY

Step 1: Place a mark on the highway to reflect your actions last week.
Step 2: Draw a little arrow toward where you'd like to be by the end of next week.
Step 3: Sign your name by the arrow as a symbol of your commitment to God.

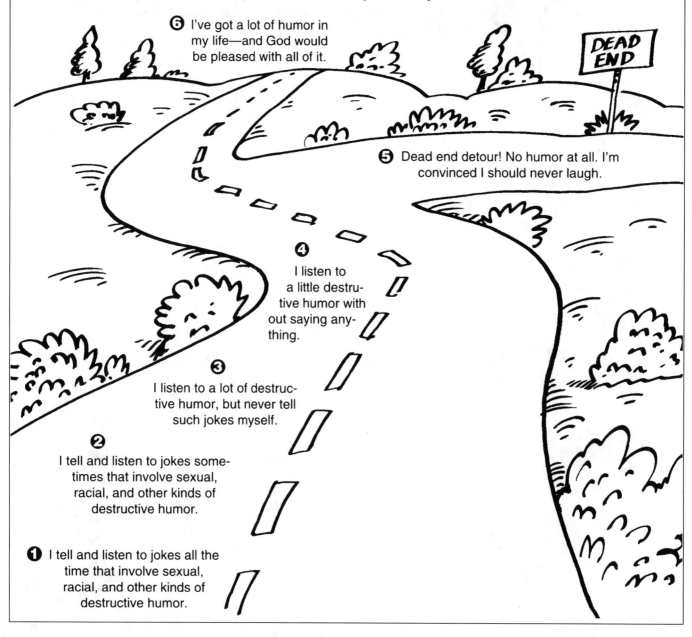

6 I've got a lot of humor in my life—and God would be pleased with all of it.

5 Dead end detour! No humor at all. I'm convinced I should never laugh.

4 I listen to a little destructive humor without saying anything.

3 I listen to a lot of destructive humor, but never tell such jokes myself.

2 I tell and listen to jokes sometimes that involve sexual, racial, and other kinds of destructive humor.

1 I tell and listen to jokes all the time that involve sexual, racial, and other kinds of destructive humor.

DEAD END

STEP 1

Try one or more of the following activities. (1) *Side-splitting Contest.* Give each team a trash bag and plenty of pillows. Have each team stuff pillows into its bag until the bag splits. The first team to "split a side" wins. (2) *Knee-slapping Contest.* Have kids sit in a circle. Slap your knees twice in a pattern (two quick slaps; one soft slap and one loud one; etc.). The next person must duplicate your pattern and add another. Work your way around the circle, with each person matching and adding. Anyone who makes a mistake is out; the last player left wins. (3) *Rib-tickling Contest.* Have your guys stand up. At your signal, girls will tickle them in the ribs. Any guy who can last for one minute without laughing gets a prize. Afterward, ask: **What kind of humor is side-splitting, knee-slapping, or rib-tickling to you? What kind of humor leaves you cold? Why?**

STEP 3

Give each person a newspaper cartoon. Let kids go outside and "turn a clean joke into a dirty one" by rubbing their cartoons in the dirt. Then challenge kids to "clean up" their jokes with soap and water—a difficult task. In Step 4, cut situations 2-6 from Repro Resource 1; put each situation in an envelope. Address each envelope to someone who could be hurt by each joke ("Female," "Jewish or African-American person," "Brother," etc.). Hide the envelopes. Explain that who-ever finds an envelope must take on the identity written on the envelope, read the situation, and consider how the joke could hurt him or her. In Step 5, have teams run a "Lighten Up" relay race. Each runner should wear a backpack filled with weights. Label each weight with a type of inappropriate humor ("sexual jokes," "racial slurs," etc.). Each runner may take out any weights whose corresponding types of humor he or she promises to avoid this week.

STEP 1

Rather than having kids form teams for the opening activity, try a different approach. Hand out paper and pencils. Instruct each person to write down his or her favorite inoffensive joke. After a few minutes, collect the papers. Read each joke aloud, trying to make it sound as funny as possible. As your impartial judge is rating the joke according to the scale described in the session plan, group members should try to guess whose joke it is. After the joke writer has been identified, have the judge reveal his or her score for the joke.

STEP 2

To expand the scope of the humorous anecdote activity for a small group, let each person tell *two* stories about himself or herself—one that's true and one that's made-up. After each person tells his or her stories, the rest of the group mem-bers should vote for the one they think is the true story. If they wish, they can keep score to see who is best at separating truth from lies. They might also want to determine who is the best (funniest) storyteller in the group.

STEP 2

With a large group, you're likely to have some "performers" in your midst. Give them a chance to put their talents to use by acting out some scenes from the funniest movies or TV shows they've ever seen. Emphasize that the scenes must be suitable (non-offensive, not suggestive) to perform in front of the group. Let kids work in pairs or small groups to prepare their presentations; then give each group one minute to perform.

STEP 3

Rather than holding up an out-of-focus picture, make the same point in another way. You'll need a music tape and a tape player with volume, bass, and treble controls. Announce that you've heard a great new song that you want your group members to hear. However, when you play the tape, turn up (or down) the bass and treble levels so that the song is completely distorted. Use this example to introduce the idea of distorted humor.

STEP 3

The Bible's opposition to certain kinds of humor probably is no surprise to kids. But they may wonder *why* these things are off limits, especially when "inappropriate" humor is used by most peers and adults. You may want to make the following points. (1) **Why is sexual humor off limits? Because sex is "dirty"? No. Sex was created by God, so it's good. But it's reserved for people who are married to each other. Most sexual jokes imply that sex outside of marriage is funny. Or they describe activities that unmarried people shouldn't be discussing with each other—either because the discussion revs up their sexual fantasies, or because it implies that it's cool to be sexually experienced whether you're married or not.** (2) **Why is "mean" humor off limits? Shouldn't people realize we're only joking? It's true that we see a lot of "funny" put-downs on TV sitcoms. If we were all fictional characters, maybe "insult" humor would be OK. But we're not. We have feelings, and feelings get hurt. Christians are supposed to put others' needs ahead of their own, even if it means having to skip a really "clever" remark about someone who's "hypersensitive."**

STEP 5

Jaded kids may mark (or ignore) Repro Resource 2 and forget the whole thing before you close in prayer. Make the exercise a little harder to forget by bringing a "smiley face" rubber stamp (or any stamp featuring a laughing or smiling character) and an ink pad. Have kids stamp their Repro Resources instead of drawing arrows, and then stamp the backs of their own hands as a reminder of what they did.

STEP 3

Explain to your kids that back in the "old" days, McDonald's promoted the Big Mac sandwich as "Two all-beef patties, special sauce, lettuce, cheese, pickles, onions, on a sesame seed bun." The promotion worked because the ads were run frequently, contests were held to see how quickly people could recite the phrase, and the slogan became a cool piece of information to know. See if any group members have memorized similarly complex, yet irrelevant information. Then explain that sometimes we (especially people with little Bible background) may assume that humor is never bad as long as no *actions* are taken. However, *words* can be wrong. Words that get embedded in our minds influence our thinking. Discuss the connection between attitudes and actions. Have kids repeat Philippians 4:8 a dozen times until it begins to stick in their minds: "Whatever is true, whatever is noble, whatever is right, whatever is pure, whatever is lovely, whatever is admirable—if anything is excellent or praiseworthy—think about such things." After kids memorize the verse, challenge them to think about what it means.

STEP 5

The Bible study in Step 3 may have been a bit jolting to kids who genuinely didn't know any better about improper joking around. To close, give kids the time and materials to make "flash cards" of the verses that most affected them and that they want to remember. Have them copy the verses on small cards to use as bookmarks, locker/mirror reminders, and so forth. Explain that change won't be easy, that they will need frequent reminders before they begin to see results.

STEP 1

Many kids—especially those who have grown up in the church—think all worship must be solemn and ceremoniously boring. They often don't see or hear that God wants us to rejoice in Him—to make a *joyful* noise unto Him. Before the session, prepare your meeting area for a worship celebration like your group members have never seen. Decorate with balloons and streamers, create a mood of celebration, and play some very upbeat worship and praise music. When the kids arrive, involve them in the music and celebration. After a few minutes, ask: **Did any of you ever think a worship service could be so joyful?** Get a few responses. Say: **God created joy and fun, just as He created everything else that's good. He wants us to have fun and enjoy life.** Then begin Step 1 in the session.

STEP 5

Set up a large paper "wall" on which kids can write "graffiti-style" their favorite jokes. Give kids markers, paint, or whatever else you have on hand. Then say: **We've just learned that God gave us the gift of humor and that there are good and not so good ways to use that gift. This wall is the "Champions Wall of Humor—proud sponsor of the U.S. Olympic Humor Team." On it, we are going to write our best fun stuff—jokes, humorous things that have happened to you, etc.** Let the kids go at it, making sure they use only appropriate humor. When they're done, hand out Good Humor ice cream bars, read the wall, and have a good laugh!

STEP 3

If your girls are open to sharing, ask: **How many of you can remember a time when you were on the receiving end of someone else's destructive humor?** Encourage those who share to describe how the experience made them feel. List the feelings that are described as group members share. Then ask: **For what purpose do you think God created humor?** As your girls share their thoughts, make another list. Afterward, compare the two lists and discuss the differences between them.

STEP 4

Change the situations on Repro Resource 1 as follows:

• 2. A bunch of girls are telling funny stories about a new girl who dresses and talks very differently than they do.

• 5. You and your friends are laughing at your youth leader's new haircut.

• 6. A Christian kid from your youth group tells a joke about the Virgin Mary.

After your group members have worked through Repro Resource 1, have them share some examples of situations they've been in that involved good or destructive humor. Discuss as a group how they reacted—or should have reacted.

STEP 4

After group members complete Repro Resource 1, focus your discussion on "locker room talk"—a problem that most guys will have to deal with. Ask: **Why do guys feel the need to get together and talk crudely about girls? Do you ever participate in locker room talk?** Point out that listening is participating. **Put yourself in the place of a girl who happened to overhear what was said about her. How would she feel? Would her feelings be justified? How would you feel about being evaluated purely on physical features?** Add other questions that you know would apply to your group of guys.

STEP 5

The application of the material covered in this session is a bit general. In many cases, guys tend to ignore opportunities unless they are spelled out clearly. So have your group members brainstorm specific ways to take one step forward on the "Humor Highway" this week. Ideas might include speaking up against the verbal abuse of others; countering negative comments with positive ones—at the risk of taking the brunt of the negative comments upon themselves; walking away from offensive people; and so on. Then ask each person to select one specific idea to put into practice this week. Close by motivating your guys with a personal challenge. Say: **What's the more manly thing to do: take part in cheap and hurtful humor or defend the dignity of someone else?**

STEP 1

Set up your room to suggest a comedy club's "Amateur Night," with a stage area and intimate seating for the spectators. Begin the meeting by letting kids take turns getting up and telling jokes. (Maintain the club atmosphere with applause, heckling, or whatever is appropriate.) You should make a list of the jokes that are told. Afterward, you can evaluate each one using the scoring system described in the session.

STEP 4

Introduce this step by showing some video clips (which you've pre-screened) from several recent movies. It shouldn't be hard to find examples of suggestive humor, put-downs of others, and so forth. After showing the clips, have kids work through Repro Resource 1. Wrap up this step by playing an audiocassette or a video of a Christian comedian performing clean humor that is truly funny. Let kids see that humor can be both enjoyable *and* uplifting if someone works at it hard enough.

STEP 1

Before the session, make an audio recording of a laughing audience (from a sound effects record or tape, a comedy album, or one of your pastor's funnier sermons). Make the recording at least a minute long, even if you have to record the same burst of laughter repeatedly. You'll be using this as a "laugh track" during your meeting. To start the session, play a one-minute, super-serious scene of a TV drama that you've recorded on your VCR; have your laugh track going at the same time and turn it up at inappropriate spots. Then ask: **How did this scene make you feel? Why? Are there some things in life that don't lend themselves to humor? If so, what? If not, why not?** You could also use your laugh track for the joke-telling contest by having your judge play the tape and turn the volume up and down to indicate scores.

STEP 3

To reinforce the idea that Christians don't have to be overly serious, play a contemporary Christian song that uses humor. Examples might include "I Want to Be a Clone" (Steve Taylor), "Fat Baby" (Amy Grant), "On One Condition" (Sonlight), and "Lookin' Out for Number One" (Wayne Watson). Or play a couple of minutes of comedy recorded by Christians such as Ken Davis, Bob Stromberg, Hicks and Cohagen, or Isaac Air Freight (check your Christian bookstore to see what's currently available).

STEP 1

Replace Steps 1 and 2 with a shorter opener called "Dueling Jokers." Before the session, cut humorous anecdotes and quotes from a copy of *Reader's Digest* or another family magazine. On a table at the front of your meeting place, put the clippings facedown in a pile. Have two group members come to the front. Each will choose a clipping and read it. The rest of the group will then vote on which item was funnier (cast tiebreaker votes yourself, if necessary). The reader of the losing item is declared "dead"; the winner picks another clipping and takes on another challenger. Keep track of who has the most wins in five minutes; give that person a prize, if you wish. Ask: **Why were some of these stories and quotes funnier than others? What kinds of humor do you like best?**

STEP 4

Instead of taking time to mark Repro Resource 1 and share results, try another option. Before the session, make a large version of a "humor meter" from the sheet, using cardboard and markers. Include the five headings and a moveable "needle" (fasten it with a brad or a piece of pipe cleaner). Have a volunteer come to the front of the room. Read the first situation from Repro Resource 1; then give kids 10 seconds to call out their responses, trying to convince the volunteer where to move the needle. Let the volunteer decide what the majority opinion seems to be. In Step 5, hand out Repro Resource 2 for kids to take with them and mark later.

STEP 2

Spend some time talking about TV shows like HBO's "Def Comedy Jam" and others that feature sexual and racial humor targeted to an urban audience. Ask: **Why do you think so many people find that kind of humor funny and enjoyable? How do you feel about that type of humor? Why?**

STEP 4

Add the following examples to Repro Resource 1:

• A guy in your class starts telling a story using an exaggerated Hispanic accent.

• To get some laughs, you make a comment about the way a homeless person in your neighborhood is dressed.

STEP 1

Ask: **What really makes you laugh?** On a large sheet of paper, make two columns—one labeled "Junior High" and the other labeled "High School." As kids begin to share what tickles their funny bones, write their responses in the appropriate columns. When they've completed their lists, spend a moment discussing their answers, noting any differences between the two columns. Then say: **Our standards and what we find funny may change from time to time, but God's standards for humor, as for everything else, never change.**

STEP 4

Change the situations on Repro Resource 1 as follows:

• 2. A bunch of guys in the locker room are laughing about a new guy, making fun of his physical development.

• 5. At a restaurant, you and your friends laugh at a waiter who appears to be gay.

• 6. A Christian kid from your youth group tells you a joke about Jesus having sex with someone.

STEP 1

Your sixth graders may be a little shy about telling jokes on their own. To ease their minds a bit, give them joke books to use. Have the team representatives choose jokes from the joke books to read. If kids use jokes from the books, they may not be quite as embarrassed if they receive few points from the judge.

STEP 5

Rather than having your sixth graders fill out Repro Resource 2, try another option. Hand out sticky notes with some kind of "just a reminder" message on the front. Have kids write on their sticky note one thing they plan to do in the coming week to avoid destructive humor. Encourage kids to keep their sticky notes handy as a reminder of their commitment.

DATE USED:

Approx. Time

STEP 1: *Funny Bone* _____
❑ Extra Action
❑ Small Group
❑ Fellowship & Worship
❑ Extra Fun
❑ Media
❑ Short Meeting Time
❑ Combined Junior High/High School
❑ Sixth Grade
Things needed:

STEP 2: *The Anatomy of Funny* _____
❑ Small Group
❑ Large Group
❑ Urban
Things needed:

STEP 3: *Distorted Funny* _____
❑ Extra Action
❑ Large Group
❑ Heard It All Before
❑ Little Bible Background
❑ Mostly Girls
❑ Media
Things needed:

STEP 4: *What's Good, What's Not?* _____
❑ Mostly Girls
❑ Mostly Guys
❑ Extra Fun
❑ Short Meeting Time
❑ Urban
❑ Combined Junior High/High School
Things needed:

STEP 5: *Moving Forward* _____
❑ Heard It All Before
❑ Little Bible Background
❑ Fellowship & Worship
❑ Mostly Guys
❑ Sixth Grade
Things needed:

Four-Letter Follies

C h o o s e   o n e   o r   m o r e

- [ ] To help kids recognize why swearing is wrong.

- [ ] To help kids understand that the language they use is a reflection of their heart and mind.

- [ ] To help kids identify at least one area of "foul intake" to eliminate from their lives.

- [ ] Other:_____
  _____

Your Bible Base:

Exodus 20:7
Matthew 12:33-34
Colossians 3:8, 17
James 1:26

STEP 1

Strange Transmission

(Needed: Copies of Repro Resource 3, pencils)

Hand out copies of "Strange Transmission" (Repro Resource 3) and pencils. Read aloud the instructions at the top of the sheet. Then have group members work in teams of three to complete the sheet. As kids work, walk around the room to make sure they understand what they're doing. The last thing you need is a group member taking home this sheet with actual swear words written all over it (unless you're hoping to get out of teaching junior high).

Give kids about five minutes to complete the sheet. When everyone is finished, have each team read the script it came up with.

Then ask: **What percent of the movies you see would you say have swearing in them? How do you feel about that kind of language in the movies you see?** Get several responses.

STEP 2

Don't Say It!

(Needed: Two copies of Repro Resource 4, watch or clock with a second hand)

Ask: **In what situations do junior highers you know swear?** (When they're surprised; when they hurt themselves; when they're mad at someone; when they want to sound tough.)

Why do you think people choose to use a swear word instead of some other word? (Because they like how the swear word sounds; because they want to shake people up; because it's the first word that comes to mind.)

Say: **It's possible that many people choose to use swear words because they're the first words that come to mind in certain situations. Most of us have probably heard people who normally don't swear get surprised or hurt themselves**

and blurt out a swear word. Maybe some of you have done that by mistake. That's a pretty normal thing to do when you hear those words all the time. We're going to play a game now in which you can't say the first words that pop into your mind.

- Have kids form two teams. Explain: **One at a time, I'll give you a card that has one word at the top written in capital letters. That's the word you will try to get your team to say. Below the word are five other words. These are five of the first words that would probably pop into your mind to describe the main word. You can't use any of these words or even any form of them. If you use one of these words, you lose the round. If your team guesses the main word in 10 seconds or less, you get three points. If you team guesses it in 10-20 seconds, you get two points. If your team guesses it in 20-30 seconds, you get one point. Thirty seconds is the maximum time. Also, you're not allowed to use any motions at all while you give clues.**

Call the first contestant from one team to the front of the room. Give him or her a card. Start the round within 10 seconds. (You don't want the person to be able to think very long.) Be sure to have an extra copy of the card that you can look at to check for violations. If a player uses any form of the five words (or the key word), make a loud buzzing sound and tell the person that his or her team has lost the round. Make sure that you remind every contestant that he or she can't use any motions—this is really hard for kids.

Continue back and forth between the two teams until you've used all of the cards. Then total the points and announce the winning team.

STEP 3

Squeaky Clean

(Needed: Bibles)

Ask: **What's wrong with swearing?** Get several responses.

What makes a swear word a swear word? Kids may offer answers like "because it's a dirty word" or "because it means something bad." These are somewhat true, but the real truth is that swear words are swear words in most cases because our culture decides they are.

If we made up a swear word, when, if ever, would it move from being a pretend swear word to a real swear word? (When our culture accepted it as a swear word.)

If someone you're passing on the street says, "Jesus Christ," how would you know if he or she is swearing or talking about God's Son?

Why does God care if we swear or not?

After several kids have responded, say: **Let's look at some verses in the Bible together.**

Have someone read aloud Colossians 3:8, 17. Then ask: **What does this passage say about swearing?** (It warns against "filthy language." Many swear words fall into this category.)

Have someone read aloud James 1:26. Then ask: **What does this verse say about swearing?** (It warns us to keep a "tight reign on [our] tongue." It also suggests that our Christianity is suspicious if we don't.)

Have someone read aloud Exodus 20:7. Many of your kids may know this verse because it's part of the Ten Commandments. Ask: **What does this verse say about swearing?** (It warns against using the Lord's name in vain. "In vain" means for no good reason.)

How would you feel if your name became a common vulgar swear word? How do you think God feels about it?

After you've gotten a few responses, say: **As you can see, God makes it pretty clear in the Bible that He doesn't like swearing. So every time we swear, it's kind of like saying to God, "I really don't care what You think."**

STEP 4

A Difference of Opinions

(Needed: Copies of Repro Resource 5, pencils)

Hand out copies of "Opinions" (Repro Resource 5). Read each opinion aloud. Then have group members check one of the boxes—"Totally disagree," "Kinda disagree," "Kinda agree," or "Totally agree"—to indicate their response. After everyone has checked one of the boxes, have volunteers share their responses. Then, as a group, discuss the responses.

Say: **Think of five of your closest friends. Which of these opinions concerning swearing do you think is closest to the opinions of your friends? Which opinion is closest to your opinion?** Volunteers may respond aloud if they wish, but you're really just asking group members to consider the questions silently.

STEP 5

Input-Output

(Needed: Bibles)

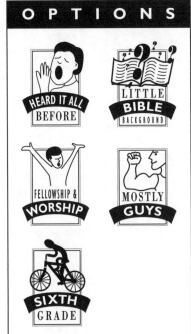
Remind group members of the game you played earlier in the session—the one in which contestants couldn't say most of the words that probably were the first to come to mind.

Say: **We've hinted at this a few times already, but we're going to take one last look at it. Simply knowing that swearing is wrong, and even deciding not to swear, may not be enough to really help some of you. Because you hear swearing so much, swear words are often the first words that come to your mind in certain situations. We take information in through our ears and keep it in two huge storage tanks—our mind and our heart.**

Have group members turn in their Bibles to Matthew 12:33-34. Ask someone to read the passage aloud. This passage tells us that what comes out of our mouths is the overflow of our hearts. Suggest that we need to examine our input in order to help control our output.

Ask: **Where are some of the places you hear swearing?** (Friends, TV, movies, videos, music, family members, etc.)

In which of these areas can you control how much input you receive? For instance, you might not be able to control the input level from a father who swears all the time, but you probably can control input from some of the other sources.

To close the session, give your kids a minute or two to pray silently to God, asking Him to help them figure out how to cut down on the foul input in their lives.

NOTES

STRANGE TRANSMISSION

Our church fax machine received a strange transmission the other day. As far as we can tell, it's a page from a movie script. But it seems to be an alien script. The fax machine must have known which words were swear words, because it left them all out. Your job is to come up with alien words to fill in the blanks. However, they can't be anything like any words you've heard here on earth.

The Torkshtuck Factor

Characters: Floit, the ultra-tough intergalactic cop; Crambot, the big-time intergalactic crime boss; Snorful, Floit's sidekick

FLOIT: Ah-hah, it's you, Crambot, you filthy _____. I knew we'd find your _____ hideout.

SNORFUL: Yeah, all I can say is _____.

CRAMBOT: Ha, ha, ha! _____! You think you little _____ scare me? Take this! *(Crambot shoots Snorful with his intergalactic zapper.)*

SNORFUL: Oh _____, he shot me. You lousy _____!

FLOIT: That's the last _____ straw, Crambot! Die, you _____!

CRAMBOT & FLOIT: Aargh! *(Both shoot each other at the same time.)*

DON'T Say It!

SCHOOL
class
building
grade
teacher
bus

TEST
quiz
paper
school
class
write

FRIEND
pal
buddy
hang out
best
talk

CHURCH
building
here
God
Sunday
(your church name)

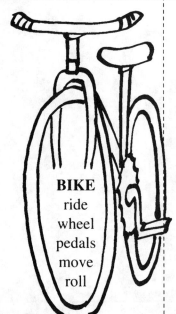

BIKE
ride
wheel
pedals
move
roll

EAT
food
mouth
drink
taste
chew

TV
show
movie
watch
videos
(name of any show)

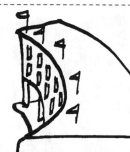

MALL
store
building
shop
food court
(name of any mall)

OPINIONS

"I try not to swear—I really do. But I'm around it all the time. All of my friends swear like crazy. So I guess I don't think it's a big deal if I slip once in a while"—James, 13

❏ Totally disagree
❏ Kinda disagree
❏ Kinda agree
❏ Totally agree

"I've never sworn—sweared—how do you say that? Anyway, I don't ever swear. I don't think you can call yourself a Christian if you swear"—Tia, 14

❏ Totally disagree
❏ Kinda disagree
❏ Kinda agree
❏ Totally agree

"I just don't see what the big deal is. They're just words—words made of letters. I don't think little alphabet letters put together can really be anything all that wrong"—Karen, 12

❏ Totally disagree
❏ Kinda disagree
❏ Kinda agree
❏ Totally agree

"Give me a pickin' break! If my swearing offends your delicate ears, then don't listen. I think God is big enough to handle any words I could come up with"—Josh, 14

❏ Totally disagree
❏ Kinda disagree
❏ Kinda agree
❏ Totally agree

NOTES

STEP 1

Play "Mouthwash Tag." Have group members form two teams—"Parents" and "Kids." Instruct both teams to take their places behind a starting line. Give the first "Parent" a bar of soap. The first "Kid" in line will make up a nonsense word and call it out; the first "Parent" should respond, "I'm going to wash your mouth out with soap!" The "Kid" will then try to run to the other side of the room as the "Parent" tries to tag him or her with the bar of soap. Repeat the process with the next "Kid" (who must make up a different nonsense word) and "Parent." Each "Kid" who makes it across the room without being tagged gets a prize; each "Parent" who tags his or her "Kid" gets a prize. Use this activity to introduce the topic of swearing.

STEP 4

Instead of handing out Repro Resource 5, have four kids play the roles on the sheet, reading their "lines" aloud. Other group members should line up behind the readers they most agree with. The catch is that kids must line up behind a reader within 15 seconds after *that* reader has read, not after all readers have read. If kids wait to line up until after the fourth reader has read, they're stuck with the fourth reader. Afterward, discuss the activity; then let kids change places if they wish.

STEP 1

In a small group, you might want to complete Repro Resource 3 as a mad-lib. In this option, you won't hand out copies of the sheet. Instead, explain that you want group members to provide you with made-up swearwords in various categories that you will provide (noun, verb, name to call someone, and so forth). If you wish, write another "act" of the play so that kids can offer a wider variety of words. You should fill in the blanks as kids respond. When you finish, read aloud the final result.

STEP 2

If you need to, you can adapt the game described in the session for your smaller group. In your version, each person can play against the clock as the rest of the group tries to guess. Keep each person's time (and make sure that everyone really tries to guess when other people are giving the clues). You might also want to add to the examples on Repro Resource 4 to provide two or three opportunities for each group member. Afterward, declare the person with the lowest time to be the winner.

STEP 1

Try another option in place of Repro Resource 3. Before the session, create three different "mad libs" based on hard-boiled dialogue from a TV police drama or from an action-adventure movie. In places where a character might use a swear word or a vulgarity, leave a blank for kids to fill in with the words they come up with while completing the mad lib (e.g., "Put your [adjective] hands behind your head, you [noun], or I'll blow your [adjective] [noun] off "). Have kids form three teams. Give a mad lib to each team. One person on each team will ask for the various kinds of words and then write down group members' suggestions in the appropriate blanks. Group members should *not* know the context of the mad lib while they're suggesting words. After about five minutes, have each team read its completed mad lib.

STEP 4

Ask for volunteers to stand up one at a time and read the statements on Repro Resource 5. After each statement is read, allow the rest of the group members to share whether they agree or disagree with the statement and explain why. You might ask your volunteers to be prepared to defend their statements as though they're the characters on the sheet. (For example, what might "Josh" say to someone who disagreed with his view of swearing?)

STEP 3

Since swearing is so widespread today, kids may feel that anyone who opposes it is simply living in the past. Keep your side of the discussion as contemporary as possible by using a recent translation of the Bible and explaining ancient-sounding terms like "profanity," "vulgarity," and "filthy language." Before getting too far into the discussion, however, get kids' attention by having an older person from your church (with whom you've arranged this before-hand) walk into your meeting. Walk up to the person and pretend to slap him or her across the face; he or she should reel with the "impact" and stagger out. Ask: **How is swearing like slapping someone in the face?** (It's offensive to many people; using God's name in vain is like slapping Him.)

STEP 5

Kids may be wary of the input-output theory, thinking it implies a "monkey see, monkey do" mentality on their part. In discussing the Matthew passage, empha-size that we need to examine not just our "audio input," but the attitudes in our hearts (out-of-control anger, prejudice, ignoring God) that overflow through our words. Say: **Ken is 14. He keeps finding himself swearing at drivers who get too close when he's riding his bike. What attitudes does he need to work on? Shannara is 13. She says "Oh my God!" whenever she's surprised, then regrets it. What attitudes does she need to work on?**

STEP 3

When you're discussing Exodus 20:7, go through the first four commandments (Exodus 20:1-11) and conduct a short Bible study on *holiness*. Introduce and explain the concept of being "set apart" for God. This comes through strongly in the first two commandments, and is continued in the third one (vs. 7). Point out that we frequently dwell on the importance of our actions and attitudes, but we need to remember that our words are just as essential to living as God wants us to live.

STEP 5

Create some tally sheets to hand out to your group members for a research assignment. Across the top of the sheet write the names of the days of the week. Down the left side, write a number of sources from which group members are likely to hear swearing: friends, family, teachers, coaches, TV, movies, and so on. Throughout the week, have kids keep up with how many times they hear swearing from these sources. (They need not write down the words and phrases—just the number of times.) Let them ask questions to clarify what constitutes swearing (heck? darn? pooh?). At your next meeting, point out that the problem may be more wide-spread and severe than they ever would have expected.

STEP 1

Before the session, set up three areas in your meeting place to serve as stations in an obstacle course. Each station must consist of an obstacle that will require teamwork to work through. Depending on the facilities available to you, these stations could include anything from a four-foot-high bar that everyone must get over without touching to a maze that kids must work through while blindfolded. Be creative! When kids arrive, divide them into three groups. Assign each group to one station. Alter your instructions as appropriate, keeping in mind special needs that any of your kids may have. Emphasize that group members may use only words that encourage each other during the activity. Place an adult at each station to monitor kids' progress. If any discouraging or inappropriate language is used, the entire group must start over. When time is up, ask kids what they thought of the process and how the words of others helped or hindered them. Then say: **As we saw by this activity, negative or cutting words can really set someone back. Today we're going to look at what God thinks of some specific negative words—swear words.**

STEP 5

As you wrap up the session, read Matthew 12:33-34 again, focusing on the image of the tree. Bring out a large piece of paper on which you've drawn the outline of a tree. At the ends of the branches, have kids write or draw what they think is the good fruit of a Christian life. When they're finished, spend a few minutes thanking and praising God for these good fruits. Then discuss as a group what your kids think the tree (the trunk) should be to produce these good fruits. In other words, what makes a good tree? Fill in the trunk with appropriate answers. Then close in prayer, thanking God again for His goodness.

STEP 1

Before the session, you'll need to come up with a list of bizarre but real words and a list of multiple-choice definitions (only one of which is correct) for each word. Instruct your girls to form teams of three or four. One at a time, read aloud the words and their accompanying multiple-choice definitions. The first team to guess the correct definition gets one point. The team with the most points at the end of the game is the winner. Afterward, say: **All words have meaning, whether we think about them much or not. Today we're going to take a look at words that we often hear, but may not think about the effects of—swear words.**

STEP 3

Gather the materials needed to make friendship bracelets (kits are available). After you talk about how swearing might make God feel, ask: **Would you want to speak to your best friend in a way that would make her feel like that?** (No.) **Why?** (I wouldn't want to hurt her. I care about her.) Remind your girls that God is the best friend they could *ever* have. Say: **To help us remember that God is our friend and that He feels hurt when we swear, we're going to make some friendship bracelets. When you wear your bracelet, remember that God wants to be your best friend and think about how He wants you to live.** After your girls have finished their bracelets, encourage them to honor God with both their friendships and their mouths.

STEP 1

After the skit, say: **Suppose that without your knowing it, all of your words and actions yesterday were filmed as a movie. Think carefully. What do you think this movie would be rated? Why? If it were shown to all of your friends and family sitting cozily around the living room TV, would you be at all embarrassed? Why? What would you be willing to do or to pay in order to "edit" the movie before other people saw it?** After your guys respond, ask: **Do you sometimes feel like "real" guys are sort of expected to swear? Why do you think swearing is considered so manly?**

STEP 5

As an ongoing reminder to try to clean up their language, have your guys start a Swearing Fund. Charge 5¢ for each "little" swear and 25¢ for major offenses. Money should be payable at each group meeting. (Make a jar or box available.) Charge double if another group member calls someone on an offense that he hasn't confessed. As guys get better at catching themselves, raise the stakes for offenses. Use the money you accumulate for special refreshments, outings, or some other good cause.

STEP 1

After you've created some swearwords for Repro Resource 3, give kids an opportunity to invent *positive* words. The catch is that the words must incorporate the names of fellow group members. For example, today we speak of brilliant ideas as being Einsteinian because Albert was so smart. And spoonerisms are named for William Spooner, a clergyman who frequently mixed up the initial sounds of his words. Ask your kids to invent positive words and use them in sentences. For example, if John is a guy who makes everyone feel at ease, someone might say, "The Johnnish attention I received when I first came to this group made me feel right at home." If Karen is a boisterous individual, someone might note, "At the concert I went to last night, the performer sang Karenly—loudly and with reckless abandon." After you give a couple of examples, it shouldn't take long for your kids to get the idea and come up with some good new words.

STEP 4

Play "Acceptable Exclamations." Explain that it's almost impossible not to say *something* when you slam your finger in the car door. See how well your kids can do coming up with inoffensive exclamations. Begin with one yourself; then designate a group member to create another one that begins with the last letter of the one you just used. Keep the chain going as long as you can. (For example: ouc*h*, *h*oo-wee, *e*eow, *w*owie zowie, and so forth.) If the chain option is too taxing on the brains of your kids this late in the session, have them select a name to misuse (if they absolutely have to) other than God's. It needs to sound good tripping off the tongue—something like "Mary Poppins!" "Ulysses S. Grant!" or "Tori Spelling!" (You get the idea.)

STEP 2

Play a scene from a video (after pre-screening for appropriateness) in which characters express strong emotions *without* swearing. Then ask: **Would this scene have been better if the character(s) had used swear words? Why or why not? Do you find it hard to express strong emotions without swearing? Why or why not?** Here are some examples of video clips you might use:

• *Searching for Bobby Fischer.* Play the school open-house scene in which the father (Joe Mantegna) lashes out at his son's schoolteacher, or a scene in which the chess master (Ben Kingsley) berates Josh, his seven-year-old student.

• *Casablanca.* Show the scene in which Rick (Humphrey Bogart) expresses anger toward Ilsa (Ingrid Bergman) when she walks back into his empty nightclub, or the scene in which Rick angrily tells piano player Sam (Dooley Wilson) to keep playing "As Time Goes By," or the climactic scene in which Rick tells Ilsa why she must get on the plane and forget him.

• *Beethoven.* Show a scene in which the hapless father (Charles Grodin) expresses his frustration over the antics of Beethoven the St. Bernard or over the desire of his family to keep the dog.

STEP 3

Play a contemporary Christian song that honors God's name. Examples might include "Emmanuel" (Amy Grant), "Sing the Glory of His Name" (Stephanie Boosahda), "Oh Holy One" (Debby Boone), "Sing unto Him" (Truth), "You Are Jehovah" (Glen Garrett), "Praise to the King" (Steve Green), "Holy Is His Name" (John Michael Talbot), and "Holy, Holy" (Kathy Troccoli). Then ask: **What names for God are used in this song? Could a person really believe the message of this song and still use God's name in vain? Explain.**

STEP 1

Replace Steps 1 and 2 with a shorter opener. Hand out pages cut from an old book or magazine (look them over beforehand for appropriateness). The pages should be all or mostly text (rather than pictures). Each person gets a page and a pair of scissors. At your signal, each person must cut out at least fifteen words that express an emotion or contain the letter S. But the cutting must be done in a way that keeps the rest of the page in one piece. The person who does so first is the winner. Then ask: **Do you think certain words should be left out of books and magazines? How about movies? Why or why not? If you cut all of the swear words out of your favorite movies, cable TV shows, or novels, would there be much left? Explain.**

STEP 3

To start Step 3, read aloud the four statements from Repro Resource 5 (don't hand it out). Let kids vote on which they most identify with. Then use Step 3 as written. Skip Step 4.

STEP 1

Rather than using Repro Resource 3, have group members brainstorm a list of slang or "street" terms that they've heard recently—words and phrases that *aren't* offensive. See how many your group members can come up with. It's likely that some of your kids will have a hard time coming up with non-offensive or non-swear words. Use this activity to lead into the questions in the last paragraph of Step 1.

STEP 4

Add the following statement to Repro Resource 5:

• "When I'm with my friends at school or with the guys on the basketball court, I use the language they use. When I'm with my friends at church, I use nicer language. Either way, nobody gets offended, so it's no big deal"—Jerome, 14

STEP 2

For the "Don't Say It" game on Repro Resource 4, play junior highers versus high schoolers. Add the following cards for your high schoolers: *Car*—drive, gas, license, keys, cruise; *Date*—car, dinner, movie, double, out; *Prom*—dance, music, tuxedo, corsage, senior; *College*—school, graduation, dorm, major, (name of any college).

STEP 4

Rather than using Repro Resource 5 as is, write out each statement on an index card, omitting the names and ages. Give each card to a volunteer. Instruct the volunteer to read the statement aloud. The rest of the group members may then decide how much or how little they agree with the statement. To jazz things up a bit, you might even want to bring in a supply of costumes and let the volunteers dress for their parts.

STEP 1

Rather than using Repro Resource 3 with your sixth graders, try a different approach. Have your kids brainstorm a list of "kinda" swear words—words that have the same meanings as swear words or that seem to suggest swear words, but aren't actually swear words. Among the words your kids might name are *gosh, geez, shoot, darn,* and *heck.* After you've got a list of words, ask: **How often are these words used in movies and TV shows?** Your kids will probably recognize that most movies and TV shows don't bother with "kinda" swear words, but instead use the real thing. Discuss the questions in the last paragraph of Step 1; then move on to Step 2.

STEP 5

Stage a "Garlic Race." Divide kids into teams. Have the members of each team pass with their hands three fresh cloves of garlic, bucket-brigade style, from one side of the room to the other. (If your group is small, have kids keep moving from the beginning to the end of the line so that the passing can continue.) Afterward, have kids smell their hands. The "sweetest-smelling" team wins. Tie this activity into the fact that contact with something—like swearing—can affect us even if we're concentrating on something else.

DATE USED:

Approx. Time

STEP 1: *Strange Transmission* _____
❏ Extra Action
❏ Small Group
❏ Large Group
❏ Fellowship & Worship
❏ Mostly Girls
❏ Mostly Guys
❏ Extra Fun
❏ Short Meeting Time
❏ Urban
❏ Sixth Grade
Things needed:

STEP 2: *Don't Say It!* _____
❏ Small Group
❏ Media
❏ Combined Junior High/High School
Things needed:

STEP 3: *Squeaky Clean* _____
❏ Heard It All Before
❏ Little Bible Background
❏ Mostly Girls
❏ Media
❏ Short Meeting Time
Things needed:

STEP 4: *A Difference of Opinions* _____
❏ Extra Action
❏ Large Group
❏ Extra Fun
❏ Urban
❏ Combined Junior High/High School
Things needed:

STEP 5: *Input-Output* _____
❏ Heard It All Before
❏ Little Bible Background
❏ Fellowship & Worship
❏ Mostly Guys
❏ Sixth Grade
Things needed:

"If You Can't Say Something Nice . . ."

YOUR GOALS FOR THIS SESSION:

Choose one or more

☐ To help kids recognize the effects that put-downs have on people.

☐ To help kids understand why putting others down is a bad habit.

☐ To help kids practice saying encouraging things to other people.

☐ Other:_____
_____

Your Bible Base:

Proverbs 18:6-7
1 Thessalonians 5:11, 15

The Average Junior Higher

(Needed: Large sheets of paper, markers, masking tape, scissors)

Have kids form groups of four. Give each group a large sheet of paper (approximately six feet long) and markers. Instruct each group to draw a life-size "average" junior higher. The junior higher may be a guy or a girl. You might suggest that each group trace an outline of one of its members' bodies to get started. (However, make sure group members don't get marker all over the clothes of the person they're tracing.) After about five minutes, have each group cut out its drawing and tape it to the front wall of your meeting area.

Ask: **How many of you heard someone get put down this week?**

How many of you got put down this week?

How many of you put down someone else this week?

After getting a show of hands for each question, say: **Let's pretend that the "average" junior highers you drew are real junior highers. Who's willing to try out a put-down on one of them?** Have volunteers come forward one at a time and put down (verbally) one of the paper junior highers. After a put down is delivered, have the volunteer tear off a portion of the "recipient" (a full limb would be an appropriate amount).

Once this activity gets going, you'll probably have plenty of volunteers, as kids will want to rip pieces off drawings other than their own. When the paper junior highers are looking fairly tattered, stop the activity.

Ask: **How do these junior highers look now? How is what we just did kind of like real life?** (When we put people down, we destroy them—even if it's only a little at a time.)

STEP 2

The 3 P's of Verbal Ripping

(Needed: Bibles, copies of Repro Resource 6, pencils, chalkboard and chalk or newsprint and marker)

Ask: **Why do you think junior highers get into put-downs so much?** (To make themselves feel superior to others; because someone's bugging them and they want that person to know it; to get attention from others; because someone ripped on them.)

Why do you think God cares if we put others down? Don't correct group members' responses here—just let them throw out any ideas they have.

Hand out copies of "The 3 P's of Verbal Ripping" (Repro Resource 6) and pencils. Explain to your group members that they're going to look at what the Bible has to say about three questions: "Why not rip?" "How should we respond to rip attacks?" and "What's a better plan?"

Write the numbers 1, 2 and 3 down the left side of the board. Write a capital "P" next to each number.

Refer to the first question on your group members' sheets. Have everyone look up Proverbs 18:6-7. Have someone read the passage aloud. This passage talks about some of the personal consequences of foolish talk (including put-downs). Next to the first "P" on the board, write "Put-downs bring trouble." Have your group members write the same thing on their sheets.

Then ask: **What might be some of the negative results if you put people down all the time?** (Loss of friends, loneliness, having people put you down all the time.)

Move on to the second question on your group members' sheets. Have everyone look up I Thessalonians 5:15. While kids are looking it up, remind them that you're looking for an answer to the "How to respond" question. Have someone read aloud the verse. Then write "Paybacks are dumb" next to the second "P" on the board. Have group members write the same thing on their sheets.

Ask: **If someone puts you down and you pay them back by putting them down, what will probably happen next?** (More put-downs.)

Have you ever been in a situation in which you and someone else put each other down all the time? Many of your group members will probably admit that they have. **If so, how did the situation finally end?** (In most cases, it either doesn't

OPTIONS

LARGE GROUP

MOSTLY GIRLS

URBAN

SIXTH GRADE

end or it escalates into more serious problems. Sometimes the relationship can just fade away into silence—ignoring each other.)

Move on to the third question on your group members' sheets. Have kids look back a few verses in their Bibles to I Thessalonians 5:11. Remind them that you're looking for "a better plan." Ask someone to read aloud the verse. Then write "Promote others" next to the third "P" on the board. Have group members write the same thing on their sheets.

Ask: **What does it mean to promote others?** (To build people up, to say good things about them.)

Before you move on to the next step, review all three questions and the "P" statements that answer them.

Promotion Plan

(Needed: Copies of Repro Resource 7, pencils, copies of the skit dialogue)

Say: **Let's pretend we've all decided we're never going to put someone down again! All we're going to do is the third "P"—promote people. There's only one small problem. How do we do this without sounding like a total idiot?**

Hand out copies of the dialogue in the following three situations to six group members (two group members per situation). Have the actors perform the brief dialogues in front of the group.

Situation 1
STUDENT A: You really are a worthless piece of filth.
STUDENT B: I really value you. You're such a special person!

Situation 2
STUDENT A *(standing alone)*: I hope I can find someone to eat with at lunch.
STUDENT B *(approaching)*: Hello. You're God's special creation, and I appreciate you!

Situation 3
STUDENT A: So, did you finish your homework?
STUDENT B: What a special question! You have such good communication skills!

Ask: **What's wrong with these situations? Is that how you think God wants us to act? Why or why not?**

After you get a few responses, hand out copies of "Promotion Plan" (Repro Resource 7). Say: **Here's what we're going to do. First, write down the names of three people you'd really enjoy putting down. These people might be your best friends or they might be people who really bug you. They might even be family members.**

Give kids a minute or two to work. Then say: **Now spend a couple of minutes writing things you could say or do to promote that person without making you sound like a total idiot.**

After a few minutes, have volunteers share their ideas with the rest of the group. However, don't force anyone to share who doesn't want to.

The Put-Up Contest

Have kids form two teams. Instruct each team to choose two representatives to compete in a contest. Have the two contestants from one team stand facing the two from the other team, about five feet apart. Explain that you're going to have a "put-up" contest, which is the opposite of a put-down contest. Announce that each team will have 10 seconds to say something positive about one of the contestants from the other team. Emphasize that all "put-ups" must be phrased in the form of a put-down. They must all start with the words "Oh yeah, well . . ."

The two contestants on a team will alternate turns for their team; but when one gets eliminated, the other must go it alone. Players are eliminated when they can't think of anything to say within 10 seconds or when they repeat a "put-up" that has already been given by someone else.

Point to one of the contestants and say: **Go.** After he or she gives a "put-up," point to a contestant on the other team. Continue back and forth, pausing only to eliminate players. At the end of the game, have everyone cheer for the winner.

Close the session in prayer, asking God to help your group members (1) avoid putting down others, (2) learn how to respond properly when others put them down, and (3) learn how to promote people.

OPTIONS

EXTRA ACTION

SMALL GROUP

HEARD IT ALL BEFORE

LITTLE BIBLE BACKGROUND

FELLOWSHIP & WORSHIP

MOSTLY GIRLS

MOSTLY GUYS

EXTRA FUN

MEDIA

JR.HIGH / HIGH SCHOOL COMBINED

THE 3 P'S OF VERBAL RIPPING

1. Why Not Rip?
(Proverbs 18:6, 7)

P

2. How Should We Respond to Rip Attacks?
(I Thessalonians 5:15)

P

3. What's a Better Plan?
(I Thessalonians 5:11)

NOTES

PROMOTION PLAN

People I'd Like to Rip

Promotion Plan

1.

2.

3.

NOTES

STEP 3

Bring in a supply of bricks or concrete blocks. Have kids form two teams. Give half of the bricks or blocks to each team. As you discuss Repro Resource 7, each team should build three steps and label them with the "P's," using stick-on labels and markers. Give a prize to the team whose steps do the best job of "lifting you up" (without falling apart) when you try a "test walk" on them.

STEP 4

Bring a supply of trite, flowery, sentimental greeting cards that gush about how wonderful the receiver is. Give each person a card. At your signal, kids should trade their cards with each other, with each person trying to end up with a less phony-sounding one than he or she started with. Kids must trade the cards they're holding every 10 seconds. Stop the game without warning after about a minute. Discuss kids' opinions of the cards they hold. Then have kids rewrite the cards they're holding to make them sound complimentary, but more "real."

STEP 1

Rather than using paper outlines, have your kids stand against the wall. Explain that you will play the role of a fellow student inviting them to visit your youth group for the first time. Then do so, but in a way that ignores their concerns and puts them down in some way. Instruct kids to stand until they decide for sure not to come. Then they should sit. You might use the following statements:

- **Please come to our group. We never have many people, so it's pretty dull.**
- **At our group, you don't have to be smart or talented.**
- **If you can't find anything better to do tonight, join the rest of us who can't either.**

Help your kids see that such invitations are essentially saying, "You should come to our youth group tonight. We've got a lot of other losers there, so you'll feel right at home." Though low-key and subtle, these invitations are put-downs all the same. Challenge kids to be more alert to how put-downs can relate to spiritual matters (and perhaps even the low number of people who attend the group).

STEP 4

As you wrap up the session, ask: **What if we built up everyone the way we've just done for each other? Do you think the size of our group would change? If so, why? Do you think the closeness of the group would change? If so, in what ways?** Try to provide a vision of better unity and perhaps numerical growth for your group in the future.

STEP 1

Before you begin the poster-tearing exercise, use another activity to introduce the topic of putting others down. You'll need a couple of foreign language dictionaries. Explain to your group members that you will read a word or phrase in another language. If kids believe that the word or phrase is a put-down, they should remain seated; if they believe the word or phrase is not a put-down, they should stand up. Read several words and phrases, pausing after each one to give kids an opportunity to respond. Then reveal what the word or phrase actually means.

STEP 2

Have kids form teams of four or five. Hand out paper and pencils to each team. Give the teams two minutes to write down as many put-downs that a junior higher might hear as they can think of. After two minutes, see which team has the longest list. Then ask: **Why do you think junior highers get into put-downs so much?** Continue through Step 2.

STEP 3

Kids may have heard many times that they aren't supposed to put each other down. But unless the underlying causes of put-downs are dealt with, the "ripping" probably will continue. Along with the "three P's," talk about "three I's" that cause put-downs. *Insecurity*, the feeling that we aren't good enough or cool enough, can lead us to tear "the competition" down so that we feel strong or important. *Impatience* can cause us to lash out at others when things aren't going our way. *Insensitivity* causes us to forget how much our "funny" put-downs can hurt others. A healthy relationship with God can develop the opposites of these "three I's" in our lives—confidence, patience, and compassion. Ask: **How did Jesus demonstrate confidence, patience, and compassion when He could have used put-downs instead?** (Examples might include when the soldiers came to get Him in Gethsemane; at His trial; and on the cross.)

STEP 4

Forced compliments may serve a purpose, but jaded kids—whether givers or receivers—won't put much stock in them. Try another option instead. Before the session, buy reward stickers—the kind teachers and parents use to affirm kids. These stickers, which bear "put-ups" like "Way to Go!" and "You're Number One!" are available at card shops, discount stores, and educational supply stores. To close the meeting, give each person at least half a dozen stickers. Say: **Put these stickers in your pocket, wallet, or purse. During the next forty-eight hours, stick them on at least three people who deserve them—three people outside of this group. Try to catch those people doing something right.**

STEP 3

A group without much Bible knowledge may not realize why put-downs are so destructive. Ask a couple of volunteers to do an impromptu skit of Adam and Eve in the Garden of Eden as it might have been if they'd begun to put down one another. This skit should show how a couple of people who refuse to get along can destroy even the most perfect relationship that God can create. It may also be that your group of kids has not had the teachings about self-image that are frequent in other groups. You may need to spend some time explaining that if we truly believe that each individual is created in the image of God and is special to Him, and if we need each other in order to function as a "body," then put-downs cannot be tolerated.

STEP 4

The "put-up" contest may be "too little too late" if your kids have never experienced the reality of God's love. While they will hear positive comments for a couple of minutes during this step, that will hardly cancel out a lifetime of put-downs, if such has been the case. So after kids have heard from their secular friends, and after they've heard from fellow youth group members, let them hear from a higher authority. Explain that you want them to see how God feels about them—no matter what other people might say. Start by having them examine passages such as Psalm 139; John 3:16-18; Romans 8:35-39; and any other passages that you think are appropriate to give kids a better understanding of their value to God—and what *should* be their value to others.

STEP 1

Before the session, create a set of name tags, half of which have positive messages such as "Hug me" or "Give me a compliment" and half of which have negative messages such as "Kick me" or "Tweak my nose." Make sure that you have at least one name tag for every member of your group. As group members arrive, stick a name tag on each person's back, making sure that no one sees his or her own tag. Play some fun, upbeat music. Encourage kids to mingle around the room, checking out each other's name tags and responding accordingly. However, make sure that no one gets carried away in responding to a name tag instruction. After a few minutes, ask: **What did you think of this activity?** Answers will vary, depending on the name tags kids had. Point out that put-downs are a lot like this activity. If you continue to get swift kicks, pretty soon you start to expect them, and either develop defenses or start to avoid people—both of which lead to loneliness and alienation.

STEP 4

Write the following on the board: "A—Adoration; C—Confession; T—Thanksgiving; S—Supplication." Briefly explain that these steps are a prayer guide—"A" involves offering praise to God for the wonderful things He is; "C" involves confessing our sins; "T" involves thanking God for what He's done; and "S" involves offering our requests to God. Give your kids an opportunity to put the ACTS method to use—adoring God for being an encourager to them, confessing times when they've put someone down recently, thanking God for giving them the strength to build others up, and making supplication for a week filled with "put-ups."

MOSTLY GIRLS

MOSTLY GUYS

EXTRA FUN

STEP 2

Put-downs are something that most junior high girls deal with every day—probably more so than guys. You may want to supplement your discussion with the following questions: **Do you think girls are more prone to putting others down than guys are? Why or why not?** (Girls learn at an early age that the tongue is an effective weapon. Many guys learn to rely on their fists.) **Why do you put others down?** (Often the reason we put others down is to make up for an area in ourselves in which we feel inferior.) Depending on the closeness of your group, your girls may or may not be willing to answer this question. **What steps can you take to change your attitude so that you'll not be so likely to put others down?** If nothing else, this question may get your group members thinking about their attitude.

STEP 4

Before your girls begin the "put-up" contest, ask for a volunteer. Have the volunteer sit on a stool at the front of the room. Announce that you're going to give her a make-over. As you begin to apply the makeup, gush on and on about how beautiful she is and how ravishing she'll be when you're finished—really lay it on thick. Then proceed to lay the make-up on thick—very thick. After you've made a real mess of her face, turn to the group and ask: **So what do you think of my encouraging words? Don't you think she feels great about herself now?** (Obviously not.) Point out that our words must be sincere and truthful in order to be of any value.

STEP 1

Begin the session by letting group members create some skits. One group should do a skit on "How my world would be different if my *friends* were always positive." Another group should do a skit on "How my world would be different if my *coach* were always positive." Other groups might try to envision ever-positive teachers, parents, bosses, and other influences in their lives. The forced focus on being positive will probably do much to remind your guys of how much negative influence they regularly have to deal with.

STEP 4

Guys traditionally aren't comfortable with verbal encouragement. So rather than using the "put-up" contest, you might want to let them work on improving their *nonverbal* methods of affirmation. ("Nonverbal" doesn't necessarily mean "silent.") Have each guy act out a way to affirm someone else that doesn't require words. For example, guys might shake hands, give a pat on the back, do a high five, buy someone a soft drink, give a good-natured punch on the arm, or whatever. Perhaps your group members might even invent a *new* method of showing admiration or affection for each other that will be special to them from now on.

STEP 3

Wrap up this step by playing and discussing the Randy Newman song "Short People." Let kids discuss why they think the writer wrote the song. (Is he really putting down short people or is he making a statement about our prejudices in general?) Encourage kids to think of other groups of people who are frequently ridiculed. They might do well to think in terms of "humor": Polish jokes, blonde jokes, lawyer jokes, and so forth. Ask: **Why do you think people stereotype and put down entire groups of people?** If kids can think of any groups they are guilty of putting down in the past, have them select one of the groups and write a positive song about those people. (Kids who can't think of specific groups can help out others who do.) When they finish, let kids sing their positive songs with all of the gusto they can muster.

STEP 4

"Saturday Night Live" frequently invents characters who have a lot of personality: Cajun Man, Opera Man, Mr. Short-Term Memory, and others. Let your group members create "Mr. (or Mrs.) Positive," who remains upbeat in spite of all of the put-downs he or she receives. Let your kids first write out some of the harshest put-downs they have recently received. Then use them against Mr. (or Mrs.) Positive to see how he or she responds. For example, one might person say, "Mr. (or Mrs.) Positive, I hear you studied all night and still couldn't pass your urine test"—to which Mr. (or Mrs.) Positive might reply, "What a witty remark! Did you hear it somewhere, or did your own inventive mind think it up?" By witnessing the always-positive nature of Mr. (or Mrs.) Positive, your kids might exercise a bit of additional strength the next time they are verbally accosted by someone.

STEP 1

Bring in a loaded video camera. Have kids stand or sit wherever they want to in your meeting place. Tell kids that you're going to work your way through the group with the camera on, giving kids a chance to hurl their best put-downs at the camera. Then do so. After bearing the brunt of kids' insults, have the group sit. Explain that you were using a "Victim-Cam"—and what you're about to play back shows what it's like to be on the receiving end of put-downs. Play back the tape and discuss the fact that most of us don't think of the victim's perspective when we're using "clever" put-downs.

STEP 4

Play one or two clips from a motivational tape—audio or video. This kind of tape is designed to "pump up" the listener's or viewer's self-esteem, usually to improve emotional health or to increase effectiveness as a salesperson. If you can't borrow such a tape from a salesperson in your church, go to a bookstore and look for tapes by speakers like Zig Ziglar, Og Mandino, Earl Nightengale, or Les Brown. Or check the "Community Service" or "Self-Help" section of a video rental store to find a motivational tape designed for teenagers—on a subject like staying off drugs or how to study. After playing one or two appropriate segments, ask: **How was this the opposite of a put-down? How did the speaker(s) try to "promote" you? How could you get the same message across, but in your own words?**

STEP 1

Replace Steps 1 and 2 with a shorter opener. Bring photos of yourself (ask a helper to take several Polaroid shots of you before the session). Have kids form teams of two to four. Give each team a photo and a laundry marker. Have the teams compete for one minute to see who can make your photo look most stupid—adding goofy hair, bow ties, zits, big ears, etc. Award prizes, if you like. Then ask: **How are put-downs designed to make people look stupid? How would you feel if we'd used your picture in this contest? What does that tell you about what it's like to be the target of put-downs?**

STEP 3

Use Repro Resource 6 for your own reference as you lead the "three P's" discussion, but don't take time to hand it out or to have kids write notes on it. In Step 3, ask kids to think of positive things to say about just one person rather than three. In Step 4, simplify the contest by giving each team one minute to come up with a single cheer that promotes the other team. If you like, give a prize for enthusiastic delivery, sincerity, or choice of words.

STEP 1

Spend some time talking about "the dozens," a popular street game in which the sole purpose is to insult your opponent as badly (and as humorously) as possible. Ask: **How do you think this game got started? Why is it sometimes fun to put down other people? How damaging do you think a game like that is? Why?**

STEP 2

To illustrate the first "P" ("Put-downs bring trouble") on Repro Resource 6, ask group members to share some examples of put-down exchanges that escalated into more serious confrontations and perhaps even resulted in violence. If possible, be prepared to share an example of your own. Ask: **How do you know if a person will respond jokingly to a put-down or whether he or she will be offended and angered by it?** (You *don't* know—that's the point. What you might think is a harmless, good-natured put-down may be offensive to the person you're putting down.)

STEP 1

Divide your kids into groups of four, making sure that you get an even distribution of junior highers and high schoolers in each group. Hand out large sheets of paper and markers. Instruct group members to create a life-sized "average" teenager (rather than specifically a junior higher). Add the following questions to your discussion of the activity: **Of the people you put down this week, what percent would you say were older than you? What percent would you say were your age? What percent would you say were younger than you?** Some of your high schoolers may think this entire session is beneath them. If so, ask them how often they hear adults putting one another down. Remind them that this is a problem that some people struggle with all of their lives.

STEP 4

Instead of using the "put-up" contest (in which you could pit your junior highers against your high schoolers, if you wish), go back to the situations presented in Step 3. Choose one junior higher and one high schooler for each roleplay. Set up the situations, using the same dialogue for Student A. However, this time, have Student B respond in a more realistic—but still positive—manner. You may wish to point out that sometimes the best response is to just walk away. After you've completed each situation, discuss as a group how it was handled and what your group members could do when they face similar situations.

STEP 2

As you work through the three "P's" on Repro Resource 6, hold your discussion on the front steps or inside stairs of your meeting place. Have kids sit on the steps as you talk. After each point, your group members should move up a step. Tie this in to the fact that the three "steps" on Repro Resource 6 lift people up rather than bringing them down.

STEP 3

Rather than having your sixth graders perform the three dialogues in Step 3, try a different approach. Ask: **How can you tell when someone's being fake or insincere in "promoting" another person?** Let group members list several ways to spot a fake. Then ask: **What do you do when you suspect that someone is giving you a fake compliment? How do you feel about people who "fake" promoting other people? Why?** Hand out copies of Repro Resource 7. In the second part of the instructions for the sheet, say: **Now spend a couple of minutes writing things you could say or do to promote that person without making you sound like a total *fake*.**

DATE USED:

Approx. Time

STEP 1: *The Average Junior Higher* _____
- ❏ Small Group
- ❏ Large Group
- ❏ Fellowship & Worship
- ❏ Mostly Guys
- ❏ Media
- ❏ Short Meeting Time
- ❏ Urban
- ❏ Combined Junior High/High School
Things needed:

STEP 2: *The 3 P's of Verbal Ripping* _____
- ❏ Large Group
- ❏ Mostly Girls
- ❏ Urban
- ❏ Sixth Grade
Things needed:

STEP 3: *Promotion Plan* _____
- ❏ Extra Action
- ❏ Heard It All Before
- ❏ Little Bible Background
- ❏ Extra Fun
- ❏ Short Meeting Time
- ❏ Sixth Grade
Things needed:

STEP 4: *The Put-Up Contest* _____
- ❏ Extra Action
- ❏ Small Group
- ❏ Heard It All Before
- ❏ Little Bible Background
- ❏ Fellowship & Worship
- ❏ Mostly Girls
- ❏ Mostly Guys
- ❏ Extra Fun
- ❏ Media
- ❏ Combined Junior High/High School
Things needed:

Did You Hear about...?

YOUR GOALS FOR THIS SESSION:
C h o o s e   o n e   o r   m o r e

☐ To help kids recognize what gossip is.

☐ To help kids understand how destructive gossip is.

☐ To help kids begin to practice "anti-gossip," saying something good about someone else.

☐ Other:_____
_____

Your Bible Base:

Romans 1:29-30
James 3:3-6

STEP 1

Say What?

Begin the session with a storytelling activity. Have kids sit in a circle. Explain to your group members that they're going to tell a story—but that they'll have only pieces of the story to work with.

Begin the story as follows: **This guy named Bill was walking home from school one day . . .** Then explain that the person with the longest hair in the group should add a sentence to the story by whispering it to the person on his or her left. That person should then add a sentence to the story and whisper the whole thing to the person on his or her left. Keep going all the way around the circle. Strongly urge your kids (especially the guys) to keep the story clean. Once the last person has heard the story, he or she should think of a final sentence to add. That person should then tell the entire story to the group.

Afterward, ask: **Isn't that how gossip works? The story starts one way and gets changed or added to along its path. The result is often not even true—that's part of the reason the Bible tells us to ignore gossip.**

O P T I O N S

EXTRA ACTION

SMALL GROUP

LARGE GROUP

HEARD IT ALL BEFORE

FELLOWSHIP & WORSHIP

MOSTLY GUYS

EXTRA FUN

SHORT MEETING TIME

Gossip Gus

(Needed: Copy of Repro Resource 8)

Ask for six volunteers to act out the skit on "Gossip Gus" (Repro Resource 8). If you have a small group, you may either double up on parts or eliminate some of the characters in the skit. Give a copy of the script only to the narrator of the skit. After you've assigned all of the roles, explain that your actors will be taking part in a "spontaneous melodrama." The narrator will read the story and the actors must act it out as they hear the lines. They should repeat all of the dialogue lines the narrator gives them with as much energy and excitement as they can muster. Encourage the actors to really "ham it up." Encourage the audience to enter into the action like a melodrama audience should—with cheers, hisses, sighs, and other reactions. Afterward, give a big round of applause to your performers.

Big Results

(Needed: Bibles, copies of Repro Resource 9, pencils)

Hand out copies of "Small Stuff, Big Results" (Repro Resource 9) and pencils. Say: **We're going to look at some really small things that have big-time results.**

Instruct group members to look at the first box on the sheet. Explain: **A spark is a tiny, tiny thing. But it can start a fire that can destroy an entire forest.**

Move on to the second box. Explain: **A ship's rudder is certainly bigger than a spark, but it's pretty small compared to the whole ship. Yet the rudder controls the direction of even the largest vessels.**

Give group members a couple of minutes to think of other examples of small things that produce big results. Instruct them to draw

pictures of their ideas in boxes 3 and 4. After a few minutes, have group members display and explain their pictures. Examples might include things like one grain of sand in an oyster being made into a big, beautiful pearl; one little blockage in an artery causing a heart attack that can kill someone; one final straw breaking a camel's back; and one little finger on a trigger ending someone's life.

Then refer your group members to the fifth box on the sheet, which has "James 3:3-6" in it. Ask group members to look up the passage in their Bibles. Have one of them read it aloud. The passage talks about the mighty destructive power of the tongue—comparing it to a ship's rudder and a spark starting a forest fire.

Ask: **Have you ever been hurt by someone's gossiping about you? If so, what happened?**

How is it that something so small as our tongue can do so much damage? If no one mentions it, point out that the "tongue" is just a way of referring to talking.

What are some of the negative effects of gossip? (Losing friends, hurting people, etc.)

Why do people gossip? (To hear juicy stories, to make themselves seem cool, etc.)

Why do you think gossip is so much more common among junior highers than among fourth and fifth graders? (Perhaps because junior highers care a lot more about what people think of them.)

Refer your group members to Box 6 on Repro Resource 9. Instruct them to draw in the box a person's face with a tongue coming out of the person's mouth. Instruct kids not to draw the tongue according to its normal size, but a size that more accurately reflects its destructive power. After a minute or two, allow volunteers to show their pictures to the rest of the group.

Have someone read aloud Romans 1:29-30. Then ask: **Did you hear "gossip" in the middle of all that? Why do you think God would include gossip with all of that really wicked stuff?** (God must think gossip is really wicked.)

What's Gossip?

(Needed: Copies of Repro Resource 10, pencils)

Say: **OK, we know gossip is a really destructive force that can do lots of damage. We also know that gossip displeases God. But some of you might not really be sure about what exactly gossip is.**

Hand out copies of "What's Gossip?" (Repro Resource 10). Instruct group members to write a definition of gossip in the first blank space. After about a minute, have a few volunteers share their definitions. Then give kids the following definition: **Gossip is talking about people in destructive ways when they aren't around.**

Lead group members through the eight examples on the sheet one at a time. Read each example aloud; then pause long enough for group members to write down whether they think the situation involves gossip or not. When kids are finished, ask them to share their responses. Use the following suggested answers to supplement your discussion of the sheet: 1—gossip; 2—gossip; 3—not gossip (but not nice); 4—not gossip; 5—gossip; 6—gossip; 7—not gossip; 8—gossip.

Anti-Gossip

OPTIONS

HEARD IT ALL BEFORE

LITTLE BIBLE BACKGROUND

FELLOWSHIP & WORSHIP

MOSTLY GIRLS

SIXTH GRADE

Say: **Now that we're a little clearer on what gossip is, let me ask you this question: "What's the opposite of gossip?"** (Saying positive things about someone when they're not around.)

Continue: **We're going to try this right now. It might seem a little weird—all right, it might seem really weird! But that's only because most of us don't do it very often.**

Ask group members to think of something positive they can say about someone in the room. After about 30 seconds, have everyone find someone to share his or her positive statement with (but it may not be the person the positive statement is about). Make sure you participate in this activity as well.

Close the session in prayer, asking God to help your group members break habits of gossiping and to give them the courage not to listen to gossip.

GOSSIP GUS

Characters: Narrator; Gossip Gus; Gus' friends—Bert, Orville, and Thurman; Prudence, the girl Gus likes

Our story takes place in the hallways of Stoobleville Public Junior High School. When we first see Gus, he's walking down Hall B with his friend Bert. "Gossip Gus," as people call him, is busy at work trying to be cool by talking about other people.

"Hey, Bert," says Gus.

"Yeah?" responds Bert.

"Did ya hear about Orville and Prudence?"

Just then, Orville walks up behind Gus and Bert and smacks them on the back. "Hi, guys," he says.

"Hey, Orville," say Bert and Gus in perfect unison.

Orville asks, "What were you saying about me and Prudence?"

Gus quickly says, "Oh, nothing." He looks down and shuffles his feet to buy some time.

Bert says, "Yeah, Gus, you were saying something about Prudence and . . ."

Before he can finish his sentence, Gus slaps his hand over Bert's mouth and says, "Prudence and Thurman—I asked if you'd heard the news about Prudence and Thurman."

Just then, Thurman walks up behind them all, smacks them all on the back and says, "Hi, guys!"

"Hey, Thurman," they all say in perfect unison.

Thurman looks at Gus and asks, "What about me and Prudence?"

"Nothing," says Gus calmly, looking up in the air to buy time.

Bert speaks up, "Yeah, Gus, you were saying something about Prudence and . . ." Gus slaps his hand over Bert's mouth and quickly says, "Prudence and some guy from Horkdale Middle School. I said, 'Did you hear the news about Prudence and some guy from Horkdale Middle School?'"

Just then Prudence walks up from the side. She says, "Hey, guys" and slaps Gus on the face.

The other guys are really excited that no one slapped them on the back. They all say, "Hey, Prudence," in perfect unison.

Prudence throws Gus against the wall and pins him there by holding her finger in the middle of his chest.

"Gus," she says, "I'd go out with any of your friends before I'd go out with a gossip like you!"

Prudence, Bert, Orville, and Thurman all walk away together arm-in-arm. And Gus is left alone without anything or anyone.

The end.

Small Stuff
Big Results

1

2

3

4

5

James 3:3-6

6

WHAT'S GOSSIP?

My definition:

1. Mary calls Meg to tell her that Bobby just broke up with Francine—which is true.

❏ Gossip   ❏ Not Gossip

2. Terrance tells Andre and Justin that he heard that Jill will make out with any guy who takes her out.

❏ Gossip   ❏ Not Gossip

3. Teresa's at lunch with Fran and Stacie. She tells Stacie that Fran got a bad grade on her test.

❏ Gossip   ❏ Not Gossip

4. Anthony tells Phil that he's really mad at him.

❏ Gossip   ❏ Not Gossip

5. Connie tells Tom that Suzie likes him. Suzie's never said anything about Tom to Connie.

❏ Gossip   ❏ Not Gossip

6. Jason tells Ben that Dave told him that Derrick said he "went all the way" with Melanie.

❏ Gossip   ❏ Not Gossip

7. Bernice tells Shawna how much the card she got from Laura meant to her.

❏ Gossip   ❏ Not Gossip

8. Jen tells Jeannie that Amy said that Tiffany said that Anita said that Penny said that Kathy said that Debbie wants to run away.

❏ Gossip   ❏ Not Gossip

NOTES

STEP 1

Instead of using the storytelling activity, have kids form two teams. Instruct each team to stand in a line, one person behind another, all facing the same direction. Tape a sheet of paper to each person's back. Give each person a crayon. Show the last person in each line a simple picture (barn, dog, fish, etc.). At your signal, that person will silently try to draw the same kind of picture on the paper taped to the person in front of him or her. That person, also silent, will try to feel what's being drawn on his or her back and attempt to draw the same thing on the paper taped to the next person. The process continues down the line. The first team to complete the process wins. Afterward, display each team's pictures in order. Discuss how the picture changed as it got further from the "source." Use this activity to illustrate how the truth can get more and more distorted as it's heard secondhand, thirdhand, etc.

STEP 3

Replace Repro Resource 9 with a "Tongue Talent Show." Let each person choose to either (1) dial a phone number with his or her tongue (put a new piece of plastic wrap over the phone before each attempt), or (2) make a star design with five toothpicks in 20 seconds, using only his or her tongue. Tie this activity into the "power" of the tongue.

STEP 1

Instead of using the opening activity, begin the session by surreptitiously calling everyone to one corner of the room. Start talking about people in and out of the group. Everything you say should be the absolute truth, but you should act as if you're clueing kids in on big juicy secrets. For example, you might say: **Pssst! Did you hear about Pastor Smith? I saw him out for a late-night walk with some woman last night. I don't need to say any more, do I?** Wink knowingly, not bothering to mention that the woman was his wife of 23 years. Afterward, ask: **Why do people seem to take such joy in sharing secrets and spreading gossip? Have you ever been guilty of spreading gossip? Have you ever been a victim of someone else's gossip?**

STEP 4

After kids complete Repro Resource 10, ask: **What's the potential effect of gossip on a small group like ours?** Help kids see the benefit of more intimate relationships that are possible in small groups, but warn them of the accompanying drawback of possibly having confidential information shared by group members at school as gossip. Read a number of statements to see how your kids feel about gossip. If kids agree with a statement, they should stand; if they disagree, they should sit. Make a list of your own, but here are a few statements to get you started:

• **I hold back facts about myself in this group because I'm afraid that people might use the information against me later on.**

• **I have passed along information shared in confidence in this group to other people outside the group—not often, but sometimes.**

• **I think more people would attend this group if they weren't afraid of gossip.**

STEP 1

If you don't think the storytelling activity would work well with your group, try another option. Ask for several volunteers to compete in a word game. On the board, write the word "cat." One at a time, have your contestants change, add, or subtract one letter in the word to make a new word. For instance, "cat" might become "bat," which might become "bait," which might become "bit," and so on. If a contestant can't come up with a new word in 10 seconds, he or she is out. Continue until only one person remains. Afterward, point out that gossip is similar to the words in the game—it starts out one way and gets changed or added to along its path.

STEP 4

After deciding which situations on Repro Resource 10 involve gossip, have kids form five teams. Assign each team one of the gossip situations (1, 2, 5, 6, 8) from the sheet. Instruct each team to come up with a scenario that describes what might happen to the person being gossiped about as a result of the gossip. For instance, for #2, how might some of the guys at school start treating Jill as a result of Terrance's gossip? After a few minutes, have each team share its scenario.

STEP 1

If kids associate the word "gossip" with chattering housewives at backyard fences, they may assume that this session doesn't relate to them and tune out. Use the following to illustrate that all of us have opportunities to gossip, whether or not we call it that. (1) **You've heard a couple of kids speculate that your music teacher is gay. Is there anyone in the world you would repeat that rumor to? Why?** (2) **A friend has just turned his back on you and joined a "cooler" group that rejects you. Another friend of yours says to forget your former friend, who is "a jerk." You happen to know the former friend is so afraid of the dark that he still sleeps with a light on. Do you mention it? Why or why not?** (3) **A new kid shows up at the youth group. You once heard someone at school say that the kid is HIV-positive. What do you do?**

STEP 5

If you used the "say something nice about each other" activity in Session 3, try another option. Have the group brainstorm a list of the "Top Five Gossip Stoppers." These would be phrases kids could use to re-route a conversation that's heading into gossipy territory. Examples might include: "Just the facts, ma'am"; "No comment"; "Can I quote you on that?" and "Please speak into the microphone." Then have kids compete to see who can say the phrases most politely, in a way that would steer a conversation in the right direction without cutting it off.

STEP 3

Prior to reading Romans 1:29-30, announce that you want group members to play "Rate-a-Sin." Explain that you will read a list of sins. After each one, kids should rate it on a scale of one (least) to ten (most) according to how "bad" it is. Then read the list, one item at a time, from Romans 1:29-30—without letting on that it's a biblical list. See how gossip compares to some of the other things. If it's rated lower, as it might well be, read the passage aloud and emphasize that gossip is just as bad as anything else on the list.

STEP 5

If your group members suddenly come to the conclusion that gossip is not something that "everybody does" and not even just a bad habit, but rather a serious sin, they may begin to feel a lot of guilt for past actions. Close with a silent prayer of confession and repentance. Assure kids that God forgives those who sincerely repent. Also challenge your kids to take the additional step of seeking forgiveness from people they may have offended in the past.

STEP 1

Write the words to a story—perhaps a favorite children's story, a Bible story, or the lyrics to a popular song—on slips of paper, one or two lines per slip. Put each slip inside a balloon; inflate the balloon. Make sure that you have one balloon for each member of your group. When kids arrive, hand out the balloons. Announce that group members will be competing in a balloon-popping contest. As kids pop their balloons by sitting on them, assign each person a number—the first person to pop his or her balloon is #1; the second person is #2; and so on. After all of the balloons are popped, have kids line up according to their numbers; then have them read the slips of paper that were in their balloons in the order in which they're lined up. It's likely that the resulting "story" won't make any sense. Afterward, say: **When we gossip—talk about people and events at random—the result is often similar to what just happened with our story. It gets all messed up and makes no sense. The story may sound funny at first, but it really isn't. That's one of the reasons the Bible tells us not to gossip.**

STEP 5

After your kids have come up with positive things to say about each other and have shared those statements, instruct them to do the same thing for God. Read Psalm 46:10 aloud; then allow a few minutes of silence for kids to think about God. Have them think of at least one thing that they really love about God—encourage them to be creative here; then allow time for them to share what they thought of with at least one other person in the room. After a few minutes, call the group back together and ask volunteers to share something they heard about God that they may not have thought of themselves. Close the session with a time of prayer, praising God for all of the wonderful things He is.

STEP 2

With a group of mostly girls, you'll probably need to make some changes to the skit on Repro Resource 8. For your purposes, Gossip Gus becomes Gossip Gertrude. Gertrude's friends are Bertha, Opal, and Thelma instead of Bert, Orville, and Thurman. Prudence, the girl Gus likes, becomes Dudley, the guy Gertrude likes. The rest of the storyline may remain the same. If your girls enjoy performing, you might want to bring in some costume clothing to help them really get into the skit.

STEP 5

Hand out pencils and slips of paper, making sure that each of your girls gets one fewer slip than the number of girls in the group. Instruct your group members to write a nice note to each person in the room (excluding themselves), sharing at least one nice thing about that person. When they're finished, allow time for them to deliver their notes to each other. Afterward, explain that we all need practice in sharing nice things about each other, both when the other person's not around and when he or she is around. The more we learn to concentrate on the positive, the more natural it will be for us to say positive things.

STEP 1

Your guys may not be adept at story-telling, but they probably like to hear stories that are incredible and barely believable. Ask: **What's the most unusual or fantastic true story you've ever heard?** If your guys don't mention any, have ready some "urban legends" to tell. (Examples include the lady who bought a "special breed of Chihuahua" that turned out to be a giant rat and the "choking Doberman"—discovered by a woman returning home and rushed to the vet where part of a finger was found stuck in his throat, leading to the discovery of a burglar passed out in the woman's home.) There are many more of these stories, and perhaps your guys will know several of them. They are almost always told as true stories, but are yet to be proven. Your guys may be especially vulnerable to this form of gossip.

STEP 2

After the skit on Repro Resource 8, ask: **Gus was a guy, but don't you think girls are really the ones who tend to gossip the most?** As group members respond, ask for specific examples. If you're clever and subtle about this, soon you can have your guys gossiping about girls, which will demonstrate that guys *are* just as prone to gossip as girls are.

STEP 1

Begin the session by having group members create a skit titled "An Average Day in the Land of Gossip." Explain that your kids have surely seen some of these natives. They're called Gossipers. So in other words, the skit should be what life would be like if everyone was a blatant gossiper. Your group members can have any job they wish in the Land of Gossip, but whenever they meet, they must act like Gossipers. This skit should be somewhat scary as kids see what could happen if gossip is allowed to occur unchallenged. It's not usually a pretty sight.

STEP 4

As you're discussing what constitutes gossip, explain that sometimes the difference between "gossip" and "not gossip" consists of only a few adjectives and adverbs. For example, take the statement "John took Mary out to dinner, to a movie, and then back home." This statement may be pure fact. But in the hands of an experienced gossiper, it can quickly become, "Smooth John took desperate Mary to a romantic movie, and then on a steamy ride back home." What began as an innocent statement can soon become juicy gossip. Let volunteers make a number of other innocent statements. After each one, work as a group to add a word or two to create gossip out of the statement. Afterward, explain (jokingly) that since group members have been able to create gossip in a nondestructive setting, perhaps they won't feel the need to do so outside the group.

STEP 2

Play one of the following video scenes:.

• *Bye, Bye, Birdie*. Play the musical number "Goin' Steady," in which a series of teenagers gossip over the phone about what happened on a date.

• *The Music Man*. Show the scene in which the River City women, who have been gossiping about the town librarian, sing "Pick a Little, Talk a Little." The number, which compares the women with chickens that are pecking at feed, concludes as a barbershop quartet joins in with "Good Night, Ladies."

After showing the scene, ask: **How does the word "gossip" apply to what these people were doing? Does the movie make gossip look dangerous, fun, silly, or what? How do kids today gossip in real life?**

STEP 4

Bring copies of "gossip columns" from newspapers or entertainment magazines. Such columns usually feature "insider" looks at who was seen with whom at a social event, whose career is in trouble, etc. Let small groups look the columns over. Ask: **Which of the items in each column might qualify as gossip? Which items could be destructive? If your school newspaper had a "gossip column," what kinds of information might it contain? If you were in charge of that column, what kinds of information would you want to keep out of it? Why?**

STEP 1

Replace Steps 1 and 2 with a shorter opener. Before the session, get three group members to agree to spread rumors as kids are arriving at your meeting place. Each rumormonger will try to spread a different rumor. All of the rumors should be believable and should at least be approved by you if you don't supply them. (Examples might include the following: "[Name of group member] isn't here this week because she got grounded"; "They got Mrs. [name of a woman in your church] to do our refreshments this week, and all she made was spinach dip"; "The church board found out that [your name] lied on his job application, and they're having a meeting to decide whether to fire him [or her]." Delay your entrance for a couple of minutes. When you finally arrive, ask how many believed each of the rumors and why. Did any of the rumors change or become more detailed as they were passed along? Be sure to dispel the rumors before moving on to Step 3.

STEP 3

Skip Repro Resource 9. Brainstorm ways in which each of the following little words could cause trouble, depending on how and when they were used: *fire*, *OK*, and *ugly*. (Examples might include the following: Yelling "Fire!" in a crowded room when there isn't any; saying "OK" to a boyfriend or girlfriend who wants to have sex; answering "Ugly," when another student asks what your math teacher is like.) Use these examples as you discuss the power of the tongue. In Step 4, use just the first five situations on Repro Resource 10.

STEP 2

To give your kids an idea of how prominent gossip is in our society, bring in some tabloid newspapers that feature outrageous stories about celebrities. Read a few of the headlines to your group members. Then say: **By now, most of us know not to believe what we read in the tabloids. But what if we didn't know that? What if people thought that these stories were true? What might be some of the effects in these peoples' lives?** As a group, brainstorm some of the far-reaching results of gossip in the lives of the celebrities featured in the tabloids. Use this activity to lead in to Step 3.

STEP 4

Ask your group members to share some examples of how gossip negatively affected someone they know. Without using names, have kids explain what happened in the person's life as a result of being gossiped about. If possible, be prepared to share an example of your own. Be careful, however, not to let this activity turn into a gossip session!

STEP 2

After the skit, divide your group into teams of five, making sure that you have a mix of junior highers and high schoolers on each team. Explain that each group member is to assume the role of one of the characters (other than the narrator) in the skit and answer the appropriate question below.

• Gus: What is it that makes you want to gossip?

• Bert: How did you feel when you kept hearing Gus change his story?

• Orville: How did you feel when you heard Gus talking about you?

• Thurman: Do you think Gus is a friend that you can trust? Why or why not?

• Prudence: Why did you say you wouldn't want to go out with Gus?

Let kids discuss their responses briefly in their teams. Then, if time permits, call the group back together and have all of the "Gus" characters share their responses, all of the "Bert" characters share their responses, and so on.

STEP 4

After working through Repro Resource 10 to make sure that your junior highers are clear on the definition of "gossip," call for some volunteer high schoolers who are willing to share some of their "gossip" experiences with the group. You may even wish to set up a panel of "experts" who would be willing to talk about how they've felt when they were the target of gossip, what's happened when they've been involved in the spreading of gossip, how gossip changes between junior high and high school, and so on.

STEP 4

To make Repro Resource 10 more interesting for your sixth graders, try the following option. Each time you read a situation from the sheet, choose one of your group members to be the first person mentioned in that situation; that person will then grab a second group member to be the second person in the situation, and so on, according to the number of people needed. These kids will then arrange themselves (linking arms, facing off, etc.) to illustrate the "chain of communication" in that situation, to help your group visualize it.

STEP 5

As you wrap up the session, give each of your group members a parting gift— a small, inexpensive squirt gun—as a reminder to put out the "sparks" caused by gossip.

DATE USED:

Approx. Time

STEP 1: *Say What?* _____
❑ Extra Action
❑ Small Group
❑ Large Group
❑ Heard It All Before
❑ Fellowship & Worship
❑ Mostly Guys
❑ Extra Fun
❑ Short Meeting Time
Things needed:

STEP 2: *Gossip Gus* _____
❑ Mostly Girls
❑ Mostly Guys
❑ Media
❑ Urban
❑ Combined Junior High/High School
Things needed:

STEP 3: *Big Results* _____
❑ Extra Action
❑ Little Bible Background
❑ Short Meeting Time
Things needed:

STEP 4: *What's Gossip?* _____
❑ Small Group
❑ Large Group
❑ Extra Fun
❑ Media
❑ Urban
❑ Combined Junior High/High School
❑ Sixth Grade
Things needed:

STEP 5: *Anti-Gossip* _____
❑ Heard It All Before
❑ Little Bible Background
❑ Fellowship & Worship
❑ Mostly Girls
❑ Sixth Grade
Things needed:

Liar, Liar

YOUR GOALS FOR THIS SESSION:

Choose one or more

☐ To help kids recognize the damage that can be caused by lying.

☐ To help kids understand why God can't stand lying.

☐ To help kids choose a lifestyle of truth.

☐ Other:_____
_____

Your Bible Base:

Exodus 20:16
Acts 4:32—5:11
Hebrews 6:18

STEP 1

Tabloid Teasers

(Needed: Tabloid newspapers, prizes [optional])

Have kids form teams of three or four. Say: **Sometimes it's hard to tell what's truth and what's not. Have you ever been in a supermarket checkout lane and seen tabloid newspapers— the ones with really weird stories?**

Explain to your group members that you'll be reading sets of five headlines to them. Four will be real headlines from tabloid newspapers (which doesn't necessarily mean the stories are true) and one will be a totally made-up headline. The task of each team is to decide which is the made-up headline. Emphasize to group members that they need to listen carefully, because you won't repeat any of the headlines.

After reading all five headlines in a set, give the teams about 30 seconds to decide; then have them verbalize their guesses. After all teams have registered their responses, announce the actual made-up headline. Have the teams keep track of how many they get right. Afterward, you might want to award prizes to the winning team.

Here are some headlines you might use (or you might want to come up with some of your own). The made-up headlines have an asterisk (*) next to them.

"2,000-Year-Old Mummy Wakes Up and Stabs Scientist"
"Do-It-Yourself Doc Operates on His Own Brain"
* "Man Bursts into Flames after Eating Mysterious Enchilada"
"Girl Hides 13 Years Over Bad Grades"
"Docs Attach Man's Foot to His Arm"

"Hubby Sues for Divorce Over Baby's Big Nose"
"U.S. Pilots Fly Captured UFO's in Nevada"
"Boy, 2, Swallowed by Giant Catfish"
"Woman Hasn't Slept a Wink in 30 Years"
* "Lovestruck Surgeon Leaves Love Letter inside Patient"

* "Housewife Cracks Egg for Breakfast and Finds Live Chirping Chick"
"Teen Sues Parents Because He's a Nerd"
"Ear Found in Jar of Spaghetti Sauce"
"Leech Saliva Is Miracle Drug for Heart Victims"
"Hungry Kitty on Death Row in Wisconsin for Stealing Food"

"Ouch! Fleeing Thief Shoves Lobster Down His Pants"

* "Flooded Raging River Carries Live Infant 30 Miles into Next State"

"World War II Bomber Found on the Moon"

"Cop Shoots Student During Gun-Control Lecture"

"Man Lives 52 Years with Axe Blade in His Head"

"Amazing Dog Girl Has 200 I.Q. and Talks with Animals"

"Five Ants Save Life of Abandoned Child"

"Hypnotized Dog's Testimony Nails Killer"

* "Woman's Wig Shrinks Until It Crushes Her Head"

"Thief Freezes in His Tracks—in Stolen Pair of Wet Jeans"

As a "bonus round," have teams guess which of the following is the real headline (indicated by an asterisk [*]).

"10 Die in Cookie Taste-Test Tragedy"

"Hijacking Terrorist Sobs, 'All I Wanted Was Another Bag of Peanuts'"

"Bank Teller Loses Arm in Drive-Thru Suction Tube"

* "Neighbors Chip in to Pay Loud Snorer $10,000 to Move Away"

"Restaurant Manager Fired for Making Mustard and Ketchup Shakes"

STEP 2

Lots-o-Liars

(Needed: Copies of Repro Resource 11, pencils)

Ask: **Do you know junior highers who lie?** (Of course!)

Then say: **It seems like lying is pretty common among junior highers. It's during the junior high years that many people get "good" at lying. And then it becomes so much a part of who they are that they end up lying all through their lives.**

Hand out copies of "Lots-o-Liars" (Repro Resource 11) and pencils. Say: **Many people agree that some lies are OK. But very few people agree on where to draw the line between an "OK lie" and a "bad lie." Read through the lies on this sheet and rank them from most OK (1) to worst (10).**

Allow group members to work in pairs to complete the sheet, if they wish. After about five minutes, have volunteers share their rankings.

OPTIONS

SMALL GROUP

LARGE GROUP

HEARD IT ALL BEFORE

MOSTLY GUYS

SIXTH GRADE

Which lies did they think were the worst? Which lies did they think were the "most OK"? Ask your volunteers to explain their rankings.

Lie 'til Ya Die!

(Needed: Bibles)

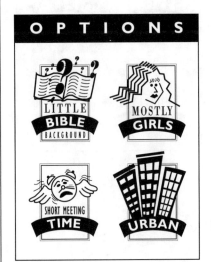
Say: **We like to think that some lies are OK and others a big deal. We even talk about "little white lies." But God makes it clear in the Bible that He's not fond of any lies!**

Have kids form small groups. Then have them turn in their Bible to Acts 4:32. As group members follow along, read Acts 4:32–5:11. This passage is the story of Ananias and Sapphira, a married couple who both lied to Peter (and to the Holy Spirit) and dropped dead on the spot as a result.

After you read the passage, give the groups about three minutes to put together a short skit depicting the story of Ananias and Sapphira. (Many junior highers will enjoy this because it's got a couple of pretty wild dying scenes.) As kids work, circulate among the groups to help them as needed. After a few minutes, have each group perform its skit.

Afterward, ask: **Why did Ananias and Sapphira die? Do you know of anyone who's ever died because he or she lied? How serious do you think God is about lying?** Get several responses.

God's Character

(Needed: Clear jar or container, water, vegetable oil)

Have group members turn to Exodus 20:16. Ask one person to read aloud the verse. (This is the "Don't give false testimony" commandment.) Point out that telling the truth is such a big deal to God that He included it in the Ten Commandments.

Ask: **Why does God care if we lie or tell the truth?** (Because lying is a sin; because the Bible says not to lie.) If no one mentions it, point out that God is truth, so non-truth (or lying) is completely opposite of everything He is.

Ask: **Do you think it's possible for God to lie?** Of course your group members know that God *doesn't* lie, but they might struggle with whether or not He *can* lie.

Have group members turn to Hebrews 6:18. Ask one person to read aloud the verse, which says that it's impossible for God to lie.

Take out a clear jar or similar container. Fill it about half full with water. Then say: **Let's pretend that this water represents God.**

Then pull out a bottle of vegetable oil. Say: **This oil represents lying.** Pour a couple inches of oil on top of the water. Then put the lid on the jar and ask a volunteer to shake the ingredients together.

Afterward, say: **Just like this oil and water, God's truth and lying can never mix and will never mix—not even a little bit. So if we want to grow in our relationship with God, we need also to separate ourselves from lying and go for truth.**

STEP 5

Truth Practice

(Needed: Copies of Repro Resource 12, pencils)

Say: **OK, so you're going to try to tell the truth. But some-times people tell the truth and are real jerks about it. Let's get a little practice in telling the truth without being jerks.**

Hand out copies of "Truth Practice" (Repro Resource 12). Group members should still have pencils from the Repro Resource 11 activity (and, by now, have probably used them to turn that repro sheet into a nice vegetable strainer). Instruct your group members to respond honestly, and not to write down simply what they think is the "right" answer. Encourage them to think about how they would actually handle the situation. After about five minutes, ask a couple of volunteers to share their responses to each situation.

Close the session in prayer, asking God for strength for your group members to pursue truth.

OPTIONS

LARGE GROUP

LITTLE BIBLE BACKGROUND

FELLOWSHIP & WORSHIP

MOSTLY GIRLS

EXTRA FUN

MEDIA

URBAN

JR. HIGH / HIGH SCHOOL COMBINED

SIXTH GRADE

LOTS-O-LIARS

Rank the following lies from the "most OK" (1) to the "worst" (10).

_____ On his tax form, a man claims that he gave $2,000 to his church. He really gave $200.

_____ A man thinks his wife's dress looks really dorky, but he tells her she looks wonderful.

_____ A seventh-grade girl tells her parents that her homework is all done. It's really not, but she'll be able to finish it tomorrow morning in study hall.

_____ A seventeen-year-old boy tells his parents that no one came over while they were out of town. He really had a wild party with about fifty other kids from his school.

_____ A pastor exaggerates a story about something that happened to him to make his sermon sound good.

_____ An eighth-grade boy tells his dad that he has no idea how the garage door got all those dents in it. Actually, the boy and his friend had been shooting a BB gun at a target on the door the day before.

_____ A woman makes a long-distance personal phone call at work, then tells her boss it was work-related.

_____ A little boy with chocolate evidence all over his face and hands tells his mom that he wasn't in the cookie jar.

_____ A man calls in sick to work so that he can go fishing.

_____ A junior high girl tells her best friend that she has to do homework tonight so her friend won't be hurt that she's having a couple of other friends over to watch a video.

TRUTH PRACTICE

Situation 1

The rule in your house is "Absolutely no friends in the house when Mom and Dad aren't home." Your best friend drops by to give you some CDs while your parents are gone and ends up staying two hours. Later, your mom asks you where the CDs came from. How do you respond?

Situation 2

Your friend has huge ears—and everybody is aware of it. She gets a new haircut that's supposed to hide them, but she's not happy with it. She says, "This haircut doesn't help at all. My ears still make me look like an ugly dork, don't they?" She's right. How do you respond?

Situation 3

You and your friend get permission to go to a really cool concert on a school night. The next morning you remember a homework assignment that's worth one quarter of your total grade. The teacher clearly said that all late assignments will be marked down a whole grade. Your friend lies and tells the teacher that he was at an uncle's funeral. The teacher believes him and gives him two extra days to finish. Now the teacher asks for your assignment. How do you respond?

NOTES

STEP 1

Have kids stand along a wall. You'll ask each person a question to which you know the answer (the person's name, state capital, etc.). As soon as you ask, the person must decide whether to tell the truth or not. If the person tells the truth, he or she must run to the opposite left corner as you run in pursuit with a stuffed sock, trying to "bop" him or her. A prize (candy bar, gum, etc.) awaits the truth-teller in the corner. If the person lies, he or she is not chased, but walks to the opposite right corner, where no prize awaits. After giving everyone a turn, ask: **Was it worth it to tell the truth, even if you might get bopped? Why? In real life, how might telling the truth get you "bopped"? How might lying seem like an easy way to avoid getting bopped? What "prize" awaits those who tell the truth?**

STEP 4

Instead of using oil and water, have kids form two teams. Put each team on one end of a length of gift-wrap ribbon. Have kids play tug-of-war. As they do, say: **Sometimes we struggle over whether to tell the truth. We go back and forth about how much truth to tell. We think we can mix a little lying with a little truth and come out OK. But God doesn't struggle. His answer is clear.** Pull out scissors and cut the ribbon in the middle, sending the teams sprawling. (If your floor is hard, pre-pad the area with mats or cushions.) **God's answer is to tell the truth.**

STEP 1

Rather than using the tabloid-headline exercise as written, let kids play as individuals and compete against each other. Don't group the headlines as is done in the session. Rather, explain that some of them are actual headlines and others are made up. Hand out paper and pencils. Instruct kids to number their papers from 1 to 30. Read one headline at a time as kids decide whether to mark it "true" or "false." Afterward, go through the items a second time, revealing which ones are true and letting kids grade their papers. Award a prize to the winner, if you wish.

STEP 2

For a small group, try to make the exercise on Repro Resource 11 more personal. Rather than having kids simply rank the statements in order, ask the questions aloud by phrasing them as follows: "Have *you* ever . . . ?" or "Might *you* ever . . . ?" To respond affirmatively, kids should stand. To answer negatively, they should sit. After each question, let group members explain and/or defend their answers. Challenge everyone to be completely truthful. (After all, you're discussing lying.) Add other situations to the list that you know are issues your group members struggle with.

STEP 2

Have kids form groups. Ask the members of each group to brainstorm some possible results of finding out that the following people are chronic liars who hardly, if ever, tell the truth: your dentist, your doctor, the writers of your history book, a driver's ed instructor, your math teacher, the mayor of your city, your parents, your boyfriend or girlfriend, your Sunday school teacher or youth group leader, etc. (add others, as desired). Encourage kids to be creative and humorous as they consider possible results. (For example, if the writers of your history book are chronic liars, then you don't know for sure who was the first president of the United States.) After a few minutes, have each group share its results. Then go through Step 2 as written in the session.

STEP 5

Have kids form three or four groups. For each situation on Repro Resource 12, instruct each group to think of a possible response for the person involved and explain what the consequences of that response might be. One group should think of a truthful response and explain what the consequences of telling the truth might be. The other groups should think of lying responses and explain what the consequences of those lies might be. After a few minutes, have each group share its responses and consequences.

HEARD IT ALL BEFORE

LITTLE BIBLE BACKGROUND

FELLOWSHIP & WORSHIP

STEP 2

Kids who have gone through "values clarification" in school may find the situations on Repro Resource 11 rather tame. For example, what if you were hiding Jews from Nazis, and some Nazis asked whether you were hiding anyone? Is it OK to lie to save someone's life? You won't be able to settle that issue in this session, but you can acknowledge it. As needed, point out that the mother and sister of Moses hid his identity to protect him (Exod. 1—2); David faked insanity to save his own life, but did not exactly tell a lie (I Sam. 21). Others who lied outright to save their own skins (like Abraham in Genesis 12 and Peter in Matthew 26) are portrayed as having sinned. Even if a rare life-and-death situation justifies lying (and Christians may disagree over whether it does), it doesn't follow that giving "false testimony against your neighbor" (Exod. 20:16) is sometimes OK. Most of us are tempted to lie to save ourselves embarrassment, loss, or punishment—not to save lives.

STEP 4

If your kids are familiar enough with the Bible to know that God opposes lying, a reading of Exodus 20:16 may not make much of an impression on them. Instead, challenge kids to prove to *you*, using their Bibles and a couple of concordances you supply, that God is against lying. Have kids work in teams. The team to come up with the greatest number of supporting passages in five minutes wins. (A few examples might include Lev. 6:1-5; Num. 23:19; Ps. 5:6; Prov. 6:19; 19:5, 9; 30:8; John 8:44; Rom. 1:25; Col. 3:9; Titus 1:2; and I John 2:21.)

STEP 3

Be sensitive to the implications of the Ananias and Sapphira story. If your kids don't know much about the Bible, it's preferable to teach the rewards of truthfulness rather than begin with a somewhat extreme liars-will-be-struck-dead passage. You might want to consider discussing Daniel's truthfulness even during desperate times (Dan. 6); the honesty of the thief on the cross (Luke 23:32-43); Solomon's heartfelt request for wisdom (I Kings 3:1-15); and similar examples.

STEP 5

If your group members are struggling a bit as they redefine their concept of lying, let them add situations from their own experience for group consideration. For example, they might ask, "Was it wrong for me to tell my parents I was at the library when I did indeed stop there for five minutes on the way to my best friend's house?" "Is it wrong for my friend to tell the teacher that his homework is his own even if he copies it from me himself?" Challenge kids to begin to deal with the *absolute* truth, but make sure to review Ephesians 4:15 and emphasize the importance of speaking that truth *in love*.

STEP 1

Begin the session by reading—and having your kids act out—the children's book *Max and the Big Fat Lie* (available from Chariot Books at your local Christian bookstore). Ask for volunteers to portray the following characters (listed in order of appearance): Max's friend Stevie, Max, Sir Fib, Max's mom, Kleever Deceiver, and Big Fat Lie. As you read the story, encourage kids to really play up their parts. Afterward, say: **Though this is a fun children's book, it contains a good truth about our topic today—lying. Often, once we start a lie, it snowballs out of control. How many of you can think of a time when that happened to you?** Get a few responses. **What are some reasons, other than the "snowball effect," that you can think of for not lying?** Allow time for responses. Then say: **Today we're going to take a look at what God thinks of lying.**

STEP 5

Read Proverbs 12:22 as further evidence that God *really* doesn't like it when we lie. Then have group members take a few minutes to brainstorm a list of all of the true things about God that they can think of. As they call out their truths, write them on the board. Encourage kids to consider the many different aspects of God and His personality. Close the session with a circle prayer. Have kids sit in a circle on the floor. One by one, have them thank God for each of the true things about Him that you listed on the board. If you run out of either kids or attributes, repeat prayers or pray-ers as needed.

STEP 3

If there are no guys in your group to play the male roles in Acts 4:32–5:11, recruit some volunteers from another group for this part of the session. If that doesn't work, bring in some props for your girls to use—old, oversized clothes; fishing gear or tools that might depict the occupations of some of the men; and so on. Be creative! Encourage your girls to really get into this story. It's an amazing account, one that is very clear about how God feels about lying.

STEP 5

Change the situations on Repro Resource 12 as follows:

• *Situation #1*—You and your best friend are going shopping. You're both trying to find a swimsuit. Ugh! You've looked in several stores. She tries on one that you think is the most hideous thing you've ever seen. She's convinced it's the one for her and tells you so. How do you respond?

• *Situation #3*—You and some of your friends are going out for pizza and then to a movie. You're planning to see the newest animated release from Disney, but when you get to the theater, your friends decide to go see a very steamy love story that your parents have specifically said you can't see. You go with your friends to see the love story. When you get home, your mom asks how the movie was. How do you respond?

STEP 2

Help your guys be more open about lying by making a contest out of it. For example, begin by having them compete to describe "The Biggest Lie I Ever Told—and Got Caught In." Then have a second round in which group members describe "The Biggest Lie I Ever Told and Got Away With." Award prizes if you wish, or perhaps create a "Forked Tongue" award for your winners. Then ask: **Why do many guys seem to take such pride in "getting away with" lying and similar behavior that isn't at all honorable?**

STEP 4

Ask: **Do you know a guy who never lies?** Most guys will probably think of at least one trustworthy person. **If so, what kind of person is he? Would you like to be that kind of person—someone whom everybody could trust? If so, how do you think you go about becoming that kind of guy?** Point out that integrity isn't established overnight. Explain that lying will eventually have results. Even if it seems like your guys are getting away with it now, lying will eventually catch up with them. If your guys ever want to be respected and have other people feel at ease to discuss problems and seek help from them, they will have to stop lying *now* and start building a trustworthy reputation.

STEP 1

Begin the session with a game of "To Tell the Truth." Call for three volunteers at a time. The three should quickly decide on something embarrassing, funny, or unique that one of them has done—and that other group members will not know about. Have them stand before the rest of the group as all three announce, "I shook hands with the president when I was six years old" (or whatever they've decided on). Let the other group members quiz each of the volunteers, trying to determine which of the three is telling the truth. For example, they might ask, "Which president was it?" "What was the temperature in Washington when you were there in April?" After a few questions, ask: **How many people think Person #1 is telling the truth? How many think Person #2 is telling the truth? How many think Person #3 is telling the truth?** Let your truth teller identify himself or herself.

STEP 5

As you wrap up the session, say: **I want to see how much you've been learning about detecting lying and the importance of telling the truth.** Before the session, write out a lengthy list of statements about yourself. Read one at a time; let kids write down whether they think each statement is true or false. (All of the statements should be true, but don't let on. To make this work, you will need to recall as many interesting and exciting things about yourself as you can. Many statements should sound so outlandish, or deal with sides of you that kids don't normally see, that they assume such statements must be false.) When you reveal that everything you said was true, point out that we need not lie to create fun and excitement in life. The truth can be plenty thrilling if we stick to it and commit to being truthful with each other.

STEP 1

Show some of the following video scenes (pre-screen them for appropriateness):

• *In the Line of Fire.* Show the scene in which John Malkovich's character opens a bank account under a false name, lying to a female employee about where he's from and what he does.

• *Dirty Rotten Scoundrels.* Play a scene in which Lawrence (Michael Caine) pretends to be an exiled king or in which Freddy (Steve Martin) claims to have an ailing grandmother.

• *The Freshman.* Show the scene in which Victor (Bruno Kirby) offers a ride to Clark (Matthew Broderick). Later, show what follows—Victor steals Clark's belongings.

• *Murder on the Orient Express.* Play a scene in which any of the suspects (Ingrid Bergman, Lauren Bacall, Sean Connery, Vanessa Redgrave, John Gielgud, Anthony Perkins, etc.) denies involvement in the murder. As it turns out, they *all* did it.

After you show each scene, have kids vote on whether the character is telling the truth (all are lying). After you've shown all of the scenes, reveal the answers and award prizes to your best "lie detectors." Ask: **How can you tell whether someone is lying? What are the advantages of being a "good liar"? What are the disadvantages?**

STEP 5

Play a song in which one person bluntly confronts another with the truth. Examples might include "You're No Good" (Linda Ronstadt), "You're So Vain" (Carly Simon), "Young Girl" (Gary Puckett and the Union Gap), "Goodbye Yellow Brick Road" (Elton John), "Mr. Big Stuff" (Jean Knight), and "These Boots Are Made for Walkin'" (Nancy Sinatra). Then ask: **What truth was the singer trying to get across? Was the truth told in a loving way? What reaction would you have if the song were directed at you? How could you change the lyrics to tell the truth in a more loving way?**

STEP 1

Try a shorter opener. As you start your meeting, announce that you can't say what the topic is. But you can give kids three hints. The first person to guess the topic will win a prize. At that point, stick a plastic fork in your mouth, tines out. Let it hang there while you tell kids that this is the first clue. Next, put down the fork and cover a group member's head with a towel for about 10 seconds. Explain that this is the second clue. Finally, have a group member (with whom you've arranged this beforehand) suddenly jump up and yell "My pants are on fire!" before he or she runs out of the room. Explain that this is the third clue. See whether anyone can guess the topic. (First clue: Speaking with a forked tongue. Second clue: Cover-up. Third clue: "Liar, liar, pants on fire." The topic, of course, is lying.) In Step 2, instead of ranking the lies, simply have kids vote on whether each is "OK" or "not OK."

STEP 3

Rather than having kids come up with Ananias and Sapphira skits, simply have volunteers act out the story as you read the passage. In Step 5, use only Situation 2 from Repro Resource 12.

STEP 3

Ask volunteers to share some examples of how lying negatively affected someone they know. It may be that the person was lied about, was caught in a lie, or believed a lie of someone else. Without using names, have kids explain what happened in the person's life as a result of lying. If possible, be prepared to share an example of your own. After several group members have shared, introduce the story of Ananias and Sapphira, who suffered the ultimate negative consequence for lying.

STEP 5

Add the following situation to Repro Resource 12:

• Last night, the apartment next door to you was burglarized. Today, on the way home from school, you overhear a couple of gang members talking about the haul they got from the burglary. One of the guys pulls out a knife and threatens to "hurt you bad" if you tell anyone about what they said. When you get home from school, a police officer is canvassing the neighborhood, investigating the burglary. He asks you if you know anything about what happened last night. How do you respond?

STEP 1

Divide kids into two teams—junior highers versus high schoolers—for the headline contest. Instead of reading the headlines aloud to the teams, give each team several sets of the "real" headlines, making sure that each gets different headlines. Allow the teams several minutes to come up with their own fake headlines to add, one per set of "real" ones. To begin the game, have a representative from one team read its headlines to the other team. If the other team can guess which headline is made up, it receives a point. The team with the most points at the end of the game is the winner.

STEP 5

To get your kids used to responding truthfully in love and not just thinking about it, have them roleplay the situations presented on Repro Resource 12. The adult roles may be played by your high schoolers, but remember, they probably need as much practice in telling the truth as your junior highers. Go through each situation a couple of times, allowing different kids to respond differently. Then, as a group, discuss some of the options that were portrayed, as well as some that may have been overlooked.

STEP 2

Have kids form pairs. Give each pair several rubber bands. Read aloud the situations on Repro Resource 11. But instead of having kids rank the lies on a scale of 1 to 10, have partners stretch a rubber band to indicate how much they think each person on the sheet is "stretching the truth." If partners think a person is doing more than stretching the truth, they should pull their rubber band until it breaks.

STEP 5

Replace Situation 3 on Repro Resource 12 with the following:

• There's a phone call for you. It's Brandon, one of your best friends. "My mom doesn't believe that I was studying at the library with you last night," he says. "She thinks that I was at some party. Would you tell her the truth?" The truth is that Brandon was at a party last night and was not with you at the library. He hands the phone to his mom, who asks, "Was Brandon at the library with you last night?" How do you respond?

DATE USED:

Approx. Time

STEP 1: *Tabloid Teasers* _____
- ❏ Extra Action
- ❏ Small Group
- ❏ Fellowship & Worship
- ❏ Extra Fun
- ❏ Media
- ❏ Short Meeting Time
- ❏ Combined Junior High/High School

Things needed:

STEP 2: *Lots-O-Liars* _____
- ❏ Small Group
- ❏ Large Group
- ❏ Heard It All Before
- ❏ Mostly Guys
- ❏ Sixth Grade

Things needed:

STEP 3: *Lie 'til Ya Die!* _____
- ❏ Little Bible Background
- ❏ Mostly Girls
- ❏ Short Meeting Time
- ❏ Urban

Things needed:

STEP 4: *God's Character* _____
- ❏ Extra Action
- ❏ Heard It All Before
- ❏ Mostly Guys

Things needed:

STEP 5: *Truth Practice* _____
- ❏ Large Group
- ❏ Little Bible Background
- ❏ Fellowship & Worship
- ❏ Mostly Girls
- ❏ Extra Fun
- ❏ Media
- ❏ Urban
- ❏ Combined Junior High/High School
- ❏ Sixth Grade

Things needed:

NOTES

NOTES

NOTES

Unit Three: Gotta Have It?

Talking to Junior Highers about Needs and Wants

by Darrell Pearson

Several months ago I received a gift certificate for an outdoors store that sells upscale clothing. When I stopped in to shop, I was amazed at how little I could buy with the gift certificate. I eventually decided to use it to buy a single shirt, reasoning that spending $75 on a casual shirt was something I had never done before. (You have to understand that this is coming from a man whose entire wardrobe consists of T-shirts from youth group trips.)

I wasn't prepared for the number of comments I got from group members who knew me well for my basic style of dress. I realized that I presented an inconsistency for them all of a sudden. The guy who downplayed clothing as an art form suddenly was in a Rembrandt.

Junior highers pick up on this sort of thing. They watch adults closely to see if their words match their lifestyles. We like to talk about being satisfied with God providing our basic needs, but we don't like to actually live that way. We're just like the kids—we have needs, and wants, too. It's pretty hard to teach others about something we're still learning ourselves.

Take a Good Look at Yourself

Where do you stand personally on the subject of needs and wants? Are you content, as Paul was, "in every circumstance"? Do you find yourself struggling with overwhelming desires to purchase the "wants" that are not critical to your life? Before you can teach kids about this tough subject, be prepared to see yourself for who you are.

I've always considered myself to be a person with a fairly simple lifestyle. Then I left the reliable paycheck of my church position to start a new youth organization, "10 to 20." That's when I began to learn about simplicity. An awful lot of things in my life went by the wayside: the *Sports Illustrated* subscription, lunches out, the daily paper. But I'm slowly learning something about what my real needs are. And I'm finding that a lot of things I thought were needs were wants. And the wants don't happen as much anymore. But amazingly enough, my needs keep getting taken care of. Has there been a time in your life when you learned the same thing? Share it with your group members. What your lifestyle preaches, they will hear.

Serve It Up

Outside of your lifestyle, a second method of getting group members to think about needs and wants is to get them involved in a service or missions experience. Many don't think of junior highers as being capable of serious mission projects; but I hear from leaders all across the country that this very thing is happening more and more. They don't have to be long trips; even a short, service-oriented project will help group members put things in perspective.

Several years ago I took two van loads of ninth graders to Mexico to participate in the increasingly popular home-building that a lot of groups are doing. When we first drove into Tijuana, I told the group members that we might stop to shop. They got very excited at the prospect of Mexican-bargaining for all those serapes and blankets. Instead, I simply drove them through the outskirts of the city for over an hour. My van became eerily quiet as kids looked out over cardboard houses and poverty they hadn't experienced before. After several days of working on our project and spending time playing with the local children, these kids had a new perspective on their lives. They realized that the Mexicans had far, far less, but were generally more satisfied, and were actually outrageously happy people. It changed those group members forever, I think. I highly recommend finding a service outlet for your junior highers. A monthly project, holiday help, a week-long trip, anything to help them see themselves in a new perspective.

The Parent's Perspective

It seems like any discussion of wants and needs is going to directly involve group members' parents—and the parents' money, as well. After all, the parents are the ones who will do most of the providing. Helping group members learn how to ask reasonably for things they need is a skill that the youth leader can help foster. Often, junior highers want just about everything they see—or see others have—even if it's totally unreasonable. The wise junior higher knows not to ask for the moon, but to use some judgment in asking parents for the things they deem important. Putting kids into their parents' shoes can be helpful here. Once young people have roleplayed parental roles (best done with parents roleplaying kids' roles) and have had to make some decisions about the limits of how far money goes, they can be more accepting of their parents' financial realities. Tackle this topic at a combined parent-group member gathering to help kids see how tough it is to provide for a family.

What Do You Want Me to Do for You?

"What do you want Me to do for you?" "What do you need Me to do for you?" The first question is one Jesus asked people in hopes of discovering the answer to the second. On the road to the Crucifixion, the disciple brothers James and John were asked the first question. Their want was to sit on the right and left of Jesus when He came into power. Jesus replies in Mark 10:38, "You don't know what you are asking. Can you drink the cup I drink...?" They wanted power; they needed to learn how to be servants.

Shortly thereafter (in vs. 51), Jesus and the disciples encounter the blind man Bartimaeus begging at the roadside. Many rebuked the man (the disciples included, I'm sure), but Jesus took time to take care of the man's needs. He asked the man the same question He asked James and John: "What do you want me to do for you?" (I can almost see Him glance at James and John as He asks it.) The response? "I want to see," said Bartimaeus. James and John learned in a poignant moment the difference between their wants and another person's needs.

There's Only So Much You Can Do

Junior highers are pretty much like James and John. They have a difficult time discerning what their needs and wants are, and how to be content without the wants that cannot be supplied. The junior high leader should be prepared for the reality that no matter what is said or taught, there is going to be a high level of disinterest in focusing on needs. In many ways, the youth leader is only planting seeds for future growth by talking with group members about needs and wants.

Is it realistic to expect kids to divorce themselves from the materialistic "want" world they live in and to live more simply? Maybe it happens once in a while, but the fact is that most junior highers won't clue in until they're older and have the maturity to process it better. And when they do—when they're in a position to evaluate their needs and wants completely—they'll likely base their decision on something taught long before by a sensitive and caring youth leader, who lived consistently with the way he or she talked.

I remember clearly my youth leaders during junior high and senior high 20 years ago. Our church always had part-time youth directors who were seminary students struggling through school. None had fancy cars. None had fancy accommodations. None wore expensive clothes. None had much of anything, except a desire to commit himself to a lifetime of service. I'll never forget those seminary students.

Modeling the life of a person satisfied with God's provision—*that's* how you talk to junior highers about needs and wants. It's loud and clear.

Darrell Pearson is co-founder of 10 to 20, an organization dedicated to presenting high-involvement events for teenagers. Formerly youth director at the First Presbyterian Church in Colorado Springs, Darrell spent most of his eleven years there directing the junior high program. He's co-authored Creative Programming Ideas for Junior High Ministry *(Youth Specialties), and written and presented the national-touring program* Next Exit. *He also speaks frequently to youth groups and leaders around the country. He lives with his wife and three daughters in Colorado Springs, Colorado.*

The images on these two pages are designed to help you promote this course within your church and community. Feel free to photocopy anything here and adapt it to fit your publicity needs. The stuff on this page could be used as a flier that you send or hand out to kids—or as a bulletin insert. The stuff on the next page could be used to add visual interest to newsletters, calendars, bulletin boards, or other promotions. Be creative and have fun!

What Do You Really Need in Life?

Is it wrong to want nice things?
How much should we spend on ourselves?
Does Jesus expect us to be poor?
We'll be looking at stuff like this in a new course called *Gotta Have It?*
Come and learn how to get what you really need!

Who:

When:

Where:

Questions? Call:

Unit Three: Gotta Have It?

(Write your own message on the note.)

Hike on over.

What do you want?

What do you need?

The oldest lie.

Wants and Needs

YOUR GOALS FOR THIS SESSION:
Choose one or more

☐ To help kids see how society and our peers can make us think we need everything we want.

☐ To help kids understand that God cares about their wants and needs, even if they don't get everything they want.

☐ To help kids choose one or more ways to cope with not getting everything they want this week.

☐ Other:_____

_____

Your Bible Base:

Psalm 37:1-11
James 2:1-13

STEP 1

Pennies from Heaven

(Needed: Masking tape, coins and/or dollar bills)

Before the meeting, you'll need to tape several coins and/or dollar bills to the ceiling of your meeting room. The more money you can tape to the ceiling, the more rewarding the following game will be to your group members. (If coins won't work, use sticks of gum or candy.)

Explain to your group members that you're going to have a contest to see who can reach the most money (in value, not in number of coins). Emphasize that group members may keep whatever money they can get off the ceiling. Make any rules necessary to safeguard your meeting place (no standing on certain pieces of furniture, for example, if you're in a home or in a room with good tables, etc.). Set a time limit and let group members go at it.

When time is up, have group members tell how much they got. Then discuss the activity, using the following questions:

How did you feel when you were trying to get the coins? (Probably most of your group members were excited about the contest. Some may have felt great because they were getting a lot of money. Others may have felt frustrated because people got to the money before they did. Still others may have felt angry at people who got greedy and pushy.)

Do you think the competition was fair? Did everyone have an equal chance to get the money? (Taller kids may have had an advantage. Smaller kids may have compensated by teaming up with other people. Others may have cheated by pushing people out of their way.)

Are you happy with the amount of money you ended up with? Let group members respond briefly.

If I had just given you that amount of money, without having you compete for it and without anyone else getting more or less than you, would you be happier? (Some group members may say no, that it was fun seeing how much they could get. Others may say that if everybody got as much as they did, they wouldn't have felt like they won anything. Still others may say yes, that they wouldn't have felt cheated if others had gotten the exact amount that they got.)

How was this game like trying to get some of the things you want in real life? (It's exciting when what you want is within reach. It's frustrating when you can't get as much as you want. Sometimes people push others out of the way when they are going after what they want.)

How were some of the unfair things we mentioned about this game like the advantages or disadvantages people have when it comes to getting stuff in real life? (Some people have natural advantages, like rich families. Some people find creative ways to improve their odds of getting things. Some people just don't seem to get the opportunities that other people have. Some people cheat to get what they want.)

How does comparing what we have with what other people have make us feel in real life? (Sometimes it makes us feel jealous or gypped because other people have more than we do. If we compare ourselves with people who have less, we might feel more grateful, or maybe superior. How you look at yourself depends a lot on who you are comparing yourself with.)

Status Symbols

(Needed: Bibles)

Say: **What kind of a Christian leader would you think I am if I gave** (name whoever got the most money in your opening activity) **special privileges for the rest of our meeting, but made** (name whoever got the least money) **do all the cleanup and stuff?** Get a few responses. **Hard as it may be to believe, that's exactly the way some people in the early church were treating others.**

Have kids turn in their Bibles to James 2:1-13. Ask a few of them to take turns reading the passage aloud. Then ask: **What are some of the status symbols at your school?** (Certain types of clothes, certain types of shoes, certain types of watches or jewelry, etc.) Compare these to the "gold ring and fine clothes" mentioned in James 2:2.

What are some ways that kids at school can make us feel like we don't have enough—or that we don't have the "right" things? (If "everybody" is wearing a certain brand of clothes—and we're not—we feel like we don't fit in. Sometimes people will come right out and be rude about what other people are wearing. If we don't have money to go skiing or some other expensive activity, we get left out.)

Can you think of any things people at your school feel like they "need" to have, but could really get along without? (Five pairs of high-tops when one pair would do; a particular brand of clothing or watch that is really different only because of its label; etc.)

What is one thing you've really wanted—that you've felt like you *had* to have—that you probably could survive without? Encourage several group members to respond. As they do, make sure you avoid judging their responses or putting down their wants.

Do you think you have most of what you really need? How about most of what you really *want?* Get responses from as many group members as possible.

STEP
3

Do Not Fret

(Needed: Bibles)

Say: **Some people say that if we don't truly need something, it's unspiritual of us to *want* it. Do you agree or disagree with that?** Get responses from as many group members as possible.

What do you think God wants us to do—and not do—when we really want something? Get several responses from your group members before you look at the following Bible verses.

Have group members form teams of three or four. Distribute paper and pencils to each team. Instruct the teams to look up Psalm 37:1-11, 16, 25 and write down as many ideas as they can find in the passage for what we should and shouldn't do when we really want something. Give the teams a few minutes to work; then have them share their responses. List the responses on the board as they are named.

Use the following suggestions to supplement the teams' answers:
- "Do not . . . be envious" (vs. 1).
- "Trust in the Lord and do good" (vs. 3).
- "Delight . . . in the Lord" (vs. 4).
- "Commit your way to the Lord" (vs. 5).
- "Be still . . . and wait patiently" (vs. 7).
- "Hope in the Lord" (vs. 9).

Use the following questions to guide your discussion of the passage:

How much does envy influence your wants? In other words, do you tend to want things that your friends or

O P T I O N S

HEARD IT ALL BEFORE

LITTLE BIBLE BACKGROUND

URBAN

people you know have? **Or do you usually want to be the first person to own certain things?**

What do you think the phrase "Trust in the Lord and do good" (vs. 3) **means?** (Depend on Him for your wants and needs; live according to His will.)

According to verse 4, what is the result of delighting in the Lord? (He will give us the desires of our heart.)

How do we "delight in the Lord"? How might delighting in the Lord affect the "desires of [our] heart"? (If we delight in the Lord, we will want what He wants. The desire of our heart will be to do His will.)

What's so hard about being "still before the Lord and [waiting] patiently for him"? (We tend to want things now. Waiting for the Lord may cause us to lose interest in what we want.)

Have group members quickly form pairs. Instruct each pair to come up with a creative, modern-day paraphrase of verse 16—something that would make the verse more understandable to today's kids. (For example: "Better the Hyundai that the righteous have than the Corvette of the wicked.") Give the pairs a few minutes to work; then have them share their suggestions.

Have someone read aloud verse 25. Then ask: **What is this verse saying? Does it make you feel any better about not getting what you want? Why or why not?**

Get Rolling

(Needed: Paper, pencils, paper bag, one assembled copy of Repro Resource 1)

Explain: **God certainly cares about meeting our needs and is certainly interested in our wants. But that doesn't mean everyone gets everything he or she wants all the time. Therefore, it's up to us to figure out ways either to get what we want or to get along without it.**

Distribute a sheet of paper and a pencil to each group member. Instruct group members to tear the sheets into three strips. Then have them write on each strip one thing that kids their age are likely to want, but may not be able to have immediately. Among the items group members might mention are a car, a bike, a skateboard, new shoes, etc.

Give group members a few minutes to work. Then collect all the strips in a paper bag.

Before the session, you'll need to assemble the cube on "Coping Cube" (Repro Resource 1). Have group members sit in a circle on the floor. Hand the bag to one of the group members and have him or her draw a slip of paper and read it to the group. Then have the person roll the cube (from Repro Resource 1) and read aloud the coping strategy that comes out on top.

Ask the person to give a specific example of how to apply that strategy to the item he or she drew from the bag, and to evaluate how well that approach might work. Invite him or her to suggest a better way if he or she cares to.

After the person responds, pass the bag to the next person and repeat the activity, going around the circle until everyone has had a turn.

Use the following information (based on the strategies listed on the cube) to supplement group members' responses.

- *Get It: Earn and save until you can buy it yourself.* (Find specific ways to earn money. This would work for smaller things, but really expensive things would take a long time to save for if parents weren't willing to chip in. This also doesn't work if parents won't permit you to have something because they don't approve of it [Nintendo, a tattoo, triple-pierced ears, etc.].)

- *Get Along Without It: Find an alternative that will do the same thing.* (If you want your own phone, but your parents say no, how about arranging a time to meet your friends after school to gab? Or how about negotiating with your parents for specific blocks of time on the family phone? If you really want certain brand name clothing, how can you keep from letting your self-esteem depend on what you wear?)

- *Get It: Negotiate to find a way you and your parents can agree.* (If you want something expensive, maybe your parents will be willing to chip in half if you pay for half. If the problem is that your parents don't approve, find a way to demonstrate that you can be trusted with whatever it is. This doesn't work if you and your parents really cannot afford it or if you secretly know they are right in forbidding it.)

- *Get Along Without It: Focus on what you have, not on what you don't have.* (Sponsoring a child or getting involved in a ministry to the poor can give you some perspective on what you really want and need. Choosing not to hang around with people who make you feel like you don't measure up materially, or not going to places where you have to have money can help.)

[NOTE: If a person rolls "Get It: You make a suggestion" or "Get Along Without It: You make a suggestion," let him or her give an original idea or pick one of the other sides of the cube to comment on.]

Coping Cubes

(Needed: Copies of Repro Resource 1, scissors, tape, pencils)

Distribute copies of "Coping Cube" (Repro Resource 1), scissors, tape, and pencils. Have group members work individually on completing the cubes. First, have them write down what they think are the best suggestions for the two blank sides of the cube. Then have them write down things they want next to the strategies on the cube that they'll try in the coming week. If you have time, ask volunteers to share what they wrote.

After group members have finished writing, have them assemble the cubes. Encourage group members to use the cubes as reminders in the coming week when they feel discouraged about not getting everything they want.

Coping Cube

Cut on the solid lines and fold on the dotted lines to form a cube. Once you've assembled the cube, secure it with tape.

Get It
Earn and save until you can buy it yourself.

Get Along Without It
Find an alternative that will do the same thing.

Get It
Negotiate to find a way you and your parents can agree.

Get Along Without It
Focus on what you have, not on what you don't have.

Get It
You make a suggestion:
_____
_____

Get Along Without It
You make a suggestion:
_____
_____

NOTES

STEP 2

Have group members form pairs. Instruct each pair to come up with a roleplay illustrating status symbols at school. In each roleplay, one person will play a kid who owns or possesses some kind of status symbol. The other person will play a kid who doesn't own or possess the status symbol. For instance, one roleplay might involve two guys in a locker room. One guy is putting on a pair of brand-new Nike Air Jordans. The other guy is putting on a pair of cheap, generic basketball shoes. The guy with the Air Jordans might be taunting or making snide remarks to the other. Give the pairs a few minutes to prepare; then have them perform their roleplays one at a time. Afterward, ask: **How do the people at your school who have certain status symbols treat those who don't? How much easier would life be at school if you had all of the status symbols that other people have? Why?**

STEP 4

Instead of using the "Coping Cube," try a more active way to present the material in Step 4. You'll need a large pair of dice. (You could dig out the fuzzy pair you had hanging from your rearview mirror in high school.) Prepare the slips of paper as described in the session. Have group members line up against a wall for a game. Explain that the object is to get to the opposite wall. One at a time, group members will roll the dice. If a person rolls an even number, he or she will get a chance to move forward. He or she will draw a slip of paper; then you will read one of the "coping strategies" from Repro Resource 1. The person will have 15 seconds to give a specific example of how to apply that coping strategy to the item on his or her slip of paper. If the person answers correctly, he or she gets to move forward the number of steps indicated on the dice. (If a person rolls an odd number, he or she must remain in place.) The first person to get to the opposite wall wins.

STEP 1

If your group is small enough, you can afford to avoid having kids go home feeling like they got gypped in the opening activity. Record how much money each person got in the opening game. Then make up the difference at the end of the session, explaining that while things don't always work out fairly in real life, when Christians give to each other, we can have a foretaste of the perfect satisfaction God has in mind for us in eternity.

STEP 2

Take advantage of your group's size by having kids share personal experiences of when they (or kids they know) were left out, made fun of, or teased for not having the "right" status symbols. You might want to share an example from your own life to get things started. Refer to group members' experiences throughout the session as you discuss status symbols.

STEP 1

If your group is so large that it would break your budget to provide coins for everyone, consider taping up certificates for special treats or privileges your group members would enjoy—seconds at refreshment time, exemption from cleanup duty, etc. When you talk about the activity, broaden your discussion to include privileges as well as more concrete material possessions.

STEP 4

Rather than having group members write down three things kids their age are likely to want, have each person write down one thing he or she wants, but may not be able to have immediately. Chances are good that many of your group members will respond similarly. Have them form teams according to their responses. (All those who wrote down a big screen TV will form one team; all those who wrote down a bike will form another team; etc.) Give each team a "Coping Cube" from Repro Resource 1 (which you've assembled before the session). Instruct each team to come up with specific examples of how to apply four of the strategies on the cube to the item its team members chose. For instance, the "big screen TV" team would come up with examples of how to earn enough money for a big screen TV; how to find an alternative to buying a big screen TV; how to negotiate with parents for a big screen TV; and how to focus on what you have, rather than focusing on not having a big screen TV. (Skip the two strategies in which kids come up with their own suggestions.) After a few minutes, have each team share its responses.

STEP 2

Jaded kids are often quick to criticize the church and other Christians for what they perceive to be hypocritical behavior. This passage from James, aimed as it is at the early church, provides a perfect opening for such criticism. Let kids air their grievances, but then turn their complaints into challenges by asking them to evaluate how they measure up in the area of treating others without favoritism and not being impressed by status symbols. Ask them whether others can tell that they are Christians by the way they spend their money, the people they favor, and so on.

STEP 3

Rather than focusing on the biblical principles concerning getting what you want, focus on what happens when biblical principles are ignored. Help your kids see the practical aspects of biblical teaching. Ask: **What happens when we get envious of someone?** (It affects our relationship with the person. We also may look petty and childish to other people.) **Rather than doing good, as instructed in verse 3, what are some bad ways to get what we want?** (Steal, threaten, pout, etc.) **What are some of the dangers of using these bad methods?** (Stealing can lead to serious trouble with the law. Threatening and pouting can negatively affect a person's relationship with the giver.)

STEP 2

Give your group members some background on the Book of James. Explain that it was written to churches who still needed guidance in how to live out what they believed in everyday life (as we still need today). In your discussion of the passage, focus particularly on verses 1-4, which provide a concrete picture most people can relate to. Don't get bogged down in questions of the law (vss. 8-13) unless you have time to explain the passage thoroughly.

STEP 3

If your group members are unfamiliar with the Bible and the Christian life, the idea of being "unspiritual" may not mean much to them. In fact, the first question may sound ludicrous to them, so you may want to skip it. After all, what's wrong with wanting something? The second question, however, should elicit some interesting responses. These responses should give you an idea of what your group members know about God. In the Bible study, focus especially on the suggestions in verses 1, 3, and 7. (Phrases like "Delight . . . in the Lord" [vs. 4] and "Commit your way to the Lord" [vs. 5] may not mean much to kids with little Christian background.) For tips on focusing on the practical aspects of the passage, see the "Heard It All Before" option for Step 3.

STEP 1

Try a brief, get-to-know-you activity to open the session. Have group members pair up (preferably with kids they don't know very well). Instruct each person to complete the following statement with his or her partner: "If I had a million dollars, here's how I would spend it: . . ." Explain that you will be giving a prize to the person who comes up with the most creative response. As each person shares, his or her partner should write down the person's responses. Then, after a few minutes, each person should introduce his or her partner to the rest of the group by saying, "This is _____ . If he (or she) had a million dollars, here's how he (or she) would spend it: . . ."

STEP 5

Have kids write their names on their cubes. Then build a "prayer tower" of the cubes by having each person say a sentence prayer and place his or her cube in the center of the circle, building on the cubes already there. Suggest that kids complete one of these sentences: "Thank you, God, for giving me . . ." or "Help me this week to (whatever they decided to do earlier in Step 5) . . ."

STEP 2

After discussing the questions in Step 2, divide group members into two teams. Give Team 1 this situation and question: **You finally have received something that you really wanted. How has your life changed because of it?** Give Team 2 this situation and question: **You have not received something that you really wanted. How has your life changed or been affected because you do not have it?** Ask each team to discuss and then present its conclusions to the other team.

STEP 5

As your group members are completing their coping cubes, ask for a volunteer to serve as a roving reporter. Give her a portable cassette recorder to tape responses from the other group members. Have your reporter ask the following questions about waiting: "Do you think you're good at waiting? Why or why not?" "What is one thing that is especially hard for you to wait for?" "When is waiting not a problem for you?" After several group members have responded, play the tape so that everyone can hear the attitudes about being "waiters."

STEP 1

After the opening activity, have each of your group members describe what life would be like without the following items:

• a television (especially during major sporting events like the World Series, Super Bowl, or NBA Championship)

• a VCR

• spending money

• soap

• school

• McDonalds

• jeans

• car radios

• junk food

Use group members' responses to lead into a discussion of what's important to them.

STEP 5

If assembling the cubes seems too much like a feminine craft to your guys, let them just jot down their ideas on Repro Resource 1 and take it home in their pockets. Or you might try another activity. Stand the guys in a circle. Give one of them the assembled cube from Step 4. Have him read one of the strategies he plans to use and toss the cube to someone else in the circle. That person must choose a strategy he plans to use, read it, and toss the cube to another person. Continue until everyone has had a turn.

STEP 1

Depending on the size of your group, bring in one or more Monopoly games. (Ideally, you should have one game for every six group members.) To open the session, have your group members play Monopoly for 10 minutes. Explain that the person with the most property and cash after 10 minutes is the winner. Afterward, say: **There's a bumper sticker that says, "He who dies with the most toys wins." What does that mean?** (The purpose of life is to acquire as many things as possible.) **Do you agree with this philosophy? Why or why not? Do you know of anyone who agrees with this philosophy?** Emphasize that you're not looking for specific names. After a few minutes of discussion, begin the money-on-the-ceiling activity.

STEP 2

Before the session, prepare several index cards. Each card should have a "status symbol" item written on it as well as an approximate price for the item. (For example: "Top-of-the-line basketball shoes—$150"; "Ski jacket—$275"; etc.) Hide the cards around the room before your group members arrive. As you begin Step 2, have your group members try to find the hidden cards. Explain that the object of the game is not necessarily to find the most cards, but to find the most expensive cards. The person with the highest dollar total on his or her cards is the winner. However, to add a twist to the game, you will periodically yell **Switch!** When you do, group members must quickly pair up. Each person will then choose (without looking) and keep one of his or her partner's cards. After a few minutes, tally up the results and declare a winner. Afterward, discuss how quickly material possessions (including various kinds of status symbols) can be lost.

STEP 2

Before the meeting, assign teams of group members with video cameras to interview kids at school, the mall, or wherever they want to go. Have them ask questions like these: "What do you think is the most in-demand item for kids your age right now?" "Do you want it? Why or why not?" "What are the status symbols at your school?" "How important are they?" "In your opinion, are Christians more likely, less likely, or just as likely as non-Christians to judge others by their clothes and possessions?" Play these interviews at your meeting to spark discussion.

STEP 4

Before your meeting, record one or more of the Pepsi "Gotta Have It" commercials or another commercial portraying a product as essential for young people. Play the clips at the beginning of Step 4 and discuss how advertising can make us think we need things that we can really get along without. If you have the Pepsi ad, focus on the conflict set up between adulthood and youth. Discuss whether youth is really a time to get everything and do everything you want. Then move into the rest of Step 4.

STEP 2

If your time is short, read only verses 1-4. Focus on the parallels between the situation in James' day and what kids encounter every day at school and elsewhere.

STEP 4

Rather than taking time to have group members write down three things kids their age want, simply have them call out their ideas while you write them on the board. After you've got a list of at least eight items, write four of the strategies from the "Coping Cube" (Repro Resource 1) on the board. (Skip the two "You make a suggestion" strategies.) Quickly go through the list of items, asking volunteers to call out specific examples of how to apply each of the four strategies to each item on the list.

STEP 1

Draw two columns on the board. Label one column "Wants"; label the other column "Needs." Then call out various areas of life—school, church, home, friends, community, etc. When you call out an area, group members should brainstorm various wants and needs associated with that area. (Emphasize that needs are those things that are absolutely essential—things that you can't do without.) For instance, school "wants" might include new clothes, school supplies with the logo of your favorite team, expensive gym shoes, a lot of money for lunch every day, etc. School "needs" might include books, teachers, a brain, etc. Use this activity to discuss the importance of separating wants from needs. If you want, you could shift the discussion to talk about social needs. Ask: **What if someone doesn't have what he or she needs because of financial or personal hardship? What could we as a group do to help such a person?** You might want to have group members identify people they know who have unmet needs. Then, as a group, you could devise ways to provide for these people.

STEP 3

Ask volunteers to talk about people they know (or have heard of) who were killed or attacked for a possession (perhaps a pair of shoes, a warm-up jacket, a hat, etc.). Ask: **Do you own any possessions that you would risk your life for? Explain.**

STEP 2

Your junior highers and high schoolers will probably have different ideas about what they consider valuable and desirable. After a junior higher names something that he or she really wants, ask one of your high schoolers to respond. Is that item something that he or she wants too? Or is it more of a "junior high thing"? After a high schooler names something he or she wants, ask one of your junior highers to respond. Use this activity to lead into a discussion of how other people's opinions affect the things we want and think we need.

STEP 4

After you've collected the slips, write group members' responses on the board. Assign your junior highers the "Get It" strategies on the "Coping Cube." Assign your high schoolers the "Get Along Without It" strategies. Instruct each group to brainstorm specific examples of how to apply their assigned strategies to each item on the list. For instance, if one of the items on the list is a bike, junior highers would brainstorm examples of how to earn enough money to buy a bike and how to negotiate with parents to get a bike. High schoolers would brainstorm examples of how to find an alternative to buying a bike and how to focus on the things you have, rather than focusing on not having a bike. After a few minutes, go through the list on the board, having each group share its strategies for each item.

STEP 2

Have your sixth graders focus on James 2:1-4, 8-9, rather than the entire passage. Have someone read aloud James 2:1. Then ask for several volunteers to pantomime verses 2-4 while it is being read aloud to the entire group. After the pantomime, ask the kids to talk about how they felt when they were judged solely by their clothing. Read aloud verses 8 and 9; then continue the discussion as written.

STEP 4

Sixth graders are more likely than older kids to be open and honest about the reasons behind their wants. After you go through the Psalm 37 passage, ask: **Which of the following usually causes you to want something more: seeing one of your friends with it or seeing it advertised on TV? Do you think it's wrong to want something your friends have? Why or why not? Do you think it's wrong to be influenced by TV advertising? Why or why not? When is it wrong to want something you don't have?**

DATE USED:

Approx. Time

STEP 1: *Pennies from Heaven* _____
- ❏ Small Group
- ❏ Large Group
- ❏ Fellowship & Worship
- ❏ Mostly Guys
- ❏ Extra Fun
- ❏ Urban
- Things needed:

STEP 2: *Status Symbols* _____
- ❏ Extra Action
- ❏ Small Group
- ❏ Heard It All Before
- ❏ Little Bible Background
- ❏ Mostly Girls
- ❏ Extra Fun
- ❏ Media
- ❏ Short Meeting Time
- ❏ Combined Junior High/High School
- ❏ Sixth Grade
- Things needed:

STEP 3: *Do Not Fret* _____
- ❏ Heard It All Before
- ❏ Little Bible Background
- ❏ Urban
- Things needed:

STEP 4: *Get Rolling* _____
- ❏ Extra Action
- ❏ Large Group
- ❏ Media
- ❏ Short Meeting Time
- ❏ Combined Junior High/High School
- ❏ Sixth Grade
- Things needed:

STEP 5: *Coping Cubes* _____
- ❏ Fellowship & Worship
- ❏ Mostly Girls
- ❏ Mostly Guys
- Things needed:

Living with Less

☐ To help kids recognize how possessions can get in the way of their relationship with God.

☐ To help kids understand that they can find happiness without having a lot of stuff.

☐ To help kids choose a group activity in which they will experience having fun with less.

☐ Other:_____
_____

Your Bible Base:

Matthew 6:19-34

Traveling Light

(Needed: Cut-apart copies of Repro Resource 2, assembled copies of Repro Resource 3, brass fastener, masking tape)

Before the meeting, you'll need to cut apart one copy of "Game Cards" (Repro Resource 2). Keep the "identity cards" and the "possession cards" in separate piles.

You'll also need to prepare the "Traveling Light Spinner" (Repro Resource 3) by cutting out the arrow and attaching it, using a brass fastener. (If you can't make the spinner, simply cut it apart and put each of the seven pieces in a hat. Have a volunteer draw one slip for each round. Put the slips back in the hat after each round.)

Make your meeting area a room-sized game board by using masking tape to mark off squares on the floor. You can make the "board" as simple or elaborate as you like; just try to have at least ten squares and make sure you have a clearly defined start and finish.

To open your meeting, ask for two volunteers (who think they are strong—or simply choose your two biggest kids) to serve as "playing pieces" on the board. Distribute the six "possession cards" from Repro Resource 2 between the two playing pieces. Ask your playing pieces what they think of their possessions. Let them trade possessions if they want.

Then ask for six volunteers to serve as "possessions." Give each one an "identity card" from Repro Resource 2. Instruct the "possessions" to find out which "playing piece" has their card and join that player on the game board, following the directions on the card. (For instance, the person with the identity card that says "leather jacket" will climb piggy-back onto his or her playing piece.)

Once all the "possessions" are distributed between the playing pieces, line the playing pieces up at the starting square. Let them take turns spinning the spinner and following the directions on it. If a player stumbles or cannot carry out the directions, he or she may not advance during that turn. Encourage the "possessions" (and the rest of the group members) to cheer the players on.

When one of the playing pieces has reached the finish square, declare him or her the winner and lead the rest of the group in a round of applause.

Then discuss the activity, using the following questions.

How did you playing pieces feel during this game? (Sore, from dragging the possessions around; overloaded; frustrated, because I had more to carry than my competitor; stupid; unable to compete because of all the stuff I had to haul around; etc.)

When you first got your possessions, did you think it was going to be good or bad to have them? (Good, at first—I thought whoever had the most would win, like in Monopoly. I started getting suspicious when they started dragging me down.)

Which possession do you think would have the most cash value? Which was the most valuable to you in this game? (The leather jacket or gold jewelry would probably have the most cash value. The person who had the "good friend" would probably say that was the most valuable possession. Instead of getting in the way and weighing the player down, the good friend helped out and supported the player.)

How is this game like real life? (Sometimes if you have too much stuff it can keep you from reaching goals because you get lazy—you figure you have it all already. If you're worried about taking care of your stuff, it can get in the way of doing other things—like when you get a new bike, but don't want to take it anywhere for fear someone will steal it. Some things can mess you up in other parts of your life—Nintendo can keep you from doing things with your friends, having your own phone can keep you from doing your homework, etc. Good friends are worth more than all the rest of our stuff put together.)

How could having a lot of stuff keep us from having a good relationship with God? (We might think we don't need Him because we have everything we want. We may not have time for Him because we're so busy with our stuff. We may not want to take risks for Him because we think we have too much to lose.)

Explain: **You probably know what it means to "travel light" when you go on a trip or go backpacking. Today we're going to see if it's possible to "travel light" in the way we live our everyday lives.**

Top Ten

(Needed: Paper, pencils)

Say: **We've listed some negative consequences of having too much stuff. But most of us probably don't feel like we have too much. In fact, most of us probably feel like we'd like to have more!**

Let's try to think of some positive things about *not* being loaded down with stuff—some good things about "living light."

Have group members form pairs. Distribute paper and pencils to each pair. Instruct the pairs to come up with a David Letterman-style list of the "Top 10 Reasons for Living Light." Get them started with a few suggestions: "Nobody tries to borrow money from you"; "You'll never have to find out your girlfriend loves you only for your Jaguar"; "You don't have to worry about finding a dependable Maserati mechanic"; etc. Encourage group members to include humor as much as possible in their lists.

Give the pairs a few minutes to work. When everyone is done, have a spokesperson from each pair read its list, starting from 10 and working up to 1.

Collage Education

(Needed: Bibles, old magazines, scissors, glue, markers, poster board or large sheets of paper, masking tape)

Have group members remain in their pairs from the previous activity. Make sure each pair has access to several old magazines, scissors, glue, markers, and poster board or large sheets of paper.

Instruct the pairs to read Matthew 6:19-34 and make a poster or collage illustrating one of the contrasting pairs found in the passage. The contrasting pairs could include earthly treasures vs. heavenly treasures, serving God vs. serving money, birds not worrying about food vs. people worrying about clothes and food, those running after material possessions vs. those seeking God's kingdom.

Encourage the pairs to be as creative as they can with their collages, mixing magazine photos and headlines with their own drawing and writing, and using contemporary images instead of trying to illustrate the text literally. Circulate among the pairs while they work to give them encouragement and help, if necessary.

When all the collages are completed, tape them to the walls in the order they are mentioned in the passage. Then have the pairs read the verses they based their work on and explain a little about the images they chose.

As you work your way through Matthew 6:19-34, stop after the appropriate verses to discuss the following questions:

Verses 19-21

What have you ever owned that got rusted, moth-eaten, stolen, or otherwise ruined? (Group members may mention bikes that rusted, sweaters that got holey, or other belongings that got stolen or just plain worn out.)

What do you think a "treasure in heaven" might be? (Love, a relationship with Jesus Christ, assurance of eternal life.)

According to these verses, why are heavenly treasures more valuable than earthly ones? (Heavenly treasures last forever.)

Which kind of treasures do you think most people are interested in? Why? (Most people are probably interested in earthly treasures because you can enjoy them right now. You can see and touch earthly treasures. People who really think about God and the future value heavenly treasures, but that doesn't mean they don't like having nice things now, too.)

Verses 22-24

What does it mean to serve God? (To do everything as if He is your boss, to obey Him and love Him.)

What does it mean to serve money? (To do whatever it takes to get more and more money, to consider money more important than God or people.)

Do you think you can serve both God and money? Explain. (Some group members will probably say no, you can't serve both God and money, because one of them will end up being more important than the other. Others may say you can love God and still enjoy things that money buys.)

Verses 25-30

What are some good ways that not worrying could make us like birds or plants? (We'd be free to enjoy ourselves. We'd depend more on God for what we need. We'd realize we aren't really in control of our lives.)

OPTIONS

EXTRA ACTION

LITTLE BIBLE BACKGROUND

MOSTLY GIRLS

MOSTLY GUYS

SHORT MEETING TIME

URBAN

JR. HIGH HIGH SCHOOL COMBINED

SIXTH GRADE

Verses 31-34

What are some things people "run after" today? (The "right" clothes, the latest "toys" or gadgets, the latest CDs, etc.)

What do you think it means to seek God's kingdom instead? (To live for God, according to His principles; to let everyone see God in you instead of some designer label on you.)

No-Frills Fun

(Needed: Paper, pencils, chalkboard and chalk or newsprint and marker)

Say: **It's easy to** *talk* **about living with less, but when it comes right down to it, most of us probably still think we'd prefer to live with more! Let's see if we can translate what we've been talking about into real-life action.**

Have group members form teams of three or four. Distribute paper and pencils to each team. Instruct each team to come up with at least five ideas for things that would be fun to do as a group that don't involve money (no admission fees or big transportation costs), expensive equipment (like skis, a boat, or someone's cottage), or the "right" clothes (like a formal for a dance or dinner). Encourage the teams to think of the most creative and enjoyable activities they can. Your goal is to show how to have fun living with less, not to point out how hard it is!

Give the teams a few minutes to work. When they're finished, have each team share its suggestions. Compile a list on the board of the teams' suggestions.

Then, as a group, choose one activity to do together. Spend some time working out the details and set a date. Wrap up the session by affirming your group's ability to have fun without "having it all."

OPTIONS

LARGE GROUP

HEARD IT ALL BEFORE

LITTLE BIBLE BACKGROUND

FELLOWSHIP & WORSHIP

MOSTLY GIRLS

EXTRA FUN

MEDIA

NOTES

GAME

CARDS

IDENTITY CARDS — *Cut these out and give one to each person who is not a playing piece.*

LEATHER JACKET: Your playing piece must wear you. Climb on his or her back and ride piggy-back.	**NEW SHOES:** Take off your shoes and stand on your playing piece's feet. You must stay on even when he or she is moving.	**GOLD JEWELRY:** Hang your arms around your playing piece's neck (you'll be a gold chain) or arm (you'll be a bracelet). Don't choke your playing piece.
WALKMAN: Your hands are ear-phones. Put them over your playing piece's ears.	**POCKET GAMEBOY:** OK, you don't really fit in a pocket. So your playing piece must carry you in his or her arms.	**GOOD FRIEND:** You don't have much cash value, but you're ready to sup-port (literally—help him or her stay on balance) your playing piece whenever needed.

POSSESSION CARDS — *Cut these out and divide them between the "playing pieces."*

LEATHER JACKET	NEW SHOES	GOLD JEWELRY
WALKMAN	POCKET GAMEBOY	GOOD FRIEND

Traveling Light Spinner

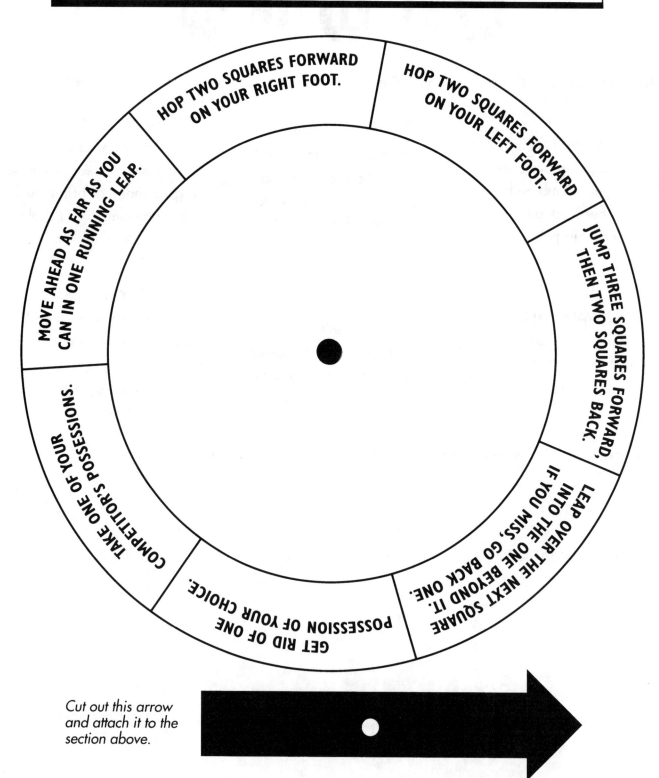

HOP TWO SQUARES FORWARD ON YOUR RIGHT FOOT.

HOP TWO SQUARES FORWARD ON YOUR LEFT FOOT.

JUMP THREE SQUARES FORWARD, THEN TWO SQUARES BACK.

LEAP OVER THE NEXT SQUARE INTO THE ONE BEYOND IT. IF YOU MISS, GO BACK ONE.

GET RID OF ONE POSSESSION OF YOUR CHOICE.

TAKE ONE OF YOUR COMPETITOR'S POSSESSIONS.

MOVE AHEAD AS FAR AS YOU CAN IN ONE RUNNING LEAP.

Cut out this arrow and attach it to the section above.

EXTRA ACTION

STEP 2

If your group members prefer more action, replace the writing exercise with a series of skits. Have group members form teams. Instruct each team to create and perform a commercial for "Life Lite." The commercial should demonstrate at least one benefit of "living light" (living without a lot of material possessions). Suggest that the teams model their commercials after the "lite" ads (for beer, diet food, diet cola, etc.) currently on TV. If your kids remember the old "Tastes great! Less filling!" ads for Miller Lite beer, they may want to follow that format. Give the teams a few minutes to prepare; then have them present their commercials. [NOTE: The intent of this activity is not to promote beer. If kids choose to mimic beer commercials, spend some time discussing ways beer commercials try to persuade people to buy the product.]

STEP 3

For a more active session, replace the poster-making activity with a game of charades. As a group, go through Matthew 6:19-34, identifying the contrasting pairs found there (earthly treasures vs. heavenly treasures, serving God vs. serving money, etc.). Write each item of the contrasting pairs on an individual slip of paper ("earthly treasures" on one slip, "heavenly treasures" on another, etc.). Then have group members form teams. One at a time, have a player from each team draw a slip and act out what is written on the slip. If the team guesses the phrase within 30 seconds, it gets a point. The team with the most points at the end of the game wins. Use the questions in the session to discuss the activity and Bible passage.

SMALL GROUP

STEP 1

If your group has fewer than six members, choose one person (preferably the biggest guy) to be a "playing piece." Assign the rest of the group members to be "possessions." Give the playing piece a series of assignments to complete within a certain time limit (perhaps two minutes). He must complete the assignments while carrying (or dragging around) the possessions. Here are some assignments you might use:

• **Shoot three paper wads into the trash can from at least 10 feet away.**

• **Step up and down on a chair three times.**

• **Run to the other side of the room and back twice.**

• **Spin around in place for 30 seconds.**

Afterward, ask: **How is this game like real life?** (Sometimes having too many possessions can "weigh you down.")

How could having a lot of stuff keep us from having a good relationship with God?

STEP 2

As long as you're talking about living with less, focus briefly on the benefits of "traveling light" as a group. Ask: **What are some of the benefits of having a small group? What kinds of things can we do that larger groups may not be able to do?** Don't spend a lot of time on this topic, but at least get your kids thinking about the special relationships that can occur among the members of a small group.

LARGE GROUP

STEP 1

Have group members form teams of five. Designate one person on each team to be the "playing piece." The rest of the team members will be "possessions." You'll need to cut apart several copies of Repro Resource 2 for this activity. Give each playing piece four possession cards. Allow a minute or two for the playing pieces to trade possession cards with each other, if they wish. (However, each should still have four cards at the end of the trading.) Have the playing pieces distribute the four cards to their teammates. Then pass out the identity cards that explain what each possession does. Play the game as described in the session—with one exception. When two playing pieces occupy the same square, they must battle for possession of the square. When you say **Go,** each must try to nudge (standing back-to-back) the other out of the square. The winner remains in the square; the loser must go back two spaces. Continue until one playing piece makes it to the finish square.

STEP 4

Rather than planning just one activity for your group to enjoy together, plan several. Have group members form teams of six to eight. Each team will plan—and actually host—a "no-frills" fun event. For instance, one team might plan a "video game night" in which group members bring their Nintendos and other computer games to the church (or someone's house) for a night of competition. To make sure everyone can compete equally, the team might plan contests to see who can get the best score playing only with one hand, who can get the best score playing blindfolded, who can get the best score while someone tries to interfere with him or her, etc. Give the teams several minutes to plan; then have each one share its ideas. Write the ideas on the board. Then have group members vote on what they'd like to do first, second, and so on, and plan your group's calendar accordingly.

STEP 2

After the pairs brainstorm their top-ten lists of reasons for living light, have them brainstorm another list—"Top 10 Reasons for Acquiring Everything You Can." Get them started with a few suggestions: "It never hurts to have a spare Porsche handy in case your other one is in the shop"; "You can pay for your parents' retirement condo when they move to Florida"; etc. Encourage the pairs to include humor in their responses— but also encourage them to be open and honest. After all, there are a lot of people who try to acquire everything they can, so there must be some good reasons for it. Afterward, have the pairs compare their two lists and determine which set of reasons are more convincing. Then have them share their opinions with the rest of the group.

STEP 4

One of the best ways to move jaded kids out of complacency is to involve them in service. Instead of (or in addition to) planning a fun event for themselves, guide your kids in planning an activity that would help them experience what it means to "seek first the kingdom." Consider these options: a workday in an inner-city ministry; a food scavenger hunt for the needy or a food pantry; pushing wheelchairs and pouring coffee at a nursing home; etc.

STEP 3

For your group members with little Bible background, you may need to explain who Solomon (vs. 29) was. Point out that he was one of the richest kings who ever lived. His reign was noted for its splendor and grandeur. That's why he is held up as an example of a splendid dresser. Explain that "pagans" (vs. 32) refers to anyone who does not know God, not just to exotic, primitive tribes in faraway countries.

STEP 4

Kids with little knowledge of Christianity or the Bible may come away from this session with the wrong idea about the Christian life. So as you brainstorm ideas for how to to have fun with less, emphasize to your kids that Christianity is a religion of joy, not of deprivation. You might want to consider closing the session by reading and briefly discussing John 10:10 as a group.

STEP 1

Have your group members form pairs. Ask each person to share with his or her partner the answers to these questions: **If your home were burning, what two possessions would you rescue? Why?** Give the pairs a few minutes to talk. Then have each person share with his or her partner the answers to these questions: **Do you think either of the two possessions you mentioned could ever come between you and God? Why or why not?**

STEP 4

Have your group members stand in a circle. Place the posters group members made in Step 3 in the center of the circle. Close the session by inviting each person to step forward and touch something on one of the posters that he or she wants to thank God for. Then, as a group, say, "Thank you, God, for the simple things. Thank you for giving us what we need."

STEP 3

As you discuss the verses and the posters or collages illustrating them, ask: **Do these verses mean that you and your parents should not work to provide clothes and food for yourselves? What's the difference between "worrying" and "being responsible"?**

STEP 4

As the teams are thinking about ideas for fun activities that don't require money, ask them to include one idea for something that can be done during this session. Keep a separate list of these in-session ideas as you compile all of the teams' suggestions on the board. Choose one idea from the list to use as you wrap up the session.

STEP 1

If you think your guys might feel self-conscious about some of the physical contact involved in the opening game, substitute another activity. You will need several stacks of books (the larger and heavier, the better) for this activity. Have group members form two teams. Instruct the teams to line up for a relay race. On the other side of the room, place two very large stacks of books (one stack per team). Explain that the contest is to see which team can move its stack of books from one side of the room to the other, using the fewest trips. When you say **Go,** the first person in line for each team will run to his team's stack, pick up as many books as he can, and carry them back to the other side of the room. Then the next person in line will do the same thing. Keep track of how many trips each team makes. Award prizes to the team that makes the fewest trips. Afterward, discuss how being "loaded down" with things can affect our performance—both in competition and in the Christian life.

STEP 3

If your guys don't express their creativity well through artistic media, send them on a modified scavenger hunt. Read through the passage, then ask each person to find one item that illustrates each contrasting pair. Allow only 5 or 10 minutes for the scavenger hunt and require that the kids stay on the grounds (no going door-to-door). The items can be as literal as a feather found outside to illustrate the birds of the air, or as symbolic as a church offering plate to illustrate giving for God's kingdom.

STEP 1

Play a game in which the winner is the person with the least amount of something at the end of the game. You might play one of your group's favorite games and award toothpicks as penalties. (For example, you might award a toothpick every time someone is caught in the middle in "Fruit Basket Upset" or with an empty chair in "Winkum.") Or you might have group members play a game like "Uno," in which the goal is to get rid of your cards first. Afterward, point out that we usually think more is better; however, sometimes less is best.

STEP 4

Point out that part of enjoying living with less involves making the most of what we have. Provide an unlikely assortment of snacks and goodies. Try to bring things that will require some ingenuity on the kids' part. (For instance, don't simply bring ingredients for ice-cream sundaes. Instead, you might bring things like peanuts, hot chocolate mix, whipped cream, granola or other cereal, etc.) Invite kids to make their own gourmet concoctions.

STEP 1

Show some clips from the video of the movie *Big*. (Make sure you preview the clips beforehand.) Focus specifically on scenes that show the things Josh accumulated as an adult. (Some of the scenes set in his apartment and his office would work well.) Then show the scene in which Josh decides to give it all up and go home. Afterward, discuss what values influenced Josh's decision and how all of his new toys and possessions affected him.

STEP 4

Before the session, record the accompaniment to the praise chorus "Seek Ye First" (or find a praise tape with the song on it), which is based on the Scripture passage for this session (Matt. 6:19-34). Close your meeting by playing this song. If your group members enjoy singing, have them sing along.

STEP 1

Rather than taking time to do the opening activity, choose two group members to compete in a race around the building. Choose the best athlete in the group to be one of the contestants; choose a non-athletic group member to be the other contestant. (Some of the other group members may comment on the seeming unfairness of the contest.) Have your contestants line up. Then, just before you start the race, hand two suitcases (filled with clothes and books) to the athletic contestant and explain that he or she must carry the suitcases during the race. After the race, discuss the advantages of "traveling light."

STEP 3

Poster-making can be time-consuming. Instead of having kids look for magazine photos to combine into a collage, provide paper and markers and let kids make simpler posters. Assure those who doubt their artistic ability that symbols, words, or campaign-type slogans are as acceptable as illustrations.

STEP 1

Try a zany alternative to the opening activity to demonstrate how possessions slow us down. Before the session, gather a number of possessions (the heavier, the better) that can be parted with—old clothes, pots and pans, books, blankets, bottles, cinder blocks, canned goods, etc.). Stack the objects in two piles, with roughly the same number and size of objects in each pile. Then mark off a difficult relay course—one that will involve running, climbing, and crawling (perhaps through many rooms). Ask for two volunteers to compete in an obstacle-course race. Hand each person a large laundry bag. Explain that the object of the race is to see who can gather the most possessions in his or her laundry bag and carry them through the relay course quickest. The first one through the course will get to keep the objects in his or her bag. At any time, the contestants may take items out of their bags to make them lighter; but once an object is taken out, it may not be put back in. Afterward, point out that we must think before we acquire certain possessions, because if we're not careful, they may slow us down in our Christian life.

STEP 3

As you start to clean up after the collage activity, pick up one of the collages that your group members made, crumple it up, and throw it away. Start to do the same to another collage. When someone objects, ask why he or she wants to keep the collage. Then ask: **How would you feel if someone came into your room and threw away your favorite CDs? What would you do? Why?** Use this illustration to begin discussing how important your group members' possessions are to them.

STEP 1

If you think your group members may find the opening activity too childish, replace it with a more athletic, sports-related competition in which the players are in some way handicapped by too much stuff. For instance, you could have group members play softball while trying to carry bowling balls. Or you might have kids try to shoot baskets while wearing several coats and balancing a shoe on their head.

STEP 3

If possible, pair up junior highers with high schoolers for the collage activity. Have one person work on one side of the collage, while the other person works on the other side. For instance, in one pair, the high schooler might work on the "serving God" side of the collage; the junior higher would then work on the "serving money" side. This is a good activity to promote mingling between the age-groups.

STEP 2

Instead of having your sixth graders form pairs, have them work in teams of three or four. Shorten the assignment by asking each team to write five reasons for living light. You might have half of the teams write "serious" lists and the other half write more humorous, nonsensical lists. After a few minutes, have each team share its list.

STEP 3

Ask your sixth graders to remain in the teams they formed in Step 2. Assign each team one of the following Scripture passages to use for its collage:

• Matthew 6:19-21 (earthly treasures vs. heavenly treasures)

• Matthew 6:24 (serving God vs. serving money)

• Matthew 6:25-30 (birds not worrying about food vs. people worrying about clothes and food)

• Matthew 6:31-34 (running after material possessions vs. seeking God's kingdom)

You might want to wander from team to team, offering suggestions and help for their collages. Afterward, display the collages around the room for a few weeks as reminders of this session.

DATE USED:

Approx. Time

STEP 1: *Traveling Light* _____
- ❏ Small Group
- ❏ Large Group
- ❏ Fellowship & Worship
- ❏ Mostly Guys
- ❏ Extra Fun
- ❏ Media
- ❏ Short Meeting Time
- ❏ Urban
- ❏ Combined Junior High/High School

Things needed:

STEP 2: *Top Ten* _____
- ❏ Extra Action
- ❏ Small Group
- ❏ Heard It All Before
- ❏ Sixth Grade

Things needed:

STEP 3: *Collage Education* _____
- ❏ Extra Action
- ❏ Little Bible Background
- ❏ Mostly Girls
- ❏ Mostly Guys
- ❏ Short Meeting Time
- ❏ Urban
- ❏ Combined Junior High/High School
- ❏ Sixth Grade

Things needed:

STEP 4: *No-Frills Fun* _____
- ❏ Large Group
- ❏ Heard It All Before
- ❏ Little Bible Background
- ❏ Fellowship & Worship
- ❏ Mostly Girls
- ❏ Extra Fun
- ❏ Media

Things needed:

The Problem with Taking What You Want

YOUR GOALS FOR THIS SESSION:

Choose one or more

☐ To help kids see how Adam and Eve paid the price for ignoring God and taking what they wanted.

☐ To help kids understand how selfish shortcuts to getting what they want usually backfire in the long run.

☐ To help kids identify one selfish action they can work to eliminate and so reduce their risk of negative consequences.

☐ Other:_____
_____

Your Bible Base:

Genesis 2:4—3:24

STEP 1

Sightless Scurry

(Needed: Chairs, prize)

To open the session, display a prize that your group members will want to win. Promise the prize to the team that wins the following game.

Have group members form two or three teams. For each team, set up a simple obstacle course using several chairs. (If you don't have enough chairs, use some of your group members as obstacles.) Designate start and finish lines.

Explain that the teams will be competing in a blindfolded relay—without the blindfolds. [NOTE: The object of this activity is to give group members an opportunity to cheat—but don't let them know that.]

Say: **When I say go, one pair from each team will run its obstacle course, with one partner keeping his or her eyes closed. When the pair reaches the end, the "seeing" partner will close his or her eyes and the "blind" partner will open his or hers to run the course back to the team. That pair will then tag the next pair, who will continue the process.** Have players run more than once, if necessary, to give the teams an equal number of pairs.

When the relay is finished, award the prize to the winning team with great ceremony. Then use the following questions to discuss the activity.

How did you feel when it looked like your team was going to win the prize? (Eager, motivated to keep going, triumphant, cocky.)

How did you feel when it looked like your team was going to lose? (Like trying harder; like giving up; angry, because the winning team was cheating; indifferent, because it's just a game.)

How many of you were tempted to cheat—maybe by peeking when you were supposed to have your eyes closed? Encourage group members to respond honestly. After all, it's hard not to open your eyes when you might ram into a chair.

Do you think I made it too easy for people to cheat by not using blindfolds? (Some group members may say yes, that the game would have been more fair if it were harder to cheat. Others may say no, that people should be able to control themselves.)

Acknowledge that, even if they weren't that motivated by the prize (your group members may feel it's not "cool" to let on that they wanted it), most people have a competitive streak in them and want to win.

Then ask: **How were some of the emotions you felt in this relay like the things you feel when you want something really badly?** (You get excited when you think you're going to get it. You get disappointed when you can't have it.)

Do you know people who will "bend the rules" to get what they want? Give some specific examples. (Some people cheat on tests to get good grades. Others lie to their parents about why they need something. Still others shoplift or steal the things they want.)

Have you ever wanted something so badly you felt like you'd do anything—even if it weren't legal or moral—to get it? Let volunteers give specific examples if they wish, but don't push the issue.

STEP 2

Forbidden Fruit

(Needed: Bibles)

Say: **Two people in the Bible wanted something so badly that they were willing to cheat big time to get it.**

Have group members turn in their Bibles to Genesis 2:4–3:24. Ask volunteers to take turns reading the passage. To add variety to a long reading like this, rather than assigning verses to people to read, assign characters. Choose volunteers to read the words of Adam ("the man"), Eve ("the woman"), God, Satan ("the serpent"), and the narrator (everything not in quotation marks).

After the passage has been read, ask: **What emotions do you think Adam and Eve had when they looked at the forbidden tree?** (They might have been curious about it. They may have thought God was being unfair to put it there and then forbid it. They may have started out intending to obey, but found that obeying just got more and more difficult.)

How did Satan, the serpent, talk Eve into taking some of the fruit? (He made her think God was being unfair and perhaps even lying to her. He played up how much she had to gain from eating it.)

If you'd been in Adam and Eve's place, do you think you would have taken the forbidden fruit? (Some group members may say no, that they would have been smart enough not to listen to Satan. Others may say it's hard to know what they would have done.)

OPTIONS

EXTRA ACTION

LARGE GROUP

HEARD IT ALL BEFORE

LITTLE BIBLE BACKGROUND

MOSTLY GIRLS

MOSTLY GUYS

MEDIA

SHORT MEETING TIME

URBAN

SIXTH GRADE

In your opinion, were the consequences of Adam and Eve's decision to take what they wanted worth it? (Obviously not—instead of good stuff, they got punished.)

Would you say God was depriving Adam and Eve by forbidding the fruit, or protecting them? (Some group members may say God was protecting them, that He didn't want them to have to leave the garden. Others may say He was depriving them, that He could have chosen not to make the tree at all, or not to punish them when they ate from it.)

STEP
3

Weighing the Risks

(Needed: Cut-apart copy of Repro Resource 4, small paper bag)

Summarize: **Adam and Eve thought they were pretty smart to get what they wanted—but their plan backfired. Selfish shortcuts almost always do, one way or another.**

Before the session, you'll need to cut apart a copy of "Worth the Risk?" (Repro Resource 4). Place the cards in a small paper bag.

Have group members sit in a circle on the floor. Pass the bag around the circle, having each person draw one card. When a person draws a card, have him or her read it aloud and then suggest ways that getting what you want by those means might backfire. Then have the rest of your group members suggest additional consequences.

Before passing the bag on, have the person decide whether that course of action would be worth the risk.

Use the following information to supplement responses.

- *You want a later curfew, but your parents are being completely unreasonable. You figure they're getting tired of hearing about it, so you launch a campaign of whining, begging, and pleading every day, hoping they'll give in just to get you off their backs.* (Consequences might include your parents seeing you as immature and deciding you really can't handle a later curfew. They might get so annoyed that they don't listen to anything you say or ask for. They might get really mad and ground you. They might give in, but feel so crabby about it that they make your life miserable. Your relationship with your parents might be weakened.)
- *You really need to boost your grade in science class or you may not be able to stay on the team. You honestly have worked hard in the class, but you just don't seem to be making any progress. So you decide to*

try to impress the teacher with your attitude. You make a point of coming to class on time, and you laugh at all the teacher's dumb jokes. You tell her that she is one of the most interesting teachers you've ever had, and you even volunteer to clean the erasers for her. Basically, you act like the nice and wonderful person you are—except you're hoping she'll be wonderful to you in return. That's not so bad, is it? (Teachers are rarely as dumb as they appear. This one will likely see right through you. She may let you clean the erasers, but she'll still probably grade you on your course work, not your charm—and she'll distrust any nice thing you ever do or say. She'll probably warn other teachers about you too. You may also get a bad reputation among your classmates.)

- *Your friend has a jacket you really like—in fact, it looks better on you than on your friend. If you could, you'd get one of your own, but you don't have the money and your parents won't buy it for you. So you ask, ever so nicely, to borrow it to wear to the game on Friday night. Your friend says no. So you don't speak to your friend all week. You manage to find a table at lunch with the rest of your friends where there is no room for your friend with the jacket. You also make sure he or she is excluded from your weekend plans. The next weekend, your friend gives in and lets you borrow the jacket. You are positively charming all week, offering to help with his or her homework, and generally finding ways to show your appreciation. Is this manipulation, or just normal give-and-take?* (Manipulation may get results at first, but eventually it will cost you friends. Your friend may find excuses to avoid you, may retaliate with the same treatment you've been dishing out, or may turn your other friends against you. You could lose a friendship that is more valuable than any jacket.)

- *You desperately, urgently want a certain something-or-other that all your friends are getting. You ask your parents to give it to you for your birthday, but they let you know that they will not. You try reasoning, but they won't listen. So you threaten to stop doing all your chores, to neglect your homework, to stop loving them, and maybe even to run away from home.* (If you stop doing your homework, you'll just hurt yourself. If you stop doing your chores, your parents will probably ground you. If you tell them you don't love them, they'll probably feel even less like doing nice things for you. If you threaten to run away, they may stop believing anything you tell them; or, if they do believe you, they may tighten their control over you or punish you in some way.)

- *You're short on cash, but you want a certain CD to play this weekend when a bunch of your friends are coming over. You go to the store hoping it's on sale, but no luck. While you're there, you start to think about the huge markup the store puts on all its merchandise, and how much money they've made off all the things you've bought there in the past. You figure they won't go bankrupt over one CD, and you know how to deactivate the alarm thing that's on it. So you slip the CD under your coat and walk out. Before you know it, you've got a new CD!* (If you get caught, you could be prosecuted. Even if you don't get caught, your parents might notice the new CD and ask embarrassing questions. Even if nobody ever finds out, your conscience may bother you. If it doesn't bother you, you might try again and risk getting caught or try to steal larger items.)

- *In your neighborhood, the only real way to get ahead—and be safe— is to be part of a gang. Some of the gang leaders have been warning you that it's time to either join with them or be considered their enemy. So you join.* (Consequences could include getting arrested, getting caught up in violence, committing a crime, or even getting killed.)

- *You really want _____ (you name it). You've asked your parents. You've tried to earn enough money for it. You've done everything reasonable. But you can't find a way to get it honestly. You can, however, think of a half dozen less-than-honorable ways to get it. Your conscience bothers you a little—you have a feeling God would rather see you do without than get what you want at any cost. But then, God has everything, and you don't. You decide to go for it.* (Depending on what means you use, you risk hurting relationships with friends or family, or risk getting in trouble with the law. Above all, you risk messing up your relationship with God, and becoming the sort of person who thinks only of yourself. If you keep this up, you may become selfish, ungodly, and totally unlikable.)

STEP 4

Risky Business

(Needed: Copies of Repro Resource 5, pencils)

Distribute copies of "Risk Profile" (Repro Resource 5) and pencils. Give group members a few minutes to complete the sheet. Emphasize that this is not intended to be a guilt trip, but rather an early warning indicator of where they may unwittingly be at risk of some of the negative consequences they listed in Step 3.

As you wrap up the session, let group members know you are available if they want to talk privately about a problem. Be prepared to listen nonjudgmentally and offer them help. If their problems are beyond your ability to help, refer your group members to someone who can help with their problems concerning parents, shoplifting, gang involvement, etc.

OPTIONS

FELLOWSHIP & WORSHIP

EXTRA FUN

MEDIA

JR. HIGH / HIGH SCHOOL
COMBINED

NOTES

W O R T H

the

RISK?

You want a later curfew, but your parents are being completely unreasonable. You figure they're getting tired of hearing about it, so you launch a campaign of whining, begging, and pleading every day, hoping they'll give in just to get you off their backs.

You really need to boost your grade in science class or you may not be able to stay on the team. You honestly have worked hard in the class, but you just don't seem to be making any progress. So you decide to try to impress the teacher with your attitude. You make a point of coming to class on time, and you laugh at all the teacher's dumb jokes. You tell her that she is one of the most interesting teachers you've ever had, and you even volunteer to clean the erasers for her. Basically, you act like the nice and wonderful person you are—except you're hoping she'll be wonderful to you in return. That's not so bad, is it?

Your friend has a jacket you really like—in fact, it looks better on you than on your friend. If you could, you'd get one of your own, but you don't have the money and your parents won't buy it for you. So you ask, ever so nicely, to borrow it to wear to the game on Friday night. Your friend says no. So you don't speak to your friend all week. You manage to find a table at lunch with the rest of your friends where there is no room for your friend with the jacket. You also make sure he or she is excluded from your weekend plans. The next weekend, your friend gives in and lets you borrow the jacket. You are positively charming all week, offering to help with his or her homework, and generally finding ways to show your appreciation. Is this manipulation, or just normal give-and-take?

You desperately, urgently want a certain something-or-other that all your friends are getting. You ask your parents to give it to you for your birthday, but they let you know that they will not. You try reasoning, but they won't listen. So you threaten to stop doing all your chores, to neglect your homework, to stop loving them, and maybe even to run away from home.

You're short on cash, but you want a certain CD to play this weekend when a bunch of your friends are coming over. You go to the store hoping it's on sale, but no luck. While you're there, you start to think about the huge markup the store puts on all its merchandise, and how much money they've made off all the things you've bought there in the past. You figure they won't go bankrupt over one CD, and you know how to deactivate the alarm thing that's on it. So you slip the CD under your coat and walk out. Before you know it, you've got a new CD!

In your neighborhood, the only real way to get ahead—and be safe—is to be part of a gang. Some of the gang leaders have been warning you that it's time to either join with them or be considered their enemy. So you join.

You really want _____ (you name it). You've asked your parents. You've tried to earn enough money for it. You've done everything reasonable. But you can't find a way to get it honestly. You can, however, think of a half dozen less-than-honorable ways to get it. Your conscience bothers you a little—you have a feeling God would rather see you do without than get what you want at any cost. But then, God has everything, and you don't. You decide to go for it.

Risk Profile

Are you at risk? Take a few minutes to honestly assess which behaviors you use to get what you want. Are you willing to risk the possible consequences if these actions backfire? And are you willing to risk becoming the kind of person—selfish, unlikeable, and untrustworthy—these behaviors might cause you to become?

Fill out your "risk profile" by circling the response that best describes you. Add up your score. Then circle one thing you want to work on correcting this week.

To get what I want, I…	often	sometimes	never
whine	2	1	0
use flattery	2	1	0
manipulate	2	1	0
threaten	2	1	0
resort to violence	2	1	0
shoplift	2	1	0
forget God and go for it	2	1	0

TOTAL RISK SCORE: _____

RATING:

0–2	You're a saint! (But are you telling the truth?)	6–8	Headed for trouble—rethink your strategies.
3–5	Low risk, but watch your danger zones.	9–11	High risk—back off or you may lose more than you gain.
		12–14	You're living too dangerously—get help!

EXTRA ACTION

STEP 2

Keep all of your group members actively involved in the Scripture reading by staging it as a mini-drama. Assign characters to read the parts as described. However, rather than just reading, have the actors stand and perform as much as they can while reading. Instruct the rest of the group to serve as an audience at a melodrama. They might boo and hiss when the snake is "onstage"; sing "Hallelujah!" when God appears; gasp as suspense builds; etc.

STEP 3

Rather than having group members draw cards individually, ask them to form teams of two or three. Instruct each team to draw a card, read it, and then come up with a roleplay illustrating how the plan on the card for getting what you want could backfire. For instance, one team might roleplay a scene in which a kid keeps nagging his or her parents for something, hoping they'll give in. Instead, they get angry and ground the kid for the week-end. After the roleplays have been presented, discuss as a group better ways to handle the situations.

SMALL GROUP

STEP 1

If team competition isn't ideal for your group size, substitute individual contests. Try simple children's games that involve blindfolds like "Blindman's Bluff" or "Pin the Tail on the Donkey." (You could add junior high appeal by changing it to "Tape the Paper Mustache on the Youth Leader.") However, group members will play the games without the blindfold. Use the questions in the session to guide your discussion of the activity.

STEP 3

If your group is small, you probably will have time not only to discuss the situations on the cards, but also to let individuals share similar challenges they have faced. Take advantage of your smaller group size to personalize each situation. If possible, share some examples from your own life to "break the ice."

LARGE GROUP

STEP 1

To keep the relay from dragging on with a large group, and to avoid having most of your group members merely watching most of the time, keep your teams small—six to eight people is ideal. If your meeting space is too small for the number of teams you would need, substitute a competition that involves everyone at the same time. A game of "Foot Locker Upset" would work well. For details, see the "Extra Fun" option for Step 1.

STEP 2

Rather than having most of your group members watch while five people read through the passage, get everyone involved. Divide the group into five teams. (A quick way to divide into teams is to have group members identify their favorite sense—sight, sound, taste, smell, or touch—and stand in a designated area according to their choice.) Assign Team 1 the role of Adam ("the man"), Team 2 the role of Eve ("the woman"), Team 3 the role of God, Team 4 the role of Satan ("the serpent"), and Team 5 the role of the narrator. Give the teams a few min-utes to look through the passage and mark their speaking parts. Then have the members of each team read in unison their parts as you go through the passage. Afterward, when you ask questions about the passage, direct your questions to the proper teams. For instance, you might ask Team 1 and Team 2: **What emotions do you think Adam and Eve had when they looked at the forbidden tree?**

HEARD IT ALL BEFORE

LITTLE BIBLE BACKGROUND

FELLOWSHIP & WORSHIP

STEP 2

Help your kids take a fresh look at this familiar story by having them consider an alternate ending for it. Have group members work in teams to write or dramatize the story as they think it might have turned out had Adam and Eve decided *not* to take the fruit. Then alter your questions to discuss the story *as it might have been.* For instance, you might ask: **How did Eve resist Satan's offer? In your opinion, were the consequences of Eve's—and later Adam's—decision not to take what they wanted worth it? Why or why not?**

STEP 3

Rather than focusing your discussion on why each of the methods on the cards is a bad idea, talk about what life would be like if those methods actually worked all of the time. Ask: **If you knew you could get anything you wanted from your parents just by whining, pleading, and begging, how often would you resort to those tactics?**

Would you be willing to become a teacher's pet if you knew it would get you better grades? Why or why not?

If you had the power to manipulate your friends for your own purposes, how often would you do it?

If your parents were swayed by threats, what things would you threaten them with to get what you want?

What kinds of things would you shoplift if you knew you wouldn't get caught?

If joining a gang were the only way to be safe in your neighborhood, would it be worth it to join one? Why or why not?

STEP 2

Group members with little Bible background may not recognize the horrible significance of the events in Genesis 2:4–3:24. Explain that this was the first sin, the act that separated people from God. Satan, the serpent, tempted Adam and Eve into disobeying God's command. As a result, they (and the whole human race) "fell." Now the only way to restore our relationship with God is through His Son, Jesus, who took the punishment we deserved for our sin.

STEP 3

If kids aren't used to applying the Bible to their own lives, they may have trouble seeing the connection between Adam and Eve's desire for a piece of fruit (which seems insignificant if you don't have the big picture) and their own desires and strategies for getting what they want. Break down the story into its simplest elements. Ask: **What did Adam and Eve want? What were they willing to do to get it?** Then, as each card is drawn, ask: **What is it that you want in the situation described on your card? What are you willing to do to get it?** Help kids see that although our wants and methods of getting those wants are different from Adam and Eve's, the underlying principle is the same.

STEP 1

Here's an activity to introduce the topic of the session and to provide an opportunity for fellowship among your group members. After the relay, have group members form pairs. Instruct each person to share with his or her partner one thing he or she really wants, but doesn't have. (It may be a bike, a skateboard, good grades, a boyfriend or girlfriend, etc.) Then have each person share a temptation he or she has faced regarding the thing he or she wants. (For instance, someone who wants a skateboard very badly may be tempted to steal someone else's; someone who wants a boyfriend or girlfriend may be tempted to lower his or her moral standards to get one; etc.) At the end of the session, have these partners pair up again and pray for each other, asking God to help the other withstand temptation regarding his or her object of desire.

STEP 4

After kids have taken an honest look at where they may be going wrong, let them affirm each other for what they are doing right. At the beginning of the session, give each group member the name of another group member and instruct him or her to watch for an unselfish action that person does during the course of the meeting. (This in itself may prompt more unselfish behavior than you're used to seeing!) Make some mental notes yourself as the meeting progresses, so that you can give suggestions to anyone who needs help. As you close the meeting, let each person share with the group the unselfish action he or she observed.

STEP 2

Broaden your discussion a little as you talk about Satan, the serpent, and his techniques in convincing Eve to take the fruit. Ask: **What are some influences in our lives that are not necessarily satanic, but that try to convince us to do something we shouldn't do? How many times have you heard other kids use the word "unfair" when they want to get something or do something? What about advertisements? Are these forms of manipulation? Why or why not?**

STEP 3

Have group members form three teams. One team should be made up of three people. The rest of the kids in the group should be divided between the other two teams. Assign Team 1 (the one with three people in it) the first situation from "Worth the Risk" (Repro Resource 4). Assign Team 2 the second situation and Team 3 the third situation. (You will discuss the other four situations on the sheet later in this step.) Ask each team to prepare and perform a roleplay for its situation. Instruct the teams to create roleplays in which each team member has a role, so that everyone is involved in the activity. After each roleplay is presented, discuss as a group the results of that situation.

STEP 2

If you choose to assign roles in reading the passage, be sensitive in choosing a guy to play Eve. This can be a fun part for a secure guy, but don't let it turn into an assault on anyone's masculinity. As you discuss the passage, don't let guys get away with laying all the blame on Eve (or women in general). Point them to Genesis 3:17, in which God specifically holds Adam accountable for his own actions.

STEP 3

If your guys showed a tendency toward "Eve-bashing" in Step 2, tie that in with the activity in Step 3. Ask your group members to describe ways in which friends (male or female) could lure them into taking selfish shortcuts to get what they want. Then ask: **Who do you think would have more of an influence on you—your guy friends or girls that you know? Why?**

STEP 1

If you have time for an additional opening game, start your meeting with a variation of an old favorite—"Foot Locker Upset" (a variation of "Fruit Basket Upset"). To play this game, assign each group member the name of one of the following brands of basketball shoes: Nike, Adidas, Reebok, Puma, and Converse. Then have kids arrange their chairs in a circle. One person, who does not have a chair in the circle, stands in the middle. He or she will call out the name of one of the shoe brands. When he or she does, group members assigned that brand must switch chairs. Meanwhile, the person in the middle tries to sit in an empty seat; so one person will be seatless at the end of the switch. That person then goes to the middle to start the next round. People in the middle also have the option of calling out more than one shoe brand or of calling, "Foot Locker Upset," at which point *everyone* must switch seats. Afterward, briefly discuss what lengths kids will go to get brand name basketball shoes or other things they really want.

STEP 4

This is the meeting in which to feature apples prominently in your refreshments! Serve apple pie, taffy apples, apples with peanut butter, Apple Jacks cereal, apple cider, or whatever else you can think of. You might even want to conduct a "Mr. Applehead" contest in which kids decorate apples with plastic facial features or various odd things (mini-marshmallows, etc.) attached with toothpicks. Remind your kids that often it isn't the *things* we want (traditionally an apple, in Adam and Eve's case) that are bad; it's the things we are willing to do to get them.

STEP 2

Before the session, search your local newspapers for stories of greed gone wrong. They shouldn't be hard to find. Look for articles on thieves who got caught, mob bosses who were convicted, etc. Bring in clippings of these articles to illustrate how taking selfish shortcuts to get what you want can backfire. When you're finished going through the articles, explain that you will read one more case study. Ask kids to listen for points of comparison with the newspaper articles. Then go through the Genesis passage.

STEP 4

As group members do their self-evaluations, set a mood of reflection by playing Wayne Watson's song "Material Magic" (from the album *Watercolour Ponies*). Afterward, if you have time, briefly discuss the song. Ask: **What is "material magic"? What kind of "spell" does it cast? In what ways do people "trade in their souls . . . for the ecstasy of the eye"?**

STEP 1

Save time in your opening activity by substituting a game that involves everyone at the same time. (You might try "Foot Locker Upset" as described in the "Extra Fun" option for Step 1). This way, you can give everyone a chance to participate in a short amount of time, rather than waiting for everyone to take a turn in a relay.

STEP 2

Rather than going through the entire description of the creation of man, begin your Bible study with Genesis 2:15. Simply explain that the events in the passage take place just after God has created Adam, the man. To save a little more time, you could end the study at Genesis 3:19, rather than going through the details of Adam and Eve's banishment from the Garden of Eden in verses 20-24.

STEP 2

After you go through Genesis 2:4–3:24 with your group, ask: **What are some of the "forbidden fruits" of today that God wants us to beware of?** Group members may suggest things like drugs, alcohol, premarital sex, etc. List the items on the board as group members name them. Then go through the list again, asking group members to consider some of the extreme lengths people will go to to acquire each forbidden fruit. For instance, some people will beg, steal, or even kill for drugs. Other people will risk getting AIDS for premarital sex. After you've finished your discussion, move directly into Step 3.

STEP 3

With an urban group, you might want to use the following scenarios to supplement the situations on Repro Resource 4.

• **There is a jacket that you want your parents to get you. However, it's the same kind of jacket that over 30 kids in your city have been killed for. Even though you promise your parents you won't wear it to school, they won't let you get it. You get angry and decide to use your allowance for the next five weeks to buy the jacket anyway.** (Consequences might include having the jacket confiscated by your parents and getting into serious trouble for disobeying them. More extreme consequences might include having the jacket stolen or even being attacked and/or killed for it.)

• **No one at school gives you any respect. You're teased and called names all the time. One day you come up with a plan to start getting respect—you'll join a gang. Your plan is to join long enough to get respect from other people and then quit.** (Consequences might include not being able to quit the gang without serious physical repercussions. You might be arrested for gang activity before you can quit. You may also be killed by a rival gang.)

STEP 3

Encourage your older group members to adapt the situations on the cards to fit the challenges that high schoolers face. For instance, someone might suggest substituting a situation involving conflict over an after-school job for the conflict on the sheet dealing with curfew. Someone else might suggest including a conflict over the use of the family car.

STEP 4

Pair up high schoolers with junior highers (or form teams with at least one high schooler on each team). Explain that the high schoolers will act as mentors for the junior highers. Instruct the high schoolers to share with their partners (or teams) one or more examples of how they fell into the trap of using "risky" behavior to try to get what they wanted, what the consequences were, and what they learned.

STEP 2

Instead of having volunteers read all of Genesis 2, instruct them to read only verses 4, 8-9, 15-18, and 20b-25. After reading these verses, ask several volunteers to explain in their own words what these verses are about. Then go through Genesis 3 by having five volunteers act out the story as described in the session.

STEP 3

Instead of passing the bag around the circle and having group members draw a slip, instruct kids to form teams. Give each team one or more of the cards from "Worth the Risk?" (Repro Resource 4). Have the teams talk about how their assigned situation(s) might backfire and what the consequences might be. After a few minutes, have each team read its situation and present its conclusions to the rest of the group.

DATE USED:

Approx. Time

STEP 1: *Sightless Scurry* _____
- ❏ Small Group
- ❏ Large Group
- ❏ Fellowship & Worship
- ❏ Extra Fun
- ❏ Short Meeting Time

Things needed:

STEP 2: *Forbidden Fruit* _____
- ❏ Extra Action
- ❏ Large Group
- ❏ Heard It All Before
- ❏ Little Bible Background
- ❏ Mostly Girls
- ❏ Mostly Guys
- ❏ Media
- ❏ Short Meeting Time
- ❏ Urban
- ❏ Sixth Grade

Things needed:

STEP 3: *Weighing the Risks* _____
- ❏ Extra Action
- ❏ Small Group
- ❏ Heard It All Before
- ❏ Little Bible Background
- ❏ Mostly Girls
- ❏ Mostly Guys
- ❏ Urban
- ❏ Combined Junior High/High School
- ❏ Sixth Grade

Things needed:

STEP 4: *Risky Business* _____
- ❏ Fellowship & Worship
- ❏ Extra Fun
- ❏ Media
- ❏ Combined Junior High/High School

Things needed:

How to Ask for What You Need

YOUR GOALS FOR THIS SESSION:
Choose one or more

☐ To help kids discover that the Book of Proverbs is a source of practical advice for everyday living.

☐ To help kids understand that when they're asking for something, how they live every day is more influential than what they say or how they say it.

☐ To help kids choose a proverb to guide them in their daily living this week.

☐ Other:_____

_____

Your Bible Base:

Proverbs 12—15

STEP 1

Smile, Honey

Open the meeting by playing the classic game "If You Love Me, Honey, Smile." Have group members arrange their chairs in a circle. Select one player to be "It." "It" has to get someone in the circle to smile. He or she does this by sitting on someone's lap (or kneeling in front of him or her) and saying, "If you love me, honey, smile." The person must reply, with a straight face, "I love you, honey, but I just can't smile." If the person does smile, he or she becomes the new "It" and must get someone else to smile. To keep anyone from being "It" too long, set a limit of three attempts per turn.

After a few minutes, compliment the players on their sweetness and politeness. Then point out that in some cases, sweetness didn't get results. Explain that next they will get a chance to try some other approaches to getting what they want.

O P T I O N S

SMALL GROUP

LARGE GROUP

FELLOWSHIP & WORSHIP

MOSTLY GIRLS

MOSTLY GUYS

EXTRA FUN

SHORT MEETING TIME

STEP 2

Smile, or Else!

(Needed: Cut-apart and assembled copies of Repro Resource 6)

Before the session, you'll need to cut apart and assemble "The Getting-What-You-Want Cube" (Repro Resource 6). If you don't want to make the cube, number the items on the sheet and have group members roll a die to determine which technique to use.

Have group members resume playing "If You Love Me, Honey, Smile." However, this time, before "It" makes the plea for a smile, have him or her roll the cube. He or she must then use the technique indicated on the cube to get people to smile.

Use the following suggestions to supplement group members' methods during the game. Included are the techniques listed on the cube as well as sample statements and actions group members might use.

- *Whining* ("If you don't smile, I'll never get out of being 'It.'")
- *Flattery* ("You have such a beautiful smile! You look so great when you smile.")
- *Manipulation* ("If you'll just smile, I'll be your friend forever.")
- *Threats* ("If you don't smile, I'll tell everyone your teeth are green.")
- *Violence* (Use good judgment here. Allow threats of violence, but no physical touch.)
- *Going for it any way possible* (These techniques may include tickling, blowing in the ear, etc.)

Play the game for a few rounds this way. Afterward, use the following questions to guide your discussion of the activity.

How did you get more success as "It"—when you asked sweetly or when you used one of the other approaches?

When were you more likely to smile—when the person asked sweetly or when he or she used one of the other approaches? Why? (Some group members may say acting nicely was more effective because they smiled out of embarrassment. Others may say one of the other methods was more effective because it was so strange they had to laugh.)

What do you think gets more results in real life—asking nicely, or whining, threatening, and so on? (Some group members may say asking nicely is more effective because people are more likely to listen to you and want to help you. Others may say whining is more effective because parents don't seem to listen until you've asked a million times. Other group members may point out that sometimes it's hard to tell the difference between asking politely and using flattery.) Don't worry too much about getting serious answers or deep insights at this point; you just want to set up the contrast between positive and negative ways to ask for things.

The Proverbial Bible Study

(Needed: Three signs, Bibles, cut-apart copy of Repro Resource 7, paper, pencils, masking tape)

Before the session, you'll need to prepare three signs. Write (in large letters) one of the following headings on each of the three signs: "What You Say," "How You Say It," and "How You Act Every Day." Post these signs in different spots around the room. You'll also need to cut apart a copy of "Proverbs for Paraphrasing" (Repro Resource 7).

Say: **The Bible is a very practical book. The Book of Proverbs, especially, is like a how-to book for getting along in life. It was written by one of the wisest people who ever lived—King Solomon. Not only did he manage to get more wealth than anyone living at the time, but he also managed to get along with one thousand wives. So you know he has some good advice for getting along with people and getting the things you need.**

Have group members form pairs. Hand out paper and pencils to each pair. Then distribute the reference cards from Repro Resource 7 as equally as possible among the pairs.

Instruct the pairs to look up their assigned proverbs, think about how those proverbs relate to the issue of asking for what you need, and then summarize the proverbs in words that are easy to understand.

As an example, have someone read aloud Proverbs 12:9. Then say: **You could summarize this proverb as "It's better to give up some self-importance to get what you need than to act like such a big shot that nobody wants to give you anything."**

Explain that some of the proverbs will deal specifically with relating to parents, some will deal with asking God for things, and some will apply to relationships in general.

Point to the three signs you posted around the room. Then say: **Some of your proverbs may give advice on what to say to get what you need. Others may give advice on how to say it. And still others may give advice on how to act every day in order to get what you need.**

After you've summarized your proverbs, decide which category each falls under, and tape it on the wall under the appropriate sign. Some proverbs may apply to more than one category. For instance, I would probably put the one we just read under "How You Act Every Day"; but it probably

could also go under "How You Say It." Use your best judgment to decide.

Give the pairs plenty of time to work. As they do, circulate among them and offer help when necessary. When everyone is finished, go through the proverbs one at a time and have the pairs share what they came up with.

Use the following suggested answers to supplement group members' responses.

What You Say
None of the proverbs deal directly with this category.

How You Say It
- *Proverbs 12:13-14*—How you talk determines what you get.
- *Proverbs 12:16*—Don't let your annoyance show; instead, have the self-control to overlook insults.
- *Proverbs 12:17, 19*—Don't lie.
- *Proverbs 13:3*—Control your tongue so that you don't speak rashly.
- *Proverbs 13:10*—Being willing to accept advice shows wisdom; being too proud to accept advice leads to quarrels.
- *Proverbs 15:1*—Speaking gently prevents you from stirring up anger.
- *Proverbs 15:18*—A hot-tempered person usually finds trouble; but a patient person calms potential quarrels.
- *Proverbs 15:23*—One of the secrets of good communication is using the right words at the right times.

How You Act Every Day
- *Proverbs 12:11*—Work, don't fantasize.
- *Proverbs 12:15*—Listen to advice.
- *Proverbs 12:24*—Be diligent, not lazy.
- *Proverbs 12:27*—Appreciate what you have.
- *Proverbs 13:1*—Listen to your parents' instructions.
- *Proverbs 13:4*—To be fully satisfied, you must be diligent, and not a sluggard.
- *Proverbs 13:11*—Dishonest money doesn't last long; money obtained gradually (and honestly) continues to grow.
- *Proverbs 13:13*—Scorning instruction and respecting instruction are both rewarded accordingly.
- *Proverbs 13:15*—Understanding what someone is saying or what someone wants from you wins brownie points with that person.
- *Proverbs 13:18*—Ignoring discipline has negative consequences.
- *Proverbs 14:23*—People who work hard will profit; people who sit around and talk will not.
- *Proverbs 15:3*—The Lord sees all of our actions.
- *Proverbs 15:5*—It's foolish to ignore parental discipline.

- *Proverbs 15:8-9*—God listens to people who pursue righteousness.
- *Proverbs 15:16*—Being poor and God-honoring is much better than being wealthy and deceitful.
- *Proverbs 15:19*—Lazy people will have a hard time accomplishing their goals.
- *Proverbs 15:20*—Wise children bring happiness to parents.
- *Proverbs 15:22*—It's wise to seek advice from others.
- *Proverbs 15:27*—Being greedy leads to trouble.
- *Proverbs 15:29*—God listens to the prayers of righteous people.
- *Proverbs 15:30*—Having a cheerful outlook on life brings joy.
- *Proverbs 15:31-33*—Wise people listen to rebuke.

Your group members may come up with a slightly different distribution than the one suggested here. That's OK—many of the proverbs overlap categories. But when everything is posted you should be able to make the point that how you live every day—what kind of a reputation you've established with parents, friends, and God—is more influential than the specific words you use when asking for something, or even the way you ask for it. This may be a disappointing revelation to those kids who were hoping for a magic formula to use tomorrow, but it's reality!

A Helpful Reminder

(Needed: Notebook paper, pencils, folders, markers, Bibles)

Remind group members that you referred to the Book of Proverbs as a how-to book for getting along in life. Instruct them to assemble their own mini how-to books so they won't forget the proverbs summarized in Step 3.

Hand out notebook paper and pencils and let kids work independently or in small teams to jot down the references and summaries that they find most helpful for their lives. Provide folders that they can put their papers in, and encourage them to design a cover using markers. See how creative they can be in the titles they use and the designs they come up with. If you have time, suggest that kids write out both the actual proverb from the Bible and the summary posted on the wall.

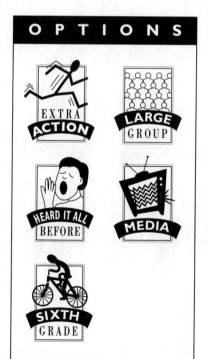

STEP 5

Proverb Cookies

(Needed: Bibles, slips of paper, pencils, fortune cookies)

Give everyone a fortune cookie (available in quantity from most Chinese take-out restaurants) and a small slip of paper. Instruct group members to choose a favorite proverb from those summarized, look up the reference, and write out the proverb as it appears in the Bible. See if anyone can remove the fortune from his or her cookie without breaking it. Then see if he or she can insert the proverb into the cookie. In some cases, this may not be possible, but kids will have fun trying. Have group members comment on their "fortunes." (Are they wise sayings, advice, or predictions?) Compare these words with the timeless truths found in Proverbs. If kids were unable to insert their proverb into the cookie, give them another cookie so they can try again at home.

Close the session in prayer, thanking God for the wisdom found in Proverbs and seeking His help when we ask for things from other people.

The Getting-What-You-Want Cube

Cut on the solid lines and fold on the dotted lines to form a cube. Once you've assembled the cube, secure it with tape.

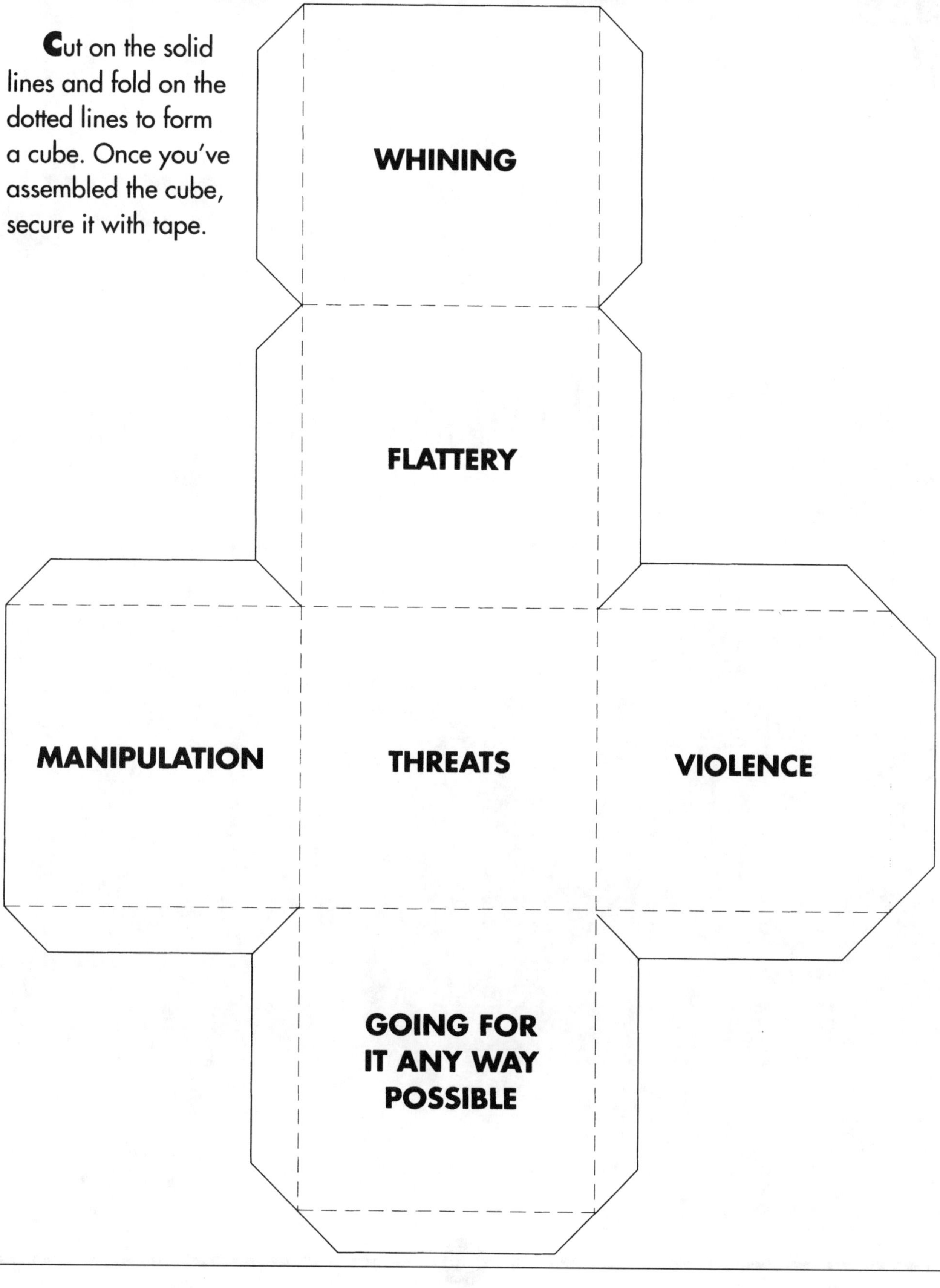

WHINING

FLATTERY

MANIPULATION

THREATS

VIOLENCE

GOING FOR IT ANY WAY POSSIBLE

NOTES

Proverbs for Paraphrasing

Proverbs 12:11	Proverbs 12:13, 14	Proverbs 12:15
Proverbs 12:16	Proverbs 12:17, 19	Proverbs 12:24
Proverbs 12:27	Proverbs 13:1	Proverbs 13:3
Proverbs 13:4	Proverbs 13:10	Proverbs 13:11
Proverbs 13:13	Proverbs 13:15	Proverbs 13:18
Proverbs 14:23	Proverbs 15:1	Proverbs 15:3
Proverbs 15:5	Proverbs 15:8, 9	Proverbs 15:16
Proverbs 15:18	Proverbs 15:19	Proverbs 15:20
Proverbs 15:22	Proverbs 15:23	Proverbs 15:27
Proverbs 15:29	Proverbs 15:30	Proverbs 15:31-33

NOTES

EXTRA ACTION

SMALL GROUP

LARGE GROUP

STEP 3

Instead of having kids tape their para-phrased proverbs to the wall, try something a little more active. Have group members form teams of six to eight. Assign each team a number. Then distribute an entire copy of Repro Resource 7 and a supply of notepaper and pens to each team. Instruct the teams to look up each proverb and write the reference down on a sheet of paper along with their team number. (If there's time, you might also have them write down their paraphrase of the proverb.) Then they should wad up the sheet and throw it into one of three boxes labeled "What You Say," "How You Say It," and "How You Act Every Day." The team that matches the most proverbs with their appropriate categories wins.

STEP 4

Instead of having kids assemble mini how-to books, try a more active option. Have group members form pairs. Assign each pair one of the following situations. Each one requires one person to ask something of another. Have the pairs roleplay two brief conversations. The first should illustrate asking for something the wrong way; the second should illustrate asking for something the right way. Here are some situations you might use:

• Asking a teacher for extra time to finish an assignment that's late because you forgot all about it.

• Asking a parent for fifteen dollars to buy a new CD.

• Asking a kid at school to stop teasing you.

• Asking a parent if you can go to the amusement park instead of to church.

• Asking a friend to help you with your homework. (This friend has helped you a lot in the past and you wonder if you're asking for help too often.)

• Asking a salesclerk at the store to help you find what you're looking for.

• Asking a new kid at school to come to your church.

STEP 1

The game "If You Love Me, Honey, Smile" might not work in a small group. Try another fun activity that will get a similar point across: Have kids communicate the following requests to one another—using only their elbows. (It's OK if kids move various objects or point to them with their elbows.) Have volunteers act out one request at a time. Here are some requests you might use:

• Could you please get me a drink of water?

• What time is it?

• What's your name?

• May I borrow ten cents?

• May I sit where you're sitting?

• Would you please clap your hands together?

After trying to guess a few requests, ask kids to name other methods (besides elbow talk) kids use to get what they want. In Step 2, choose a couple of the preceding requests and have kids act out ways to ask for those things using the approaches suggested on the "Getting-What-You-Want Cube."

STEP 3

If your group is small, don't feel you have to load kids up with 10 or 12 verses each just to get through all of the proverbs listed on Repro Resource 7. Either distribute the passages equally and work for a set amount of time, or choose only a portion of the passages to paraphrase. (If you do the latter, refer to the list in Step 3 to make sure you choose passages from each category.) You'll find enough overlap among the proverbs that your students will get the point without having to examine each one.

STEP 1

Here's a way to combine Steps 1 and 2 with a large group. As kids arrive, secretly assign them to one of the following teams: The Whiners, The Flatterers, The Manipulators, The Threateners, The Violencers, or The Sweeteners. Bring in a treat and explain that you'll give it to only one team—the one that does the best job of using its particular technique to get the treat from you. (You'll need to set some limits on what The Violencers can do.) For example, The Whiners might all complain about how they're really hungry, how their stomachs are growling, how hard it is to pay attention when they're hungry, etc. Have kids try to guess what technique each of the other teams is using. After awarding your treat to one team (or declaring a tie), discuss ways kids try to get what they want from others. Ask: **What's the most effective way to ask for something? What's the best way?**

Have group members remain in the same teams for the proverb-paraphrasing activity in Step 3, rather than work in pairs.

STEP 4

If it's too much work to assemble individual mini-books, you could assemble one how-to manual for the entire group—using an overhead projector. Have group members work in teams of three. Give each team a blank piece of acetate and some transparency pens. Have one team design and illustrate a cover with a title like *How to Ask for What You Need*. The other teams should each choose one of the proverbs from Step 3 to illustrate in some way. For example, if the members of a team chose to illustrate Proverbs 12:24, they might draw two kids, each thinking about a new bike. One could be mowing a lawn (or doing some other kind of work for money); the other could be lying in a hammock. After a few minutes, collect the pages and show them to the entire group.

HEARD IT ALL BEFORE

LITTLE BIBLE BACKGROUND

FELLOWSHIP & WORSHIP

STEP 3

If your kids think they know everything there is to know about the Book of Proverbs, give them a quick quiz to test their awareness. Read them some of the proverbs from Repro Resource 7, but leave certain key words blank. Have kids guess what the right words are. You could make a game out of this by having each group member write down his or her guess on a slip of paper, collecting the papers, reading them (along with the actual words), and having kids vote on which one is correct. Here are some examples you might use:

• "He who works his land will have abundant food, but he who chases _____ lacks _____" (fantasies/judgment) (Prov. 12:11).

• "An evil man is trapped by his _____ _____" (sinful talk) (12:13).

• "Pride only breeds quarrels, but _____ is found in those who take _____" (wisdom/advice) (13:10).

• "All hard work brings a profit, but mere _____ leads only to _____" (talk/poverty) (14:23).

• "The way of the sluggard is blocked with _____, but the path of the upright is a _____" (thorns/highway) (15:19).

STEP 4

Help your kids get a fresh perspective on King Solomon and his wisdom by casting him in the role of an advice columnist. Remind kids that people came from all over the known world to consult with Solomon; today he would probably hold his audience in the daily newspaper. Rather than having kids assemble books for themselves, have them write "Dear Abby" type letters, asking for advice on how to negotiate with parents, how to get requests through to God, etc. Have group members exchange letters and write replies based on the proverbs they've paraphrased.

STEP 3

Proverbs is a great book for kids new to the Bible because it's so practical and the instructions come in manageable, bite-sized pieces. Help your group members appreciate the section of Proverbs you're looking at (chapters 12–15) by sharing some of the following information:

• The author is Solomon, son of David and Bathsheba. Solomon was a very wise man who didn't always practice what he preached. (See I Kings 3:1-28; 4:29-34; 10:14-29; 11:1-13 for some of the highlights of Solomon's life.)

• Proverbs is primarily a book about wisdom. Proverbs 1:4-5 states the purpose of the book.

• Most of the proverbs in chapters 10–22 are two lines long, with some sort of contrast between two opposites.

• A sluggard isn't someone who can really hit a baseball; it's someone who's very lazy.

If you have time, you might want to have group members call out some popular sayings that sound like they might come from Proverbs, but don't. Examples might include the following: "No pain, no gain"; "Haste makes waste"; "Early to bed, early to rise makes a man healthy, wealthy, and wise"; "The Lord helps those who help themselves"; etc.

STEP 5

The idea of taking a specific verse to focus on and live by may be a new one to your kids. Take some time to talk about ways to incorporate the verses they've chosen into their daily lives: by reading the verse nightly; by memorizing it; by planning each morning one specific way to live out the verse that day; by using the verse as a checkpoint against which to measure their actions at the end of each day; etc.

STEP 1

Keep your meeting from becoming too "needs" centered by opening with a time of thanksgiving to God. You can do this spontaneously with sharing and prayer, or facilitate it by having kids find one thing in or around the room that reminds them of something they're thankful for (a friend, nature, a textbook symbolizing making it through midterms, etc.). Remind kids that even though this session focuses on asking, saying "thank you" is at least as important.

STEP 5

Provide extra fortune cookies and slips of paper. Have kids affirm one another by making personalized fortune cookies for each other. You can assign each person one other person to affirm, or have all group members personalize cookies for everyone. Suggest some possible formats and positive statements in the fortune-cookie style. ("You are energetic and will go far in life.") You might even provide some partially completed "fortunes," already written out, for those who have trouble thinking of their own fortunes. (For instance, you might write "Your _____ [personal quality] wins you many friends.") Let kids slip their personalized "fortunes" into cookies and give the cookies to each other to open during the week when they need a boost.

MOSTLY GIRLS

MOSTLY GUYS

EXTRA FUN

STEP 1

Adapt the game as follows: (1) Have the players stand, facing each other, rather than sit on each other's laps. (2) Instead of saying "If you love me, honey, smile," have players say "If you're my friend, smile." (3) The responding person should say "I'm your friend, but I just can't smile."

In Step 2, follow the same rules, but let the girls ham it up more. An example of whining might be "If you're my friend, smile; but if you're not, I'll start crying, and my tears will cause all of us in this room to have a bad hair day."

STEP 5

After the girls have chosen favorite proverbs, ask them to write some new proverbs that deal with asking others for things they want or need. Discuss some of the paraphrased proverbs and how they were written. Then have group members apply the biblical principles they know to write additional sayings. The sayings could involve two contrasting statements like some of the biblical proverbs do. Here's one example: "A wise daughter asks her father if she can stay out later after she clears the table and fills up the dishwasher; but a foolish daughter asks if she can stay out an hour later after yelling at her little sister and putting her sister's cat in the dishwasher."

STEP 1

If your guys like sitting on one another's laps and calling each other "Honey," use Step 1 as is. But if they'd rather do something else, try adapting a sport in which players communicate plays. You might have them play a quick game of touch football, and then discuss whether or not they followed the plays given in the huddle. Later, at the end of Step 3, you can point out that just as they listened to their teammates because they were all on the same team, so parents and others are more likely to listen to them if the parents feel like their kids are on their side.

STEP 2

Adapt whatever game or sport you chose for Step 1 by having players communicate in the styles on the cube. Don't worry too much about results—how other players respond. Just have a good time illustrating how ludicrous some of these ways of making "requests" can be.

STEP 1

Combine Steps 1 and 2 by playing a game of "Simon Says." Ask for several volunteers to be Simon. The first Simon should act as sweetly as possible. ("Simon says stand up, pretty please. Oh, how nicely you all stood up. You can sit down now.") The second Simon should whine. ("I hate doing this, but Simon says turn around one time. I can't believe how stupid this is. Simon says stand on one foot.") The third Simon should use threats. ("Simon says hop up and down or you'll have to do 10 push-ups. Stop jumping right now or you'll have to sing a solo.") Afterward, point out that most of us don't get our way just by saying "Simon says." Ask kids to name some of the techniques people use to try to get their own way. Continue with the final question in Step 2.

STEP 5

After the session, order a pizza. But first, have kids write down their two favorite toppings. (Cheese and tomato sauce don't count.) Have kids work together to try to agree on what to order. The object is for each group member to have a pizza with his or her two favorite toppings on it. Obviously some compromise will be needed. Stipulate that each pizza ordered must have at least two toppings. This will give kids an opportunity to express their "needs" to one another. Put everyone's name into a hat. Select one name and have that person call the pizza place with the order.

STEP 2

Before the session, tape a segment of a TV show in which a teenager is trying to get his or her way by some selfish or negative means (like those listed on Repro Resource 6). If you don't come across anything on TV, show a clip from a contemporary teen movie or an older one like *Ferris Bueller's Day Off* or one of the *Back to the Future* movies. In most cases, the teenager probably will be portrayed as succeeding by somewhat shifty means. Ask: **What would happen if you tried something like this with your parents/teachers/principal?**

STEP 4

Have kids summarize what they've learned by recording an "infomercial" on the topic of how to ask for what you really need in life. Have group members write a simple script (or outline) and improvise the rest. The infomercial might show right and wrong ways to ask for something, include interviews with kids who have or haven't gotten what they asked for, etc. Spectators should applaud any time something positive is said. If you don't have a camcorder, group members could simply perform the infomercial live.

STEP 1

Combine Steps 1 and 2 with the following activity: Offer a small sum of money (or some other prize) to the group member who asks you for it in the proper way. Let kids take turns rolling the cube from Repro Resource 6. They must ask for the item (verbally) in the manner indicated by the cube. Here's the trick: Award the prize to the first person who doesn't say "me," "my," "I," or some other personal pronoun. If no one gets it after several tries, explain what you were looking for. Point out that our motivations for asking for things are usually very selfish. Explain that in this session, you're going to be discussing some better ways to ask for things we need in life.

STEP 3

You may not have time to look up and paraphrase all of the proverbs on Repro Resource 7. Put three signs ("What You Say," "How You Say It," and "How You Act Every Day") on the wall as suggested in the session. Then, as you read selected proverbs, have kids run to the sign that best describes that proverb. After each proverb is read, ask a few kids why they are standing where they are. After reading several proverbs, point out that none of them tells us what to say; rather, the proverbs give us principles for how to speak and how to act. After making this point, hand out copies of Repro Resource 7. Assign one passage to each group member to paraphrase. After sharing and discussing the paraphrases, skip Step 4 and move directly to Step 5.

STEP 3

Try having your group members paraphrase the proverbs listed on Repro Resource 7, using slang. This is a creative way for them to show how well they really understand the verses. For instance, here's one way that Proverbs 12:9 could be rendered: "Better to slug hard at Mickey-D's 9 to 5 with no rep, than with funky-fresh threads and still not fill your hunger hole." King James might turn over in his grave once or twice, but these slang translations might help your kids see the proverbs in a new way.

STEP 5

If you don't have the resources to buy or find fortune cookies, here are three alternatives for making "urban fortunes":

(1) Write a fortune on a piece of paper; then put the paper in a balled-up piece of newspaper.

(2) Write a fortune on a piece of paper; then put the paper between two crackers held together with peanut butter.

(3) Write a fortune on a piece of paper; then slip the paper between the paper wrapper and foil of chewing gum.

STEP 2

Make a second cube from Repro Resource 6, covering the words with the following six items: (1) Asking someone out for a date; (2) Asking to borrow something very expensive; (3) Asking for a job; (4) Asking a teacher to reconsider a grade you think is unfair; (5) Asking a younger brother or sister to be quiet; (6) Asking a parent if you can go to Florida over spring break with some friends. Have pairs take turns rolling the cubes and roleplaying conversations between two people who fit the descriptions on the cubes. For example, one pair might roleplay a conversation between a parent and a kid who uses flattery to try to borrow the parent's car. Another pair might roleplay a conversation between a teacher and a student who uses whining to try to get the teacher to reconsider a grade. After several pairs finish their conversations, talk about the various ways kids ask for things. Ask: **What do you think people you ask things of pay the most attention to—your words, your tone of voice, your nonverbal gestures, or something else? Why?**

STEP 3

After reviewing the proverbs, ask which verse or verses might have something to say to the following individuals:

• Someone who is contemplating whether to shoplift something he wants.

• Someone who is hesitant to ask a favor of her mother because her mother seems to be in an especially bad mood.

• Someone who gets home an hour after his curfew because he was having so much fun, he lost track of time.

• Someone who accidentally bumps into another person in the hall and hears the person yell, "Watch where you're going, you little twit!"

• Someone who finds out a supposed friend has been spreading malicious rumors behind her back.

• Someone who planned a big outdoor party that's just been rained out.

STEP 3

Since paraphrasing can be difficult for sixth graders, limit the number of verses from "Proverbs for Paraphrasing" (Repro Resource 7). Have the kids work in teams of two to four. Give each team no more than three reference cards. If you need to eliminate some of the reference cards, be sure not to eliminate all of the proverbs from one category, but have an even distribution between verses for "How You Say It" and "How You Act Every Day."

If you don't think the paraphrasing activity will work, and you're a good typist (or know someone who is), try the following activity. Type out several of the proverbs on separate slips of paper. The proverbs should be from at least three different Bible translations (perhaps the Living Bible, the New International Version, and the King James Version). Whatever translations you use, try to include at least one modern-day paraphrase (like the Living Bible). Don't include the chapter and verse designations. Shuffle the verses, keeping them in three piles. Have kids work together to match up the same verse in each translation. This will help kids think about what the verses mean without having to paraphrase them themselves.

STEP 4

As your sixth graders make their own mini how-to books, have them begin the project by choosing six verses each. Ask them to look for proverbs that are especially significant to them personally. Give the kids the option of drawing a picture or cutting pictures from old magazines to illustrate each verse they've chosen. If you don't have time to make individual books, have each group member choose just one or two especially meaningful verses to illustrate. Compile them into one book. Ask a couple of kids to work together on the cover. Display the book somewhere visible so kids will see it often.

PLANNING CHECKLIST

DATE USED:

Approx. Time

STEP 1: *Smile, Honey* _____
- ❏ Small Group
- ❏ Large Group
- ❏ Fellowship & Worship
- ❏ Mostly Girls
- ❏ Mostly Guys
- ❏ Extra Fun
- ❏ Short Meeting Time
- Things needed:

STEP 2: *Smile, or Else!* _____
- ❏ Mostly Guys
- ❏ Media
- ❏ Combined Junior High/High School
- Things needed:

STEP 3: *The Proverbial Bible Study* _____
- ❏ Extra Action
- ❏ Small Group
- ❏ Heard It All Before
- ❏ Little Bible Background
- ❏ Short Meeting Time
- ❏ Urban
- ❏ Combined Junior High/High School
- ❏ Sixth Grade
- Things needed:

STEP 4: *A Helpful Reminder* _____
- ❏ Extra Action
- ❏ Large Group
- ❏ Heard It All Before
- ❏ Media
- ❏ Sixth Grade
- Things needed:

STEP 5: *Proverb Cookies* _____
- ❏ Little Bible Background
- ❏ Fellowship & Worship
- ❏ Mostly Girls
- ❏ Extra Fun
- ❏ Urban
- Things needed:

Waiting for What You Need

YOUR GOALS FOR THIS SESSION:
Choose one or more

☐ To help kids recognize that God cares about their needs even when He lets them wait.

☐ To help kids understand that good things can come from having to wait.

☐ To help kids identify ways to make waiting easier.

☐ Other:_____

_____

Your Bible Base:

1 Samuel 1:1-20
John 5:1-15
Romans 8:18-27

STEP 1

Suspended Animation

OPTIONS

SMALL GROUP

FELLOWSHIP & WORSHIP

EXTRA FUN

SHORT MEETING TIME

JR. HIGH HIGH SCHOOL COMBINED

Begin the session with a game of freeze tag. Choose a group member to be "It." That person will then try to tag as many people as possible. Once tagged, a player must "freeze" in position until another player taps him or her to break the freeze. If "It" is able to freeze three people (or a number appropriate to the size of your group) at once, the last person frozen becomes "It." Give group members a few minutes to play.

Afterward, use the following questions to discuss the activity.

How did you feel when you were frozen? (Uncomfortable, because I was stuck in one position; bored, because I couldn't play until someone tapped me; fine, because I could take a break instead of being chased around.)

How was the experience of being frozen like waiting for something in real life? (It's like you're stopped in mid-stride. You can't do anything about it. You get tired of it if you have to wait too long.)

What are some of the things you've really wanted that you had to wait for—or are still waiting for? (Some group members may be waiting to be old enough to drive. Others may be waiting for a special event to arrive. Others may be waiting to save up enough money for something. Still others may be waiting for their parents to decide whether or not they may have something.)

STEP 2

Wait Watchers

(Needed: Bibles)

Have group members form two teams. Assign one team to read 1 Samuel 1:1-20; assign the other team to read John 5:1-15. After the teams have read their assigned passages, have them prepare short dramatizations of the passages to present to the other team.

The dramatizations can be as elaborate or as simple as the teams want to make them. One team may want to assign roles and have the actors physically move about as they perform. The other team may want to do a "reader's theater" presentation and have different people just read the text while facing the audience.

Give the teams a few minutes to prepare; then have each team perform. Afterward, discuss the passages using the following questions.

Which character did you identify with in these passages? Explain. (Some of your group members may identify with Hannah—not that they want a baby, but that sometimes they feel like their friends rub it in that they don't have the things other people have. Other group members may identify with Eli—they'd be suspicious of someone who acted like Hannah was acting. Others may identify with Elkanah, Hannah's husband—they sometimes get tired of hearing people whine about what they can't have. Others may identify with Peninnah, Elkanah's other wife, because they've never really had to wait for anything major. Still others may identify with the man at the pool—they may feel that nobody cares enough to help anybody else.)

Why do you think God let Hannah and the man at the pool wait so long? (Perhaps He wanted them to really appreciate it when they finally got what they wanted. Perhaps He wanted to use their waiting to do a miracle. Sometimes it's hard to know why people have to wait.)

Why do you suppose God lets you wait for the things you want or need? (Some group members may say that sometimes it seems like the things they want aren't important to God. Others may say that God may be trying to teach them how to get along without the things they want. Others may say that God wants them to learn patience. Still others may say that, for some reason, God doesn't want them to have what they want.)

OPTIONS

LARGE GROUP

HEARD IT ALL BEFORE

LITTLE BIBLE BACKGROUND

MOSTLY GUYS

MEDIA

URBAN

Wait Limits

(Needed: Two kinds of prizes or treats, Bibles, cut-apart copies of Repro Resource 8)

Hold up two prizes or treats—both should be good, but one should be obviously better than the other. Offer group members the choice of having the good one now, or the better one later (perhaps later today, perhaps next week). Distribute the "good" prizes to those who want theirs now and hold on to the better prizes for those who choose to wait.

Have group members form teams of three or four. Distribute one cut-apart copy of "Waiting out of Line" (Repro Resource 8) to each team. Make sure each team has at least one New International Version of the Bible.

Explain that the cards from Repro Resource 8 contain the text of Romans 8:18-27. When you give the signal, the teams will open their Bibles to Romans 8:18-27 and try to put their cards in order. The first team to do so wins. Ask the members of the winning team to read aloud the ordered passage to verify that they did it correctly. Use the following to check their answers:

"I consider that our present sufferings are not worth comparing with the glory that will be revealed in us. The creation waits in eager expectation for the sons of God to be revealed. For the creation was subjected to frustration, not by its own choice, but by the will of the one who subjected it, in hope that the creation itself will be liberated from its bondage to decay and brought into the glorious freedom of the children of God. We know that the whole creation has been groaning as in the pains of childbirth right up to the present time. Not only so, but we ourselves, who have the firstfruits of the Spirit, groan inwardly as we wait eagerly for our adoption as sons, the redemption of our bodies. For in this hope we were saved. But hope that is seen is no hope at all. Who hopes for what he already has? But if we hope for what we do not yet have, we wait for it patiently. In the same way, the Spirit helps us in our weakness. We do not know what we ought to pray for, but the Spirit himself intercedes for us with groans that words cannot express. And he who searches our hearts knows the mind of the Spirit, because the Spirit intercedes for the saints in accordance with God's will" (Romans 8:18-27).

Afterward, ask: **What similarities do you see between this passage and the choice you just had between the two prizes?**

(If you wanted the better prize, you had to wait for it. In the same way, God has better things ready for us in the future, even though the waiting seems hard now.)

How would you say it helps to have hope when you're waiting for something? If you need a hint, look at verses 24 and 25. (Hope is something that gives us patience to wait. Hope keeps us going even when we can't see any signs of what we're waiting for.)

Do you have hope? (Some group members may say they have hope for some things, but not for everything. Others may say it's hard to keep hoping if you have to wait too long. Still others may point out that it's one thing to have hope for stuff like eternal life—for which we have guarantees; it's another thing to have hope for stuff we want now—for which we don't have guarantees.)

Do verses 26 and 27 give you hope? (Some group members may say yes, that the verses give them hope—at least for spiritual things. Others may say the verses give them hope for other things because they know the Holy Spirit is helping them pray for those things. Others may say the verses give them hope because even if what they want isn't in God's will, they trust that God knows what's best for them. Still others may say no, the verses don't give them hope, because you could explain away disappointments as not being "God's will.")

STEP 4

Wait Training

(Needed: Paper, pencils)

Distribute a piece of paper and a pencil to each group member. Then have group members form teams. If possible, try to have the same number of group members per team as you have teams (three teams of three people, for example).

Instruct group members to list, with their teams, as many things as they can think of that help people who are waiting for something. Suggestions might include things like marking off days on a calendar, distracting your mind from your wait, making plans for the thing you're waiting for, etc. Make sure each group member writes down every suggestion his or her team comes up with.

After a few minutes, have group members form new teams—with each new team consisting of one member of each of the previous teams. (An easy way to do this is to have group members number off

OPTIONS

EXTRA ACTION

SMALL GROUP

MOSTLY GIRLS

MOSTLY GUYS

SHORT MEETING TIME

SIXTH GRADE

in their first teams. Then, when it's time to form new teams, you could have the "ones" form one team, the "twos" form another team, and so on.)

Then have each group member read to his or her new team the list his or her previous team came up with. Suggest that group members add to their lists any new ideas that are mentioned.

STEP
5

Wait Lifters

(Needed: Prizes)

As you wrap up the session, assure your group members that God—and our Christian friends—can help us get through times of waiting. Remind them that the Holy Spirit is lifting their needs before God, and that we can lift up one another too. To demonstrate this, one by one, have the group lift each person as high as possible, while shouting the person's name.

Then close the session by awarding the prizes to those who chose to wait for the better prize.

NOTES

WAITING OUT OF L·I·N·E

I consider that our present sufferings are not worth comparing with the glory that will be revealed in us.

The creation waits in eager expectation for the sons of God to be revealed.

For the creation was subjected to frustration, not by its own choice, but by the will of the one who subjected it ...

... in hope that the creation itself will be liberated from its bondage to decay and brought into the glorious freedom of the children of God.

We know that the whole creation has been groaning as in the pains of childbirth right up to the present time.

Not only so, but we ourselves, who have the firstfruits of the Spirit, groan inwardly as we wait eagerly for our adoption as sons, the redemption of our bodies.

For in this hope we were saved. But hope that is seen is no hope at all. Who hopes for what he already has?

But if we hope for what we do not yet have, we wait for it patiently.

In the same way, the Spirit helps us in our weakness. We do not know what we ought to pray for, but the Spirit Himself intercedes for us with groans that words cannot express.

And He who searches our hearts knows the mind of the Spirit, because the Spirit intercedes for the saints in accordance with God's will.

NOTES

STEP 3

Try a more active approach to putting the verses in the correct order. Tape one of the slips from Repro Resource 8 to each person's back. (If you have fewer than 10 kids, tape two or more consecutive slips to each person's back.) Have kids line up in the correct order, according to the verses. However, group members must do so without speaking at all. The challenge is that no group member will know what's on his or her own back. Don't let group members look in their Bibles during the activity. After they line up, check their order against the Bible. If you have 20 or more kids, this would be a great contest between two or more teams.

STEP 4

Turn the list-making into a contest among teams. Give the teams a certain amount of time to list as many ways as possible to make waiting easier. Then have each team read its list. As the other teams listen, they should check the items on their lists that occur on other teams' lists as well. Award one point for every valid (according to your judgment) item on each list; award five points for every valid item that no other team had.

STEP 1

Freeze tag may not work well in a small group. Try another activity instead. Bring in a corn popper, popcorn, and some oil. Put one kernel of popcorn into the popper for each member of the group. Spread out the kernels so that each person knows which kernel belongs to whom. Have a contest to see whose kernel pops first. Use this activity to introduce the concept of waiting. Ask: **When do you have the hardest time waiting for something? What's the longest you've had to wait for something you really wanted? What was the hardest part about waiting? Was it worth the wait?**

STEP 4

Instead of making lists of things people wait for, have kids offer advice to the following people. Encourage kids to draw upon some of the biblical principles you discussed earlier in the session. What would they say to each of the following people?

• A kid who wants to get bigger muscles so that he can be better at football

• A kid who wants to be a good pianist, but hates to practice

• A kid who wants a new stereo system, but can't afford one

• A kid who is embarrassed because other kids her age are showing more signs of physical maturity

• A kid who just moved to a new community and feels totally friendless

• A kid who's having a lot of difficulty getting along with her parents

• A kid who's doing poorly in school and hates going

• A kid who hates the way she looks and wants to lose a lot of weight

STEP 2

Instead of looking at the two passages listed in this step, introduce a number of Bible characters who patiently waited for something. To do this, play "The Waiting Game." Have several adult volunteers assume the identity of one of the following characters. Have kids form two teams. Let teams alternate asking yes-no questions of each character to find out who the person is and what he or she waited for. Award ten points for guessing in 5 or fewer questions, three points for guessing in 6 to 10 questions, and one point for guessing in 11 to 15 questions. Select some of the following characters or use some others that you think of.

• Noah—waited for the rain to come— and go

• Abraham—waited for a son

• Jacob—waited for a wife

• Moses—waited for Israelites to inhabit the promised land

• Gideon—waited for a sign

• Ruth—waited for a husband

• Hannah—waited for a child

• David—waited for God to make him king

• Simeon—waited for the Messiah

• Blind man—waited for healing

STEP 5

Turn the "lifting up" activity into a game. Have group members form teams of eight to ten. The first team to get all of its members to touch the ceiling (or sign all of their names on a piece of paper you've taped high up on a wall) wins.

STEP 2

Ask kids to think of contemporary parallels to these familiar stories—people they know who have faced similar struggles. If they can, have them go beyond simple identification with the specific need (wanting a baby; a long-term illness; etc.) to deal with the whole concept of hope deferred. Discuss where these people are in the process (still waiting? hope answered?), how their needs have been met, whether they were met in the way the people expected (perhaps receiving a baby through adoption rather than conception), and whether kids think God worked in those solutions as He did in the more obvious answers in the passages. Don't be afraid to wrestle with questions about people who died without their hopes ever being realized—you can use those questions to lead into the Romans passage.

STEP 3

Your kids may have *heard* this passage before, but they probably don't understand it completely. To help them better understand it, write the following headings on the board and have kids list examples under each one:

• Present sufferings

• How creation is frustrated

• Things we groan about

• Things we hope for

• How the Spirit helps

Another way to look at the passage is to photocopy it from the session. Then you could have kids underline all negative and circle all positive words in the passage. Afterward, discuss what group members discover and address any questions that are raised.

STEP 2

Work with the teams to pronounce tricky names. You might also want to give them a little background to the stories. Explain that motherhood was the main status symbol in Old Testament times, so Hannah's desire for a child was much more than the simple wish to be a mother. Her "churchgoing" neighbors would all assume that God had punished her for some terrible sin by keeping her from having children. (The neighbors probably speculated about what her sin was.) Her husband's other wife (another detail that takes some explaining) was socially correct in jeering at Hannah. Explain that the pool referred to in John 5 was not just a comforting hot tub: when the water was "stirred" (vs. 7), people who got in expected to be healed. Explain that the Jewish religious leaders had strict rules about what was acceptable on the sabbath (somewhat equivalent to our Sunday). That's why they chided the man for carrying his mat.

STEP 3

The Romans passage is a rather difficult one and may be completely over the heads of some kids. You could simply focus on verses 24 and 25 and talk about the connection between hope and patience. If you tackle the whole passage, make sure you explain these phrases:

• sons of God (vs. 19)—a reference to the end times (see I John 3:1-2)

• subjected to frustration (vs. 20)—a reference to the Fall (see Gen. 3:17-19)

• liberated (vs. 21)—God's ultimate plan for creation (see I Pet. 3:13; Rev. 21:1)

• firstfruits (vs. 23)—the Holy Spirit is sort of a down payment for our future inheritance (see 2 Cor. 1:22; 5:5; Eph. 1:4)

• adoption (vs. 23)—see Romans 8:15

• redemption (vs. 23)—occurs at the final resurrection (see 2 Cor. 5:1-5)

STEP 1

Instead of asking the last question to the whole group, facilitate personal sharing by having kids form pairs. Ask each person to share with his or her partner the answer to these questions: **When you were little, what was one of your favorite birthday or Christmas presents? What is one thing you remember having a hard time waiting for as a child? What is one thing that you're having a hard time waiting for now?**

STEP 5

Guide a time of worship, using the theme of hoping in God to meet our needs and help us wait. Remind kids that the Holy Spirit, who appeared at Pentecost in the form of a flame, now offers our prayers to the Father. Give each person a candle. Go around the circle, asking each group member to commit a need to God or ask for help in a specific situation. After each person prays, he or she will turn to the next person and light his or her candle.

MOSTLY GIRLS

STEP 4

Before the teams talk about things that make it easier to wait, ask them to plan and present skits (or stories) about how not to wait. Allow two minutes for each presentation. Talk about some specific things kids wait for and then have each team choose something different to do so there will be a variety of examples presented. You might want to assign some of the following specific situations to get kids started: how not to wait for the right guy; how not to wait for a better body; how not to wait for the Lord to answer your prayers; how not to wait for test results at school; etc.

STEP 5

Instead of lifting each other up, have your group members think of at least three different ways to support each other physically, such as leaning against someone, helping someone walk, or giving someone a hug. Then let each group member choose and experience how she wants to be "supported" by her friends. Discuss ways friends can support each other in the following situations:

• when one girl is having a difficult time with her parents.

• when one girl is rejected by a guy she really likes.

• when one girl does poorly on a test.

• when one girl feels particularly unattractive.

MOSTLY GUYS

STEP 2

Instead of looking at the account of Hannah, guys might relate better to the familiar story of Abraham. Review some of the key events in his life by looking only at the first five verses of the following chapters. Ask: **What do you suppose was going through Abram's/Abraham's mind at this point? What do you suppose he learned about waiting?** (1) Called by God at age seventy-five (Gen. 12:1-5); (2) God's covenant with Abram (15:1-5); (3) had a child by Hagar (16:1-5); (4) circumcision and name change (17:1-5); (5) birth of Isaac (21:1-5); (6) Abraham tested (22:1-5); (7) death (25:1-5).

STEP 4

List the following items on the board. Have group members rank them from 1 (easiest to wait for) to 10 (hardest to wait for). Afterward, discuss the ranking.

• Getting a driver's license

• Having sex

• Growing more physically mature

• Getting a job

• Having a steady girlfriend

• Getting test results

• Summer vacation

• Christmas

• The release of a certain movie on video

EXTRA FUN

STEP 1

Instead of playing freeze tag, try the following activity to get kids thinking about the subject of waiting. Decorate your room for Christmas. Be as simple or as elaborate as you choose. Consider playing some Christmas music, hanging some lights, setting up a tree—whatever will create the atmosphere you want. As kids arrive, have them make paper stockings to hang on a "fireplace" you've created on the wall. Have them write things they want or are waiting for on their stockings. Talk about what it's like to wait for Christmas. How is it different now from when they were younger? Is it still exciting, or no big deal? Bring out an attractively wrapped package. Explain that there's something so wonderful inside, it defies description. Build up the excitement as much as possible about the package. Then, just as you're ready to open it, two thieves should appear (possibly with nylon stockings over their heads and armed with super-soaker squirt guns) to steal the package. After they leave the room, apologize and move on with Step 2. During Step 3, skip the part about the gifts. But during your discussion of the Romans passage, point out that sin robs us of what God really intends us to have—much like the thieves robbed you of your package. However, someday God will abolish sin and death completely and usher His children into His glorious presence. After Step 5, have your thieves return the gift. There should be something great to eat inside, along with a balloon for each group member. Have kids blow up their balloons to remind them of the Holy Spirit, who gives us hope for an eternal future.

STEP 5

If you used the Christmas option in Step 1, wrap up the session with a full-blown Christmas party, complete with eggnog, cookies, caroling, mistletoe, etc.

STEP 2

Before you read the Scripture passages, distribute magazines, newspapers, and scissors. Have kids cut out ads for anything "instant" or "quick" (foods, weight-loss plans, investment schemes, etc.). Discuss what the prevalence of these products says about our impatience as a society. Have group members form teams to read the Scripture passages. Then have the teams create ads for products that would solve Hannah's or the man's problems without waiting.

STEP 3

After reading the passage, play a contemporary love song that has the theme of "I can't live without you; I have to have you now." (You shouldn't have trouble finding one!) If your kids are into classic rock, you might want to consider playing "Love the One You're With" by Stephen Stills, a song that captures how impatient some people are. Discuss the differences in perspective between the song and the passage in Romans. Ask which emotion seems more natural, and which one would lead to more contentment.

STEP I

Combine Steps I and 2 with the following activity. Cover any clocks in your room. Have your group members stand. Tell them to sit down when they think two minutes are up. (They may not look at watches!) To make it more challenging, have them recite the alphabet backward or sing a simple song while they wait. Have an official timekeeper keep track of the two minutes and watch to see who sits down closest to the actual time. Award a small prize to that person. Then talk about the difficulty of waiting for things and the positive and negative aspects of waiting. Instead of acting out the passages in Step 2, simply read them and talk about which characters kids most identify with and why.

STEP 4

Instead of making lists, have kids write down how long they would be willing to wait for each of the following:

• their next meal.

• to have sex. (Don't use this one if it's inappropriate for your group.)

• to learn how to drive.

• to see a new movie that everyone's raving about.

• to buy a new cassette or CD that they really want.

• to spend some time alone with God.

• for a friend to return a phone call.

• for a friend to return the $10 he or she borrowed from you.

Explain to group members that they don't need to write their names on their papers. When they're finished, collect the papers and see how much variation there is among responses. Then ask: **What tips would you offer to someone who's having a hard time waiting for something?**

STEP 2

Here's a different way to introduce the two Bible passages. Tape several very light objects to the ceiling at different lengths. Objects must be light so that if one falls off prematurely, no one is in danger of getting hurt. Have some of the items placed high enough so that few will be able to reach them. If your room allows for it, at least one item should be out of the reach of everyone by at least a foot. Ask kids to go around and determine how many objects they think they can touch—first by standing on tiptoes, and then by jumping. Then have them see how many they can actually touch. Afterward, discuss why they couldn't reach some of the items. Some may say they were too short or couldn't jump high enough. Then ask: **Do you think you'll ever be tall enough to touch all of these objects?** Point out that sometimes God intentionally keeps things out of our reach. Ask for examples. Then ask: **Why does God sometimes keep things from us?** After several kids respond, move into your study of the two Scripture passages, in which people had to wait a long time for something that was beyond their grasp (at least for a while).

STEP 3

When looking at the Romans passage, discuss particular ways in which this country's cities are "groaning." Ask: **Can you give me some examples of people who seem to have lost hope for the future? How can you tell they've lost hope? What are some problems we face because people are so impatient? How can you bring hope to someone who seems to have lost it? How can you help someone be more patient?**

STEP 1

High schoolers may feel that a game of tag is beneath them, so try something else. Play a short segment of any video that won't be too familiar to your kids—in the fast-forward mode. After a minute or two, ask your kids a few questions about what they saw—who the characters were, what they were talking about, etc. Then have group members form teams. Instruct each team to come up with a list of ways people try to speed things up in life. After a few minutes, have each team share its list. Then, as a group, discuss the difficulty people seem to have waiting for things. Ask: **Why is this? What can be learned from waiting? Describe a time when you had to wait a long time for something. What did you learn?**

STEP 3

Your older students may be better able to wrestle with some of the cosmic implications of the first part of Romans 8:18-27. Address these points in your discussion:

• We are not alone in waiting.

• The whole world—not just the human race—is frustrated by the sin in the world that leads to unfulfilled needs.

• Just as humanity is responsible for creation's frustration (through the Fall), so too, somehow, we are involved in its restoration (vs. 21).

• We have an advantage—the Holy Spirit is a "down payment" of things to come.

STEP 3

Before looking at the Romans passage, have each group member complete the following statement: "Hope is . . ." After group members share their answers, discuss the dictionary definitions of hope: "(1) to long for with expectation of obtainment; (2) to expect with desire; trust." Ask kids to name the opposite of hope (despair). Instead of looking at the entire Romans passage, focus only on verses 24 and 25. Give kids an opportunity to change their definitions in light of the passage. Point out that hope involves a certainty of fulfillment, a solid trust that God will come through for us. It's not wishful thinking, like "I hope it doesn't rain tomorrow" or "I hope this session isn't boring."

STEP 4

Before the teams begin working, discuss as a group some things that sixth graders may have to wait for. List the suggestions on the board. You might also want to list some things sixth graders fear about the future. Are any items on both lists? Have the kids refer to these lists as they work in their teams on ideas for good ways to help the waiting process.

DATE USED:

Approx. Time

STEP 1: *Suspended Animation* _____
- ❑ Small Group
- ❑ Fellowship & Worship
- ❑ Extra Fun
- ❑ Short Meeting Time
- ❑ Combined Junior High/High School
Things needed:

STEP 2: *Wait Watchers* _____
- ❑ Large Group
- ❑ Heard It All Before
- ❑ Little Bible Background
- ❑ Mostly Guys
- ❑ Media
- ❑ Urban
Things needed:

STEP 3: *Wait Limits* _____
- ❑ Extra Action
- ❑ Heard It All Before
- ❑ Little Bible Background
- ❑ Media
- ❑ Urban
- ❑ Combined Junior High/High School
- ❑ Sixth Grade
Things needed:

STEP 4: *Wait Training* _____
- ❑ Extra Action
- ❑ Small Group
- ❑ Mostly Girls
- ❑ Mostly Guys
- ❑ Short Meeting Time
- ❑ Sixth Grade
Things needed:

STEP 5: *Wait Lifters* _____
- ❑ Large Group
- ❑ Fellowship & Worship
- ❑ Mostly Girls
- ❑ Extra Fun
Things needed:

CHECK OUT OUR OTHER BOOKS!

WWW.INSPIREDTOGRACE.COM

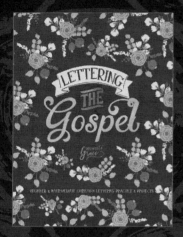
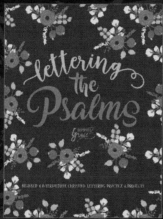

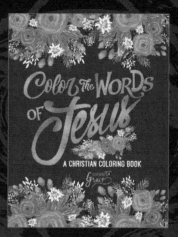

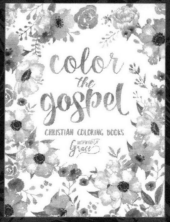

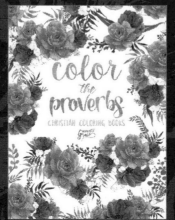
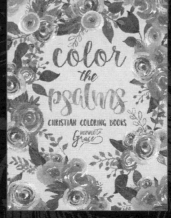

BE SURE TO FOLLOW US
ON SOCIAL MEDIA
FOR THE LATEST NEWS,
SNEAK PEEKS, & GIVEAWAYS

ADD YOURSELF TO OUR
MONTHLY NEWSLETTER FOR FREE DIGITAL
DOWNLOADS AND DISCOUNT CODES

www.inspiredtograce.com/newsletter

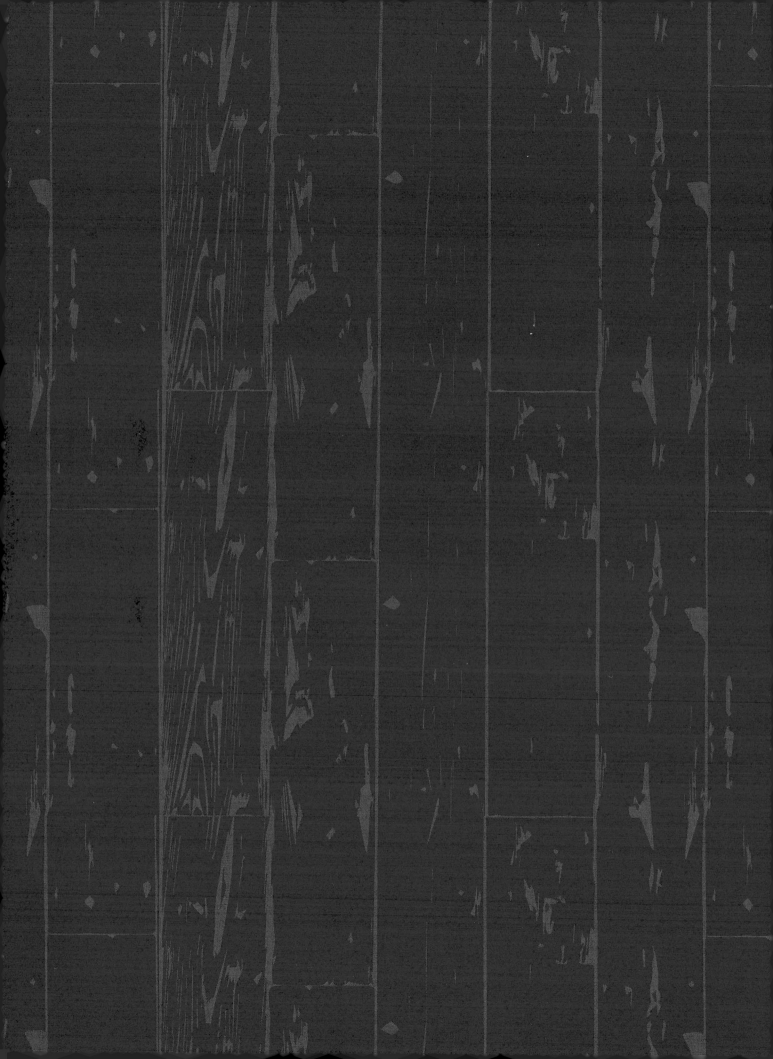

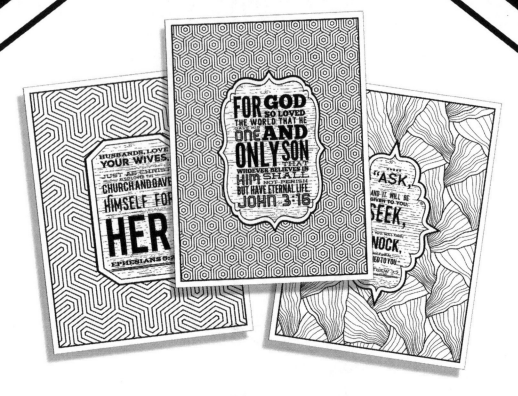

FREE DOWNLOAD LINK
VERSES FOR MEN
WOODGRAIN EDITION
WITH WOODGRAIN FRAME CENTERS

www.inspiredtograce.com/usvfm

DOWNLOAD CODE: VFM1572

 @INSPIREDTOGRACE

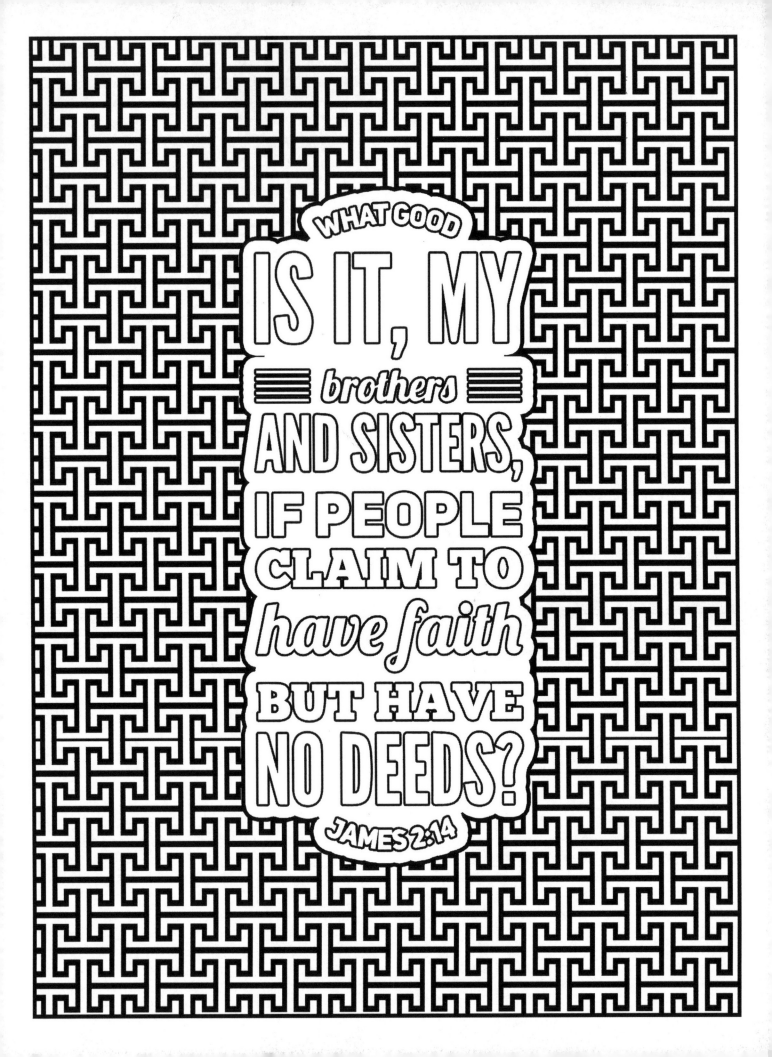

What good is it, my brothers and sisters, if people claim to have faith but have no deeds? Can such faith save them?

James 2:14 (NIV)

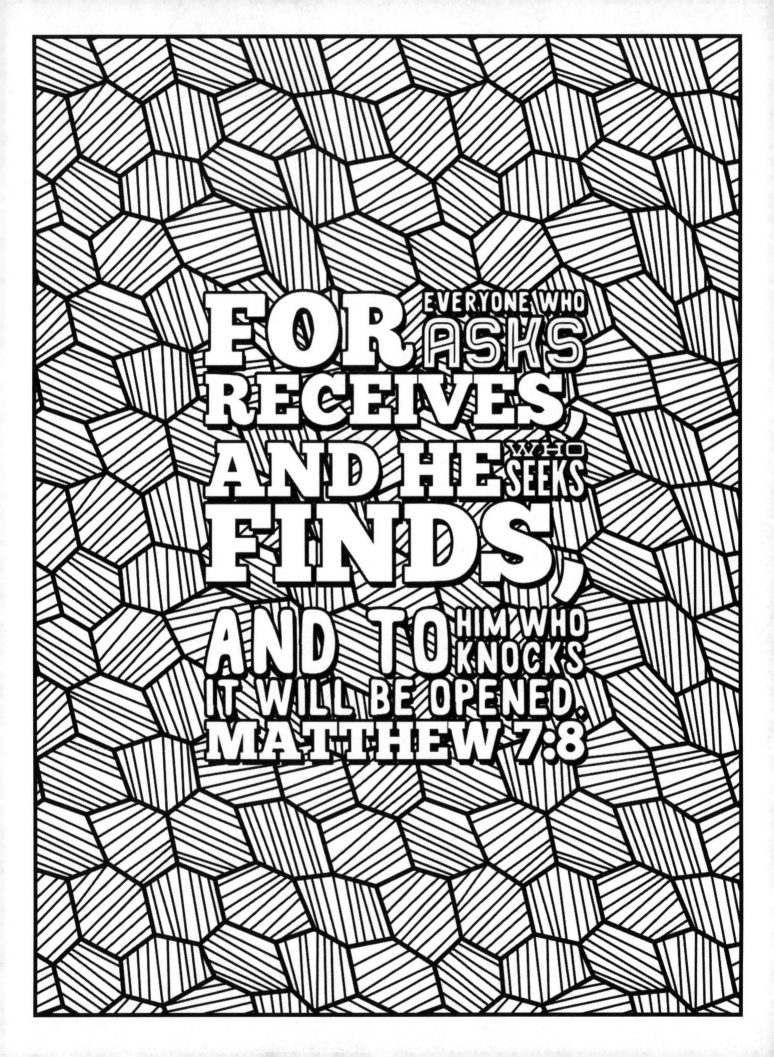

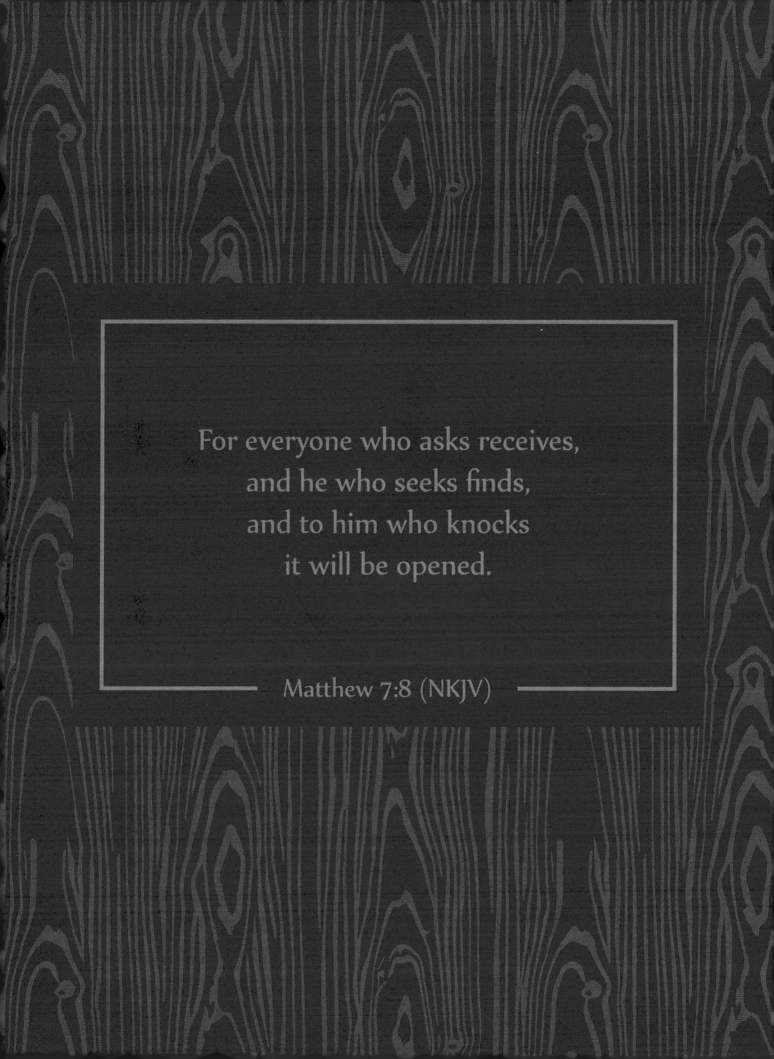

For everyone who asks receives,
and he who seeks finds,
and to him who knocks
it will be opened.

Matthew 7:8 (NKJV)

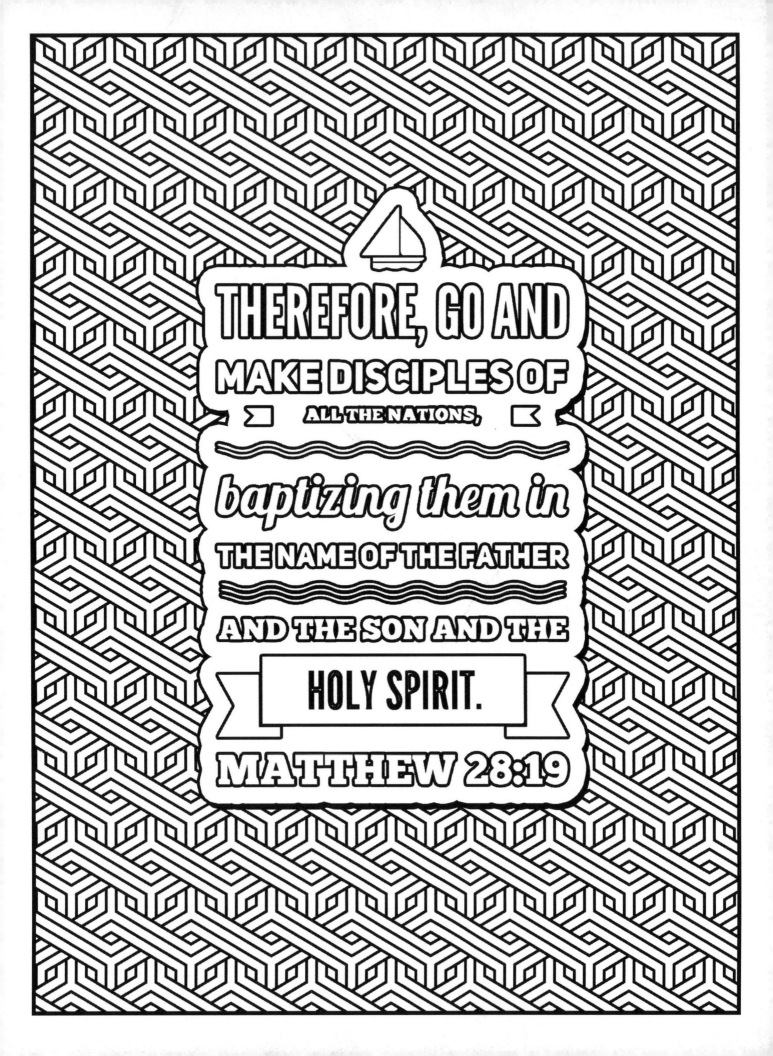

THEREFORE, GO AND MAKE DISCIPLES OF ALL THE NATIONS, baptizing them in THE NAME OF THE FATHER AND THE SON AND THE HOLY SPIRIT. MATTHEW 28:19

Therefore, go and make disciples
of all the nations, baptizing them
in the name of the Father
and the Son and the Holy Spirit.

Matthew 28:19 (NLT)

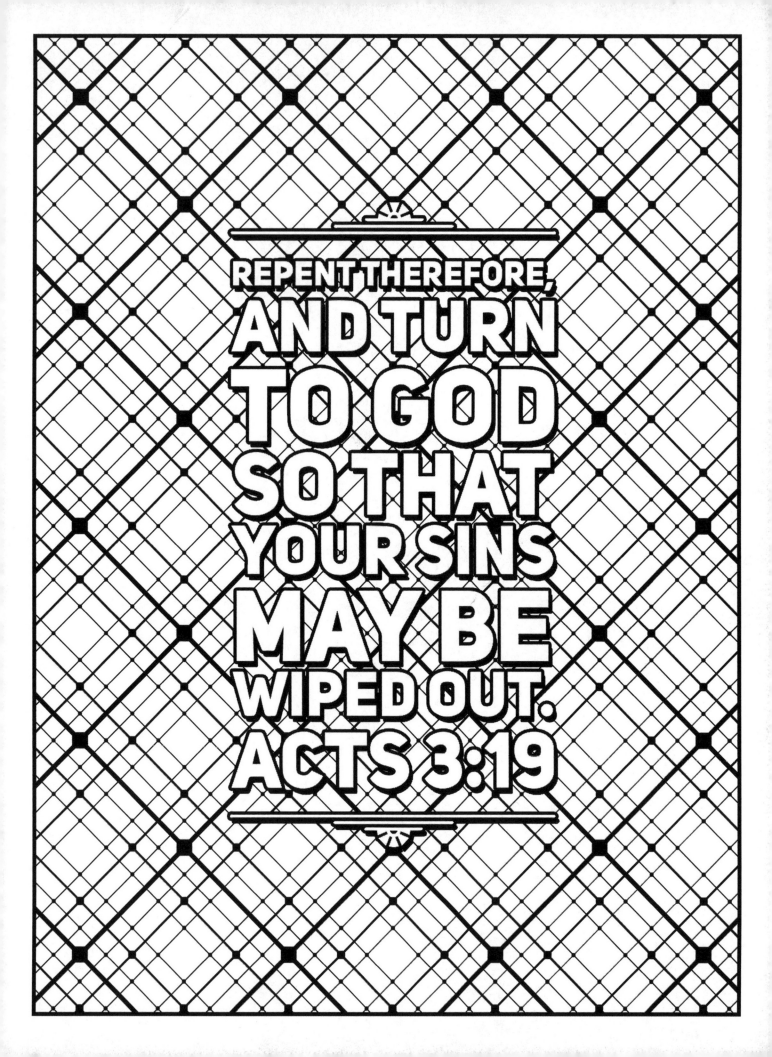

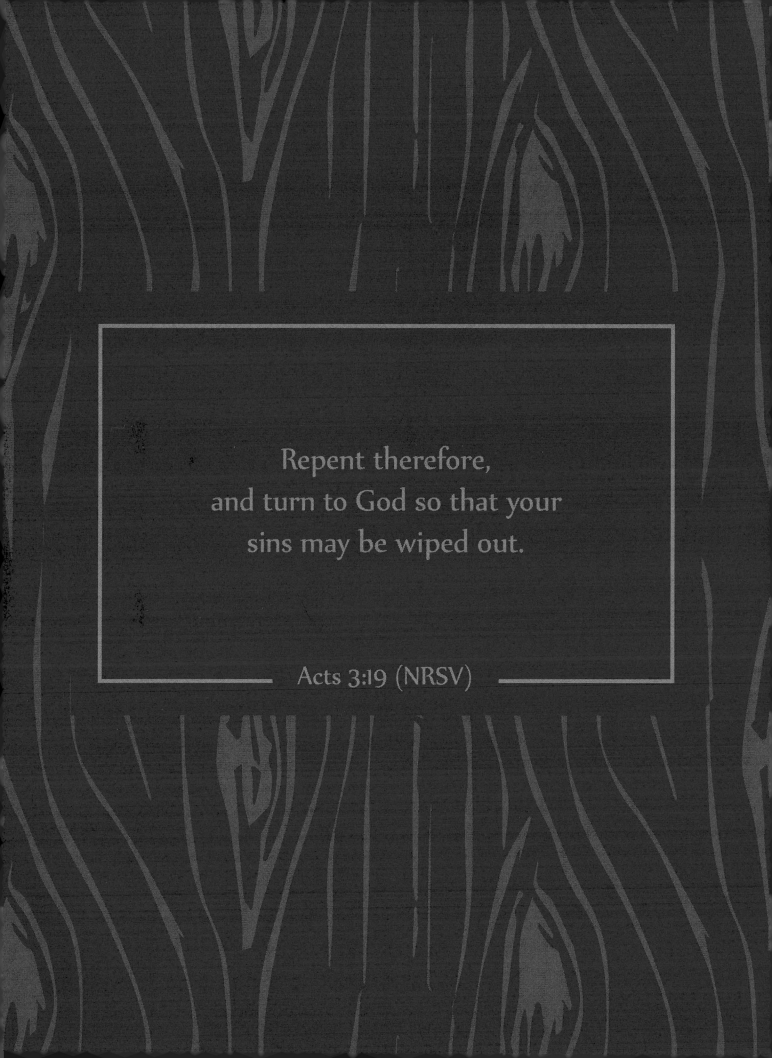

Repent therefore,
and turn to God so that your
sins may be wiped out.

Acts 3:19 (NRSV)

Do not store up for yourselves treasures
on earth, where moth and rust destroy,
and where thieves break in and steal.

Matthew 6:19 (NIV)

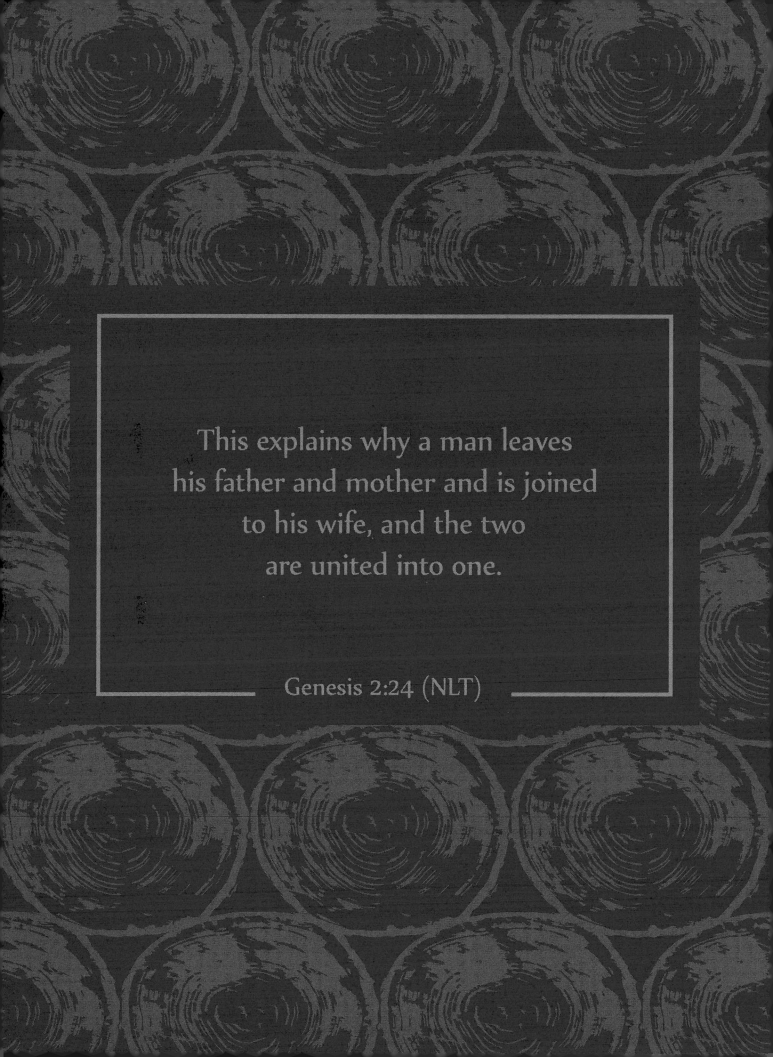

This explains why a man leaves
his father and mother and is joined
to his wife, and the two
are united into one.

Genesis 2:24 (NLT)

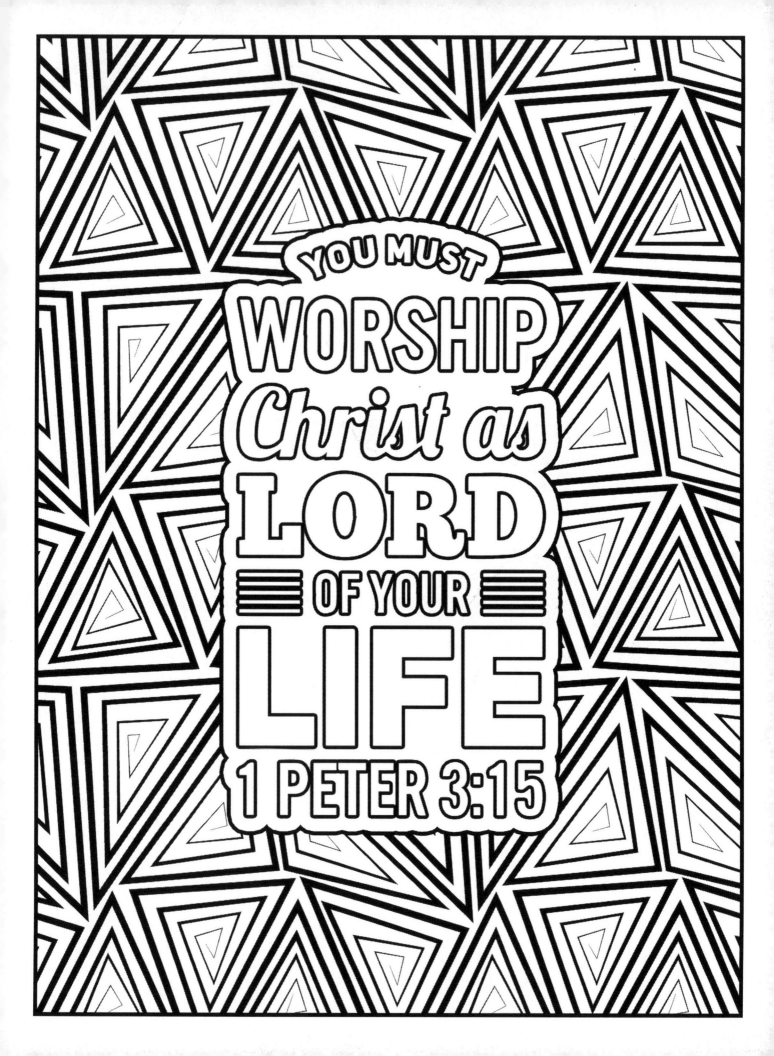

Instead, you must worship Christ as Lord of your life. And if someone asks about your hope as a believer, always be ready to explain it.

1 Peter 3:15 (NLT)

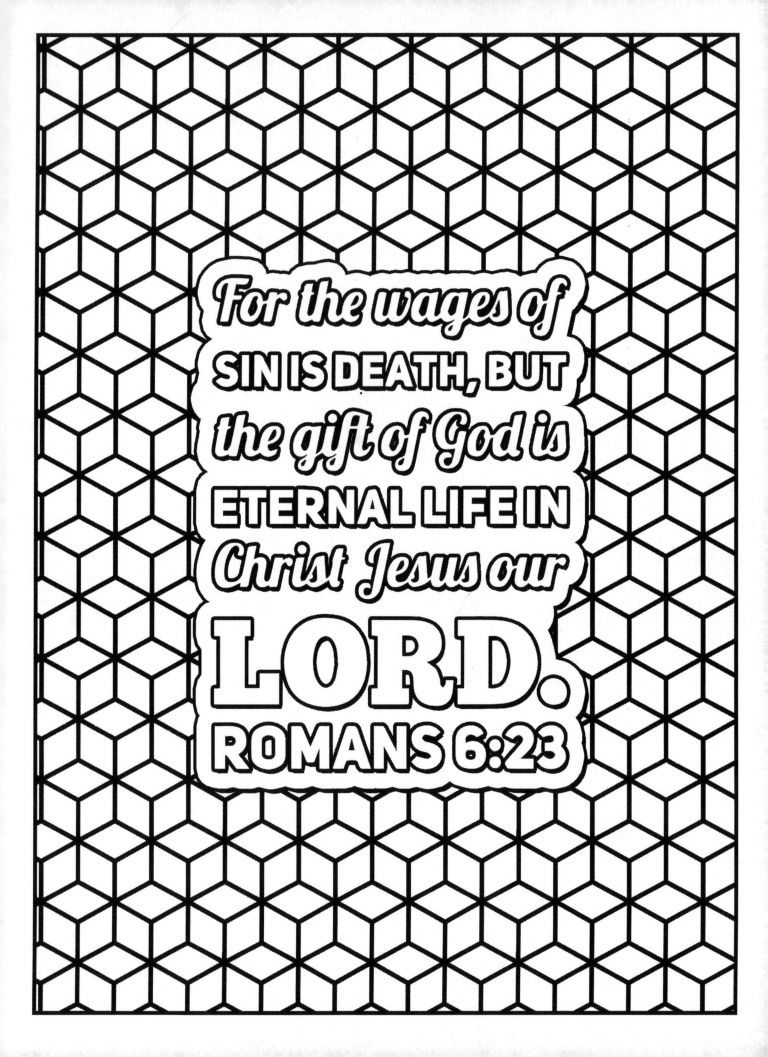

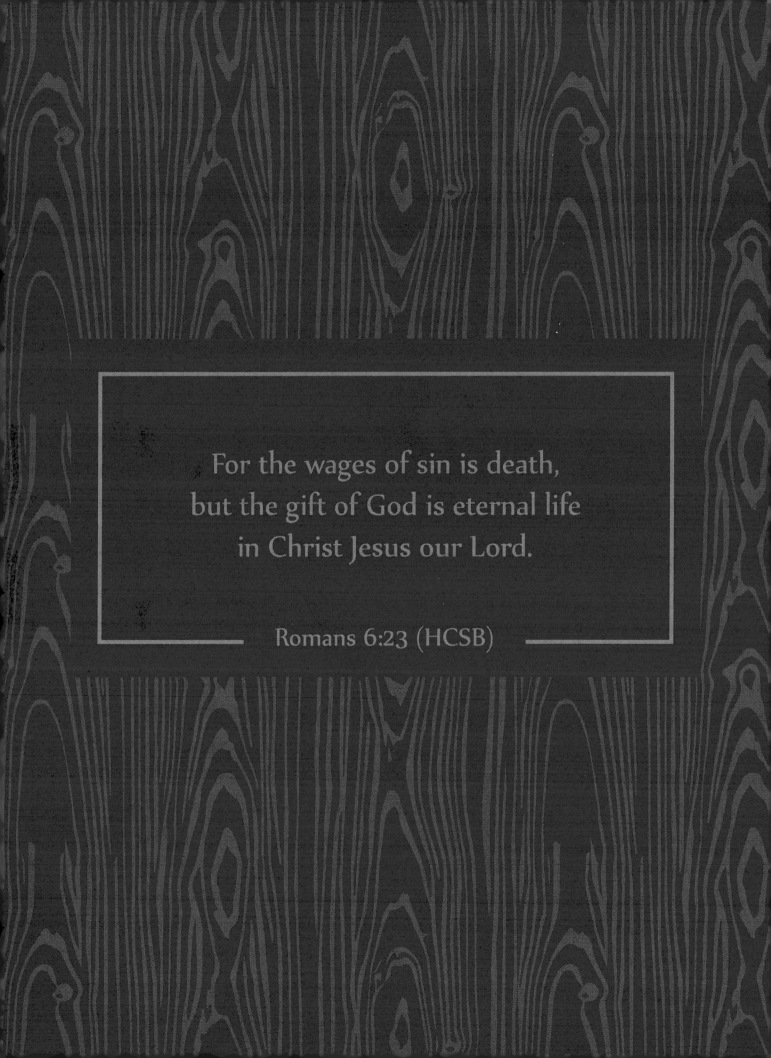

For the wages of sin is death,
but the gift of God is eternal life
in Christ Jesus our Lord.

Romans 6:23 (HCSB)

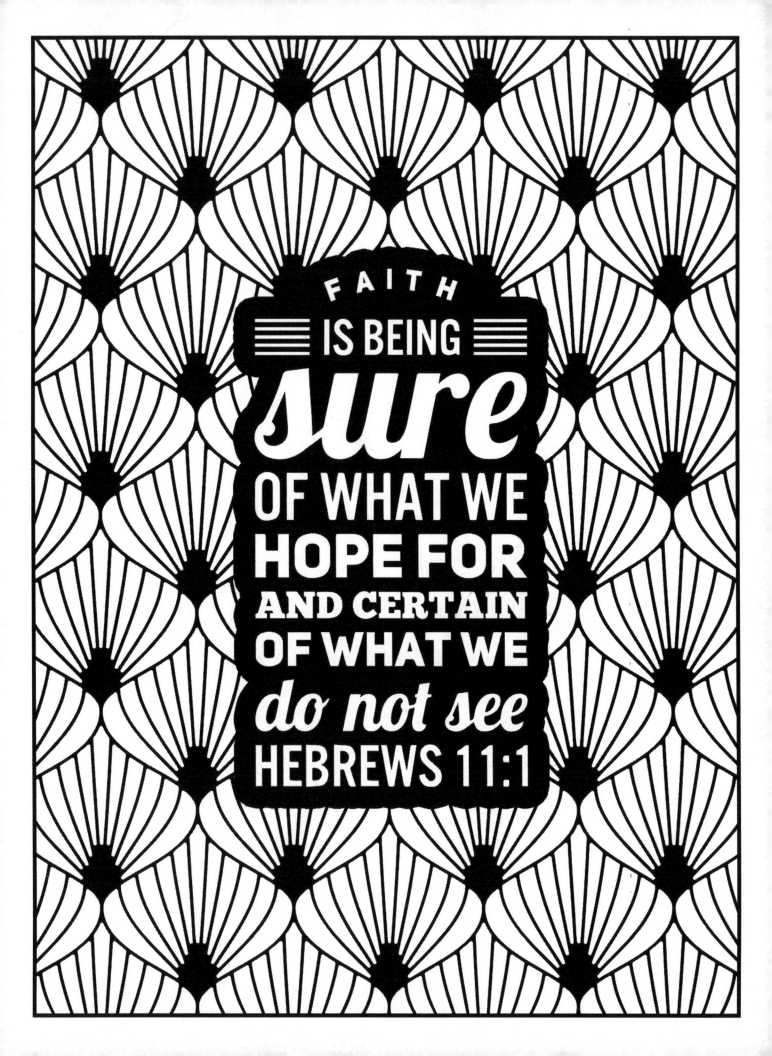

FAITH IS BEING *sure* OF WHAT WE HOPE FOR AND CERTAIN OF WHAT WE *do not see* HEBREWS 11:1

Now faith is being sure of what we hope
for and certain of what we do not see.

Hebrews 11:1 (NIV)

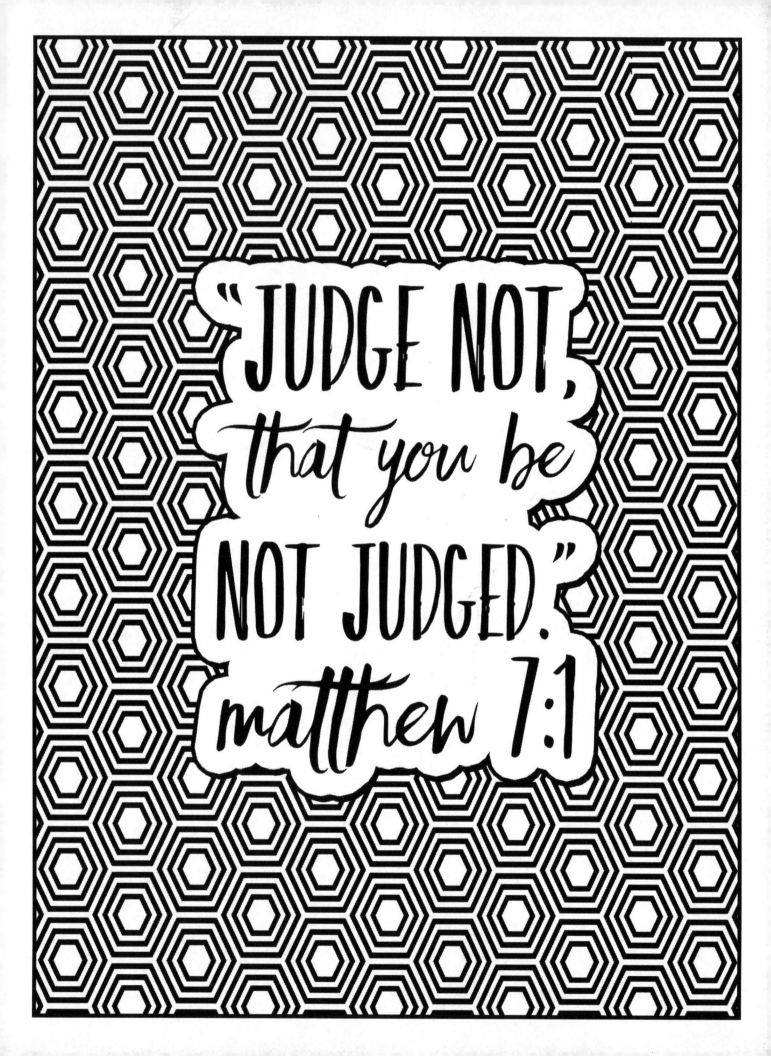

Judge not,
that you be not judged.

Matthew 7:1 (NKJV)

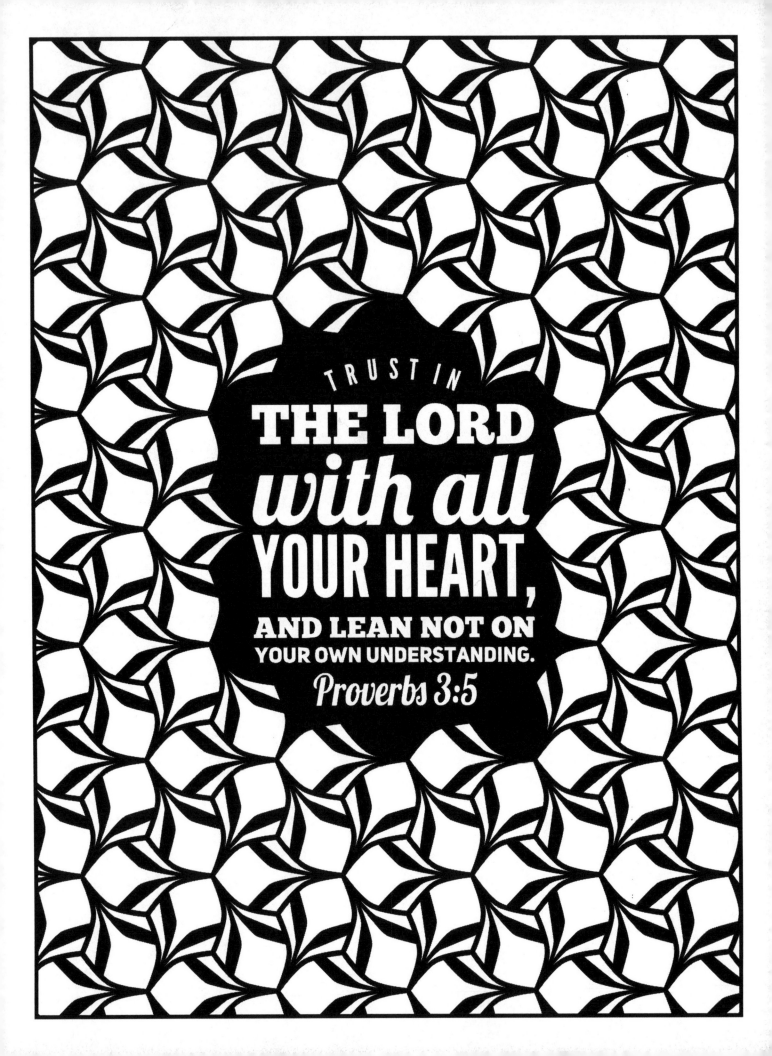

TRUST IN
THE LORD
with all
YOUR HEART,
AND LEAN NOT ON
YOUR OWN UNDERSTANDING.
Proverbs 3:5

Trust in the Lord with all your heart,
and lean not on your own
understanding.

Proverbs 3:5 (NKJV)

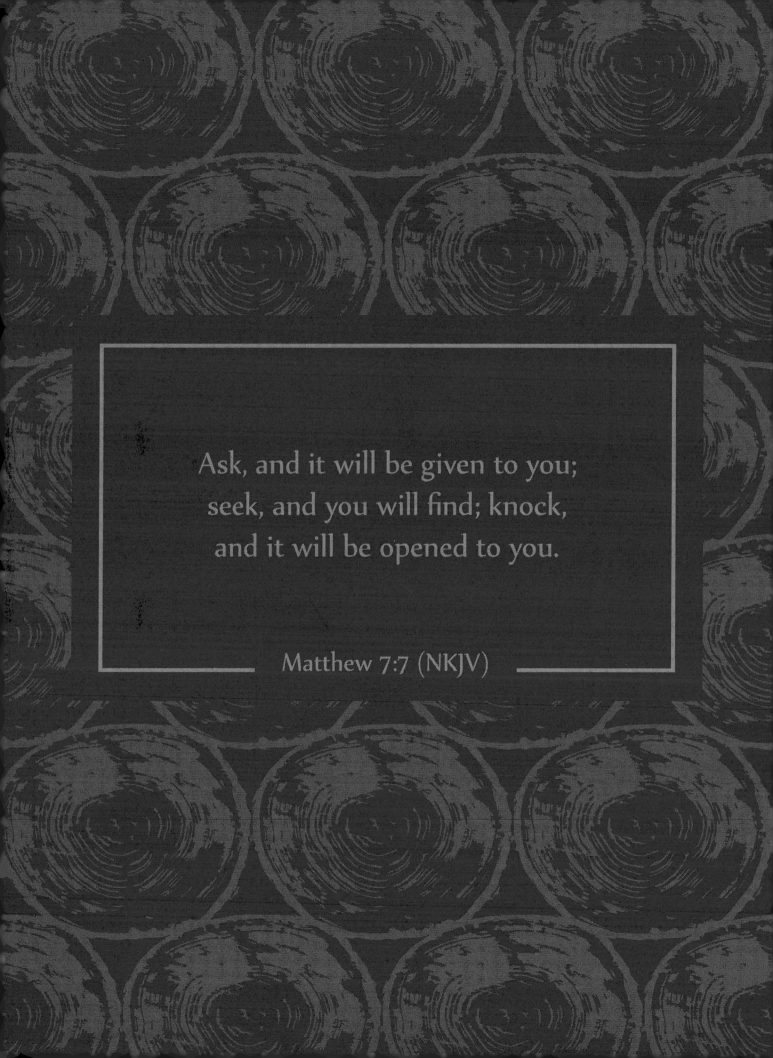

Ask, and it will be given to you;
seek, and you will find; knock,
and it will be opened to you.

Matthew 7:7 (NKJV)

The Lord does not delay his promise,
as some understand delay, but is patient
with you, not wanting any to perish
but all to come to repentance.

2 Peter 3:9 (HCSB)

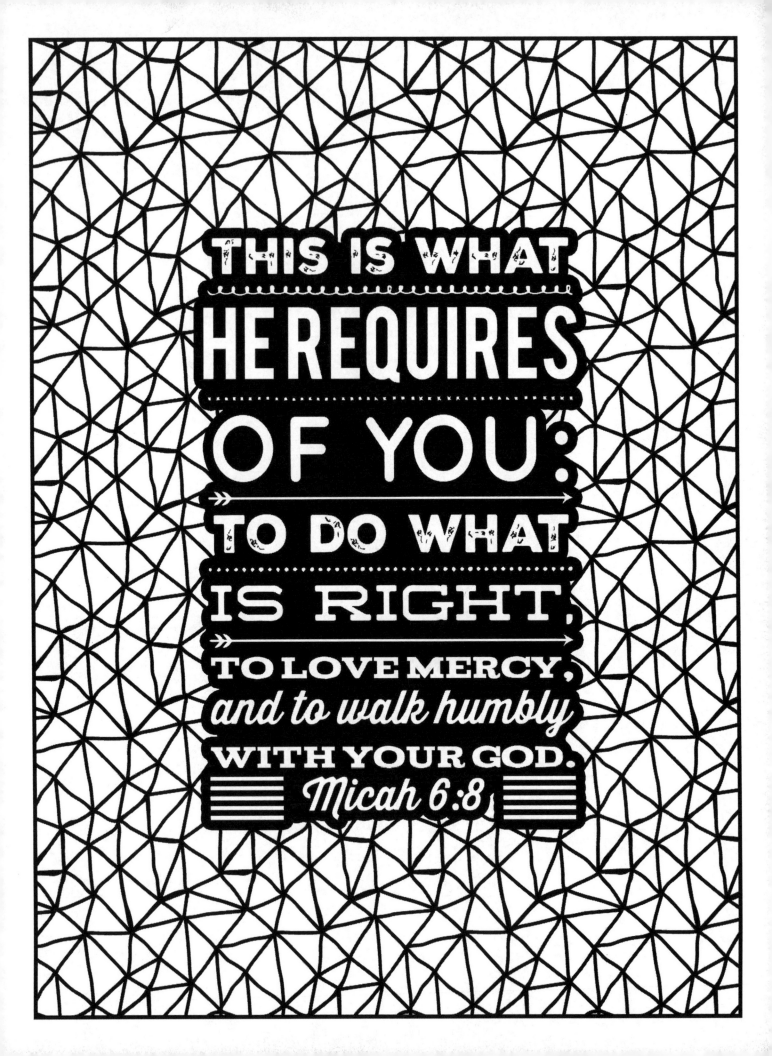

No, O people, the Lord has told you what
is good, and this is what he requires
of you: to do what is right, to love mercy,
and to walk humbly with your God.

Micah 6:8 (NLT)

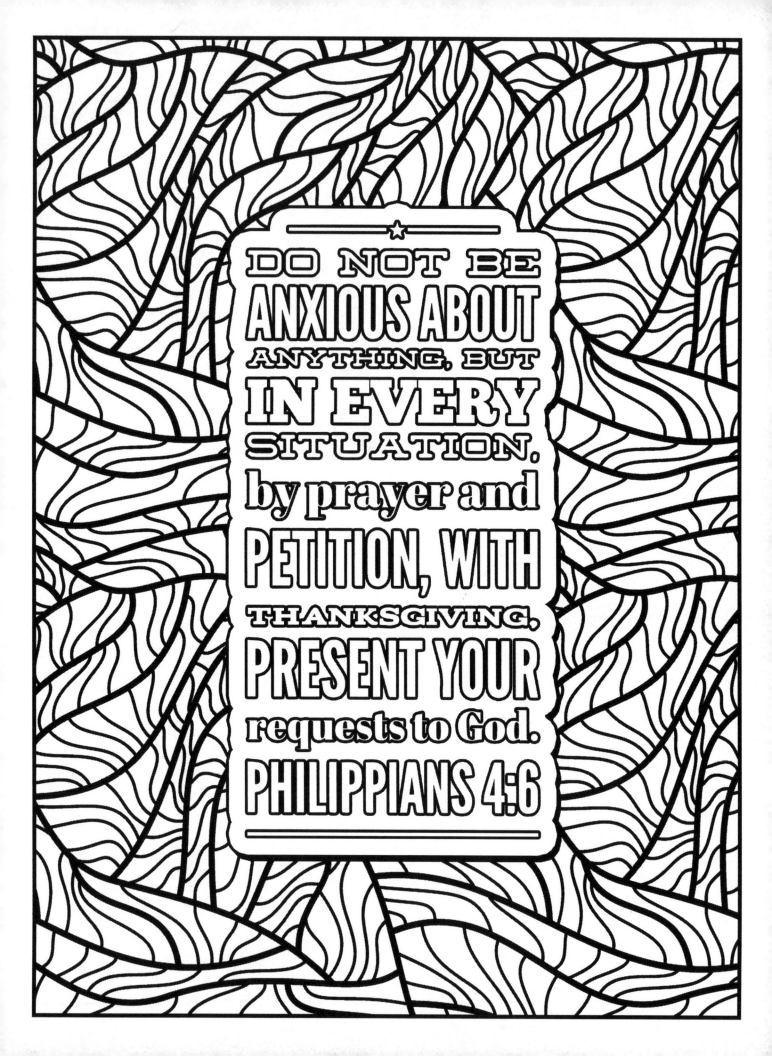

Do not be anxious about anything,
but in every situation, by prayer
and petition, with thanksgiving,
present your requests to God.

Philippians 4:6 (NIV)

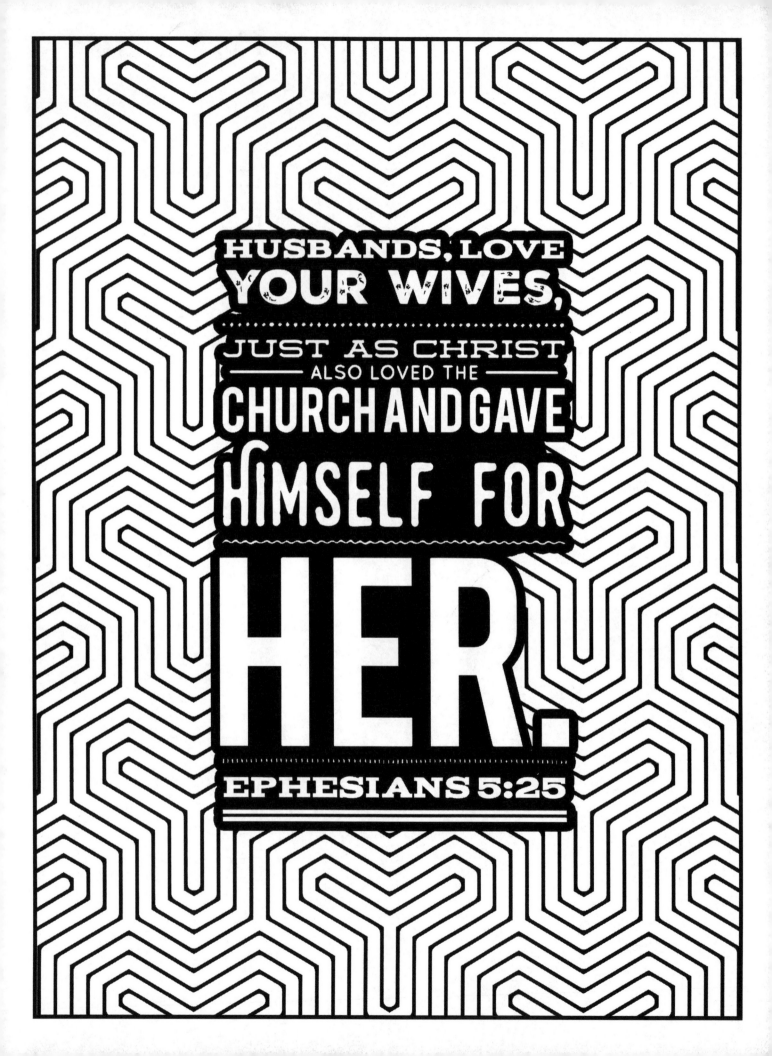

Husbands, love your wives,
just as Christ also loved the church
and gave himself for her.

Ephesians 5:25 (NKJV)

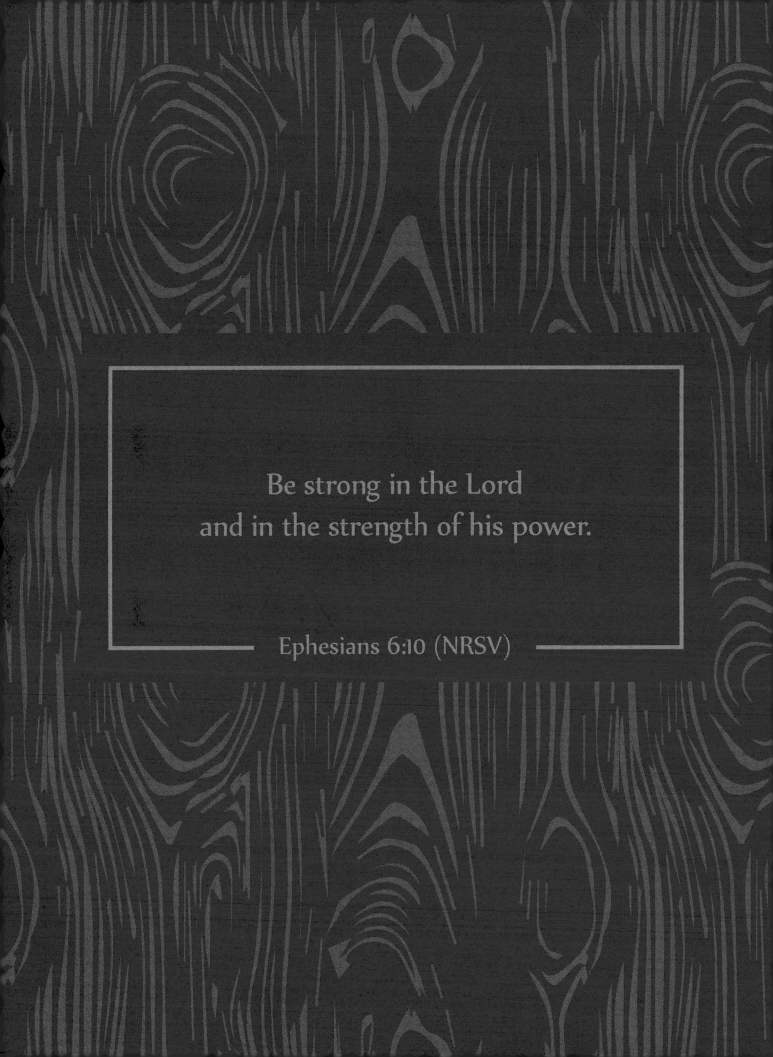

Be strong in the Lord
and in the strength of his power.

Ephesians 6:10 (NRSV)

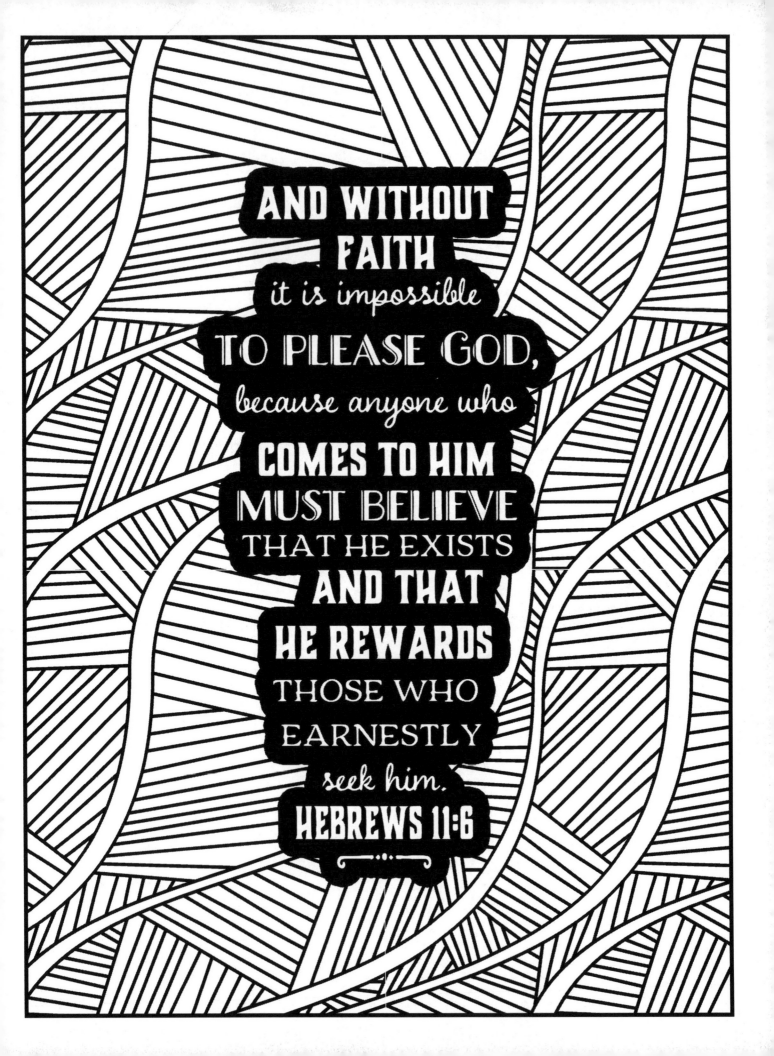

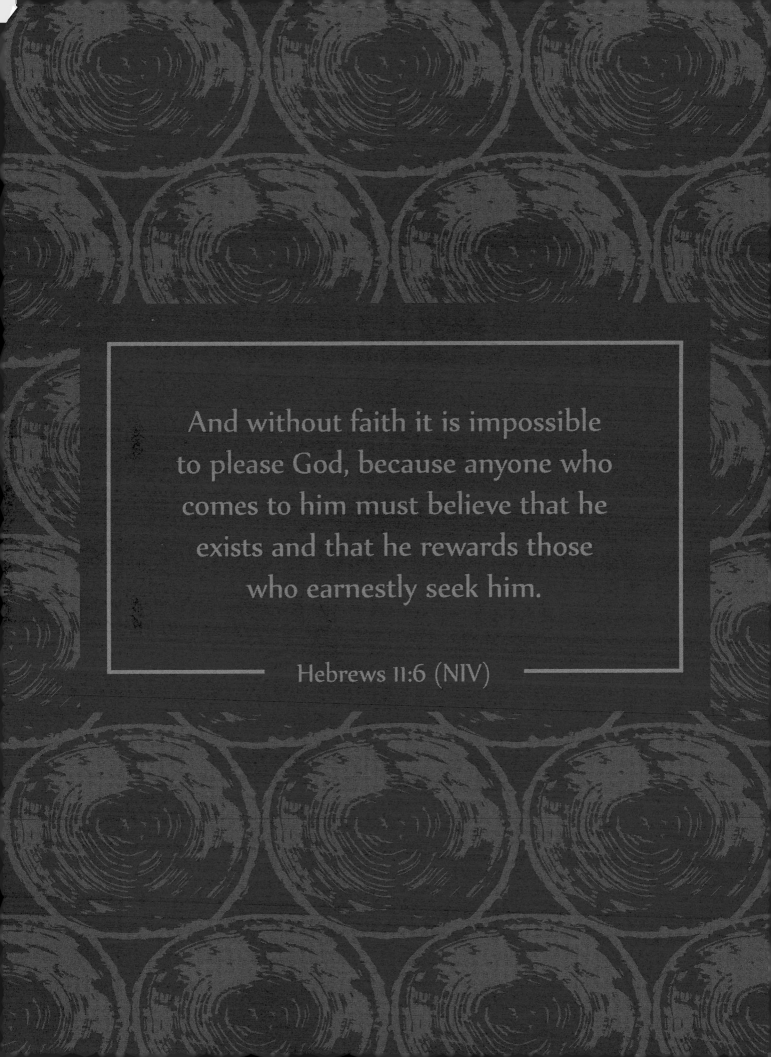

And without faith it is impossible
to please God, because anyone who
comes to him must believe that he
exists and that he rewards those
who earnestly seek him.

Hebrews 11:6 (NIV)

Keep your lives free from the love of money, and be content with what you have; for he has said, "I will never leave you or forsake you."

Hebrews 13:5 (NRSV)

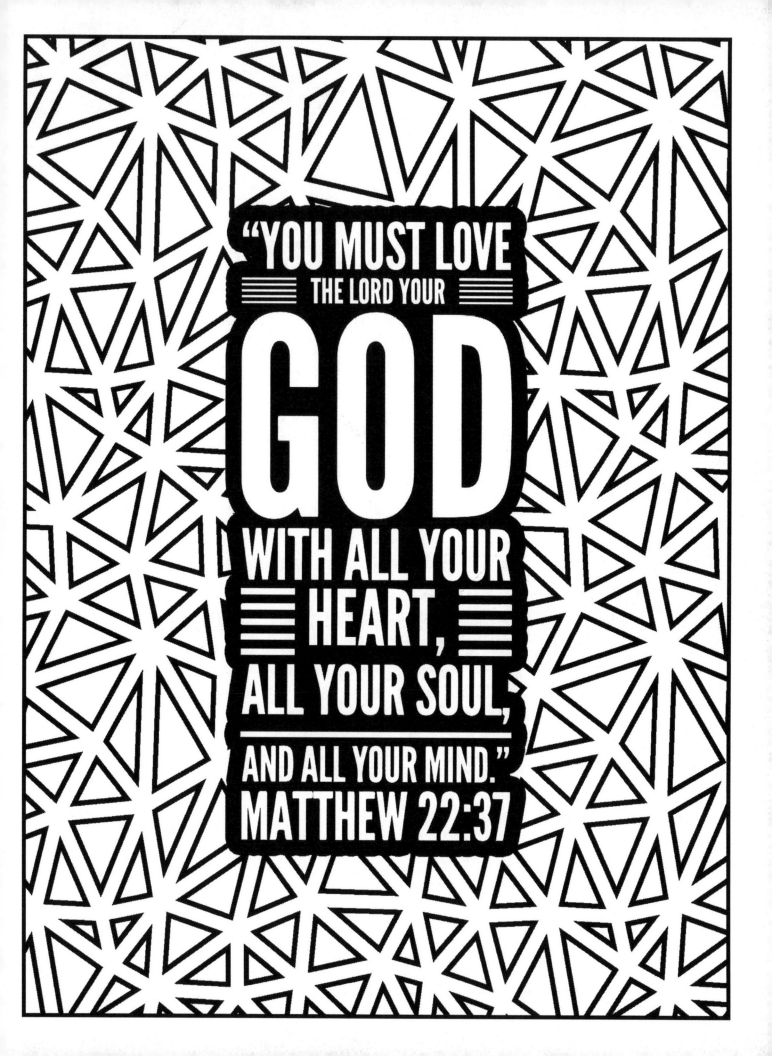

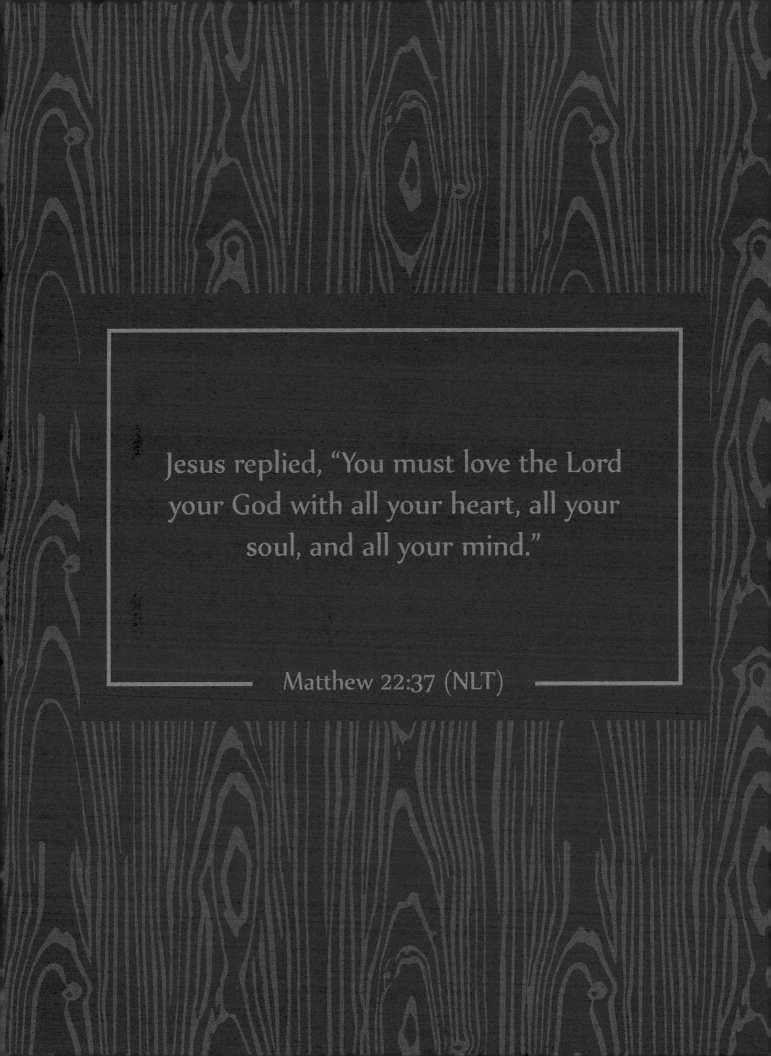

Jesus replied, "You must love the Lord your God with all your heart, all your soul, and all your mind."

Matthew 22:37 (NLT)

Finally brothers, whatever is true,
whatever is honorable, whatever is just,
whatever is pure, whatever is lovely,
whatever is commendable – if there is
any moral excellence and if there is any
praise – dwell on these things.

Philippians 4:8 (HCSB)

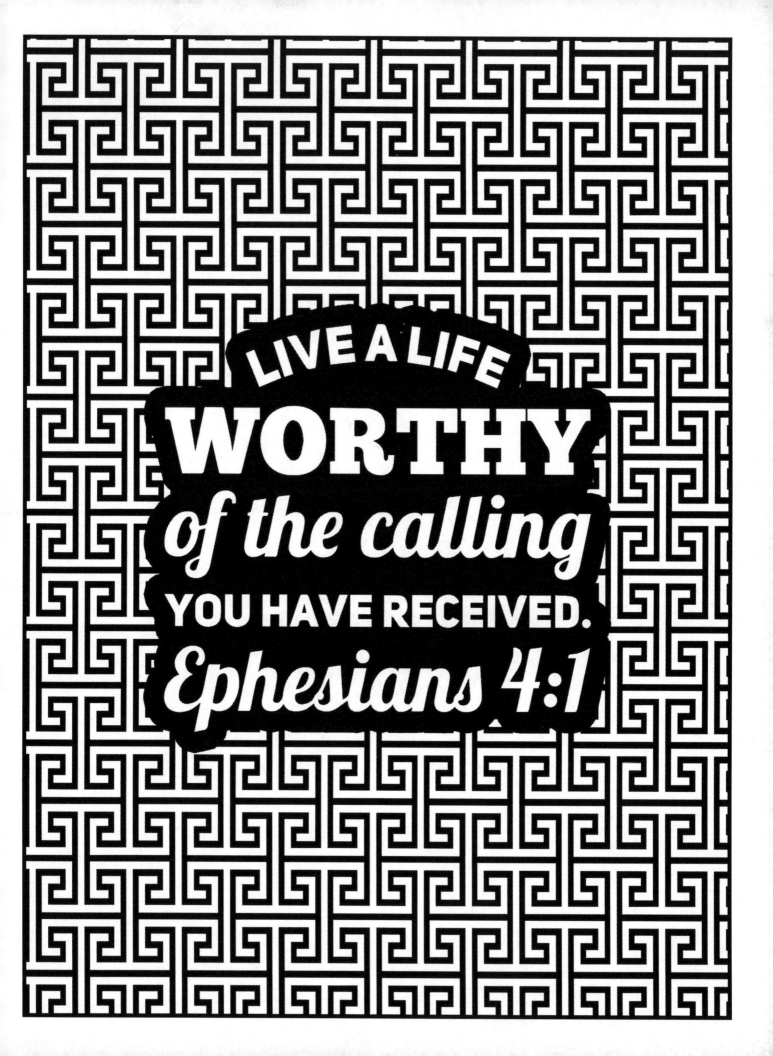

As a prisoner for the Lord, then,
I urge you to live a life worthy
of the calling you have received.

Ephesians 4:1 (NIV)

I can do all things through
Christ who strengthens me.

Philippians 4:13 (NKJV)

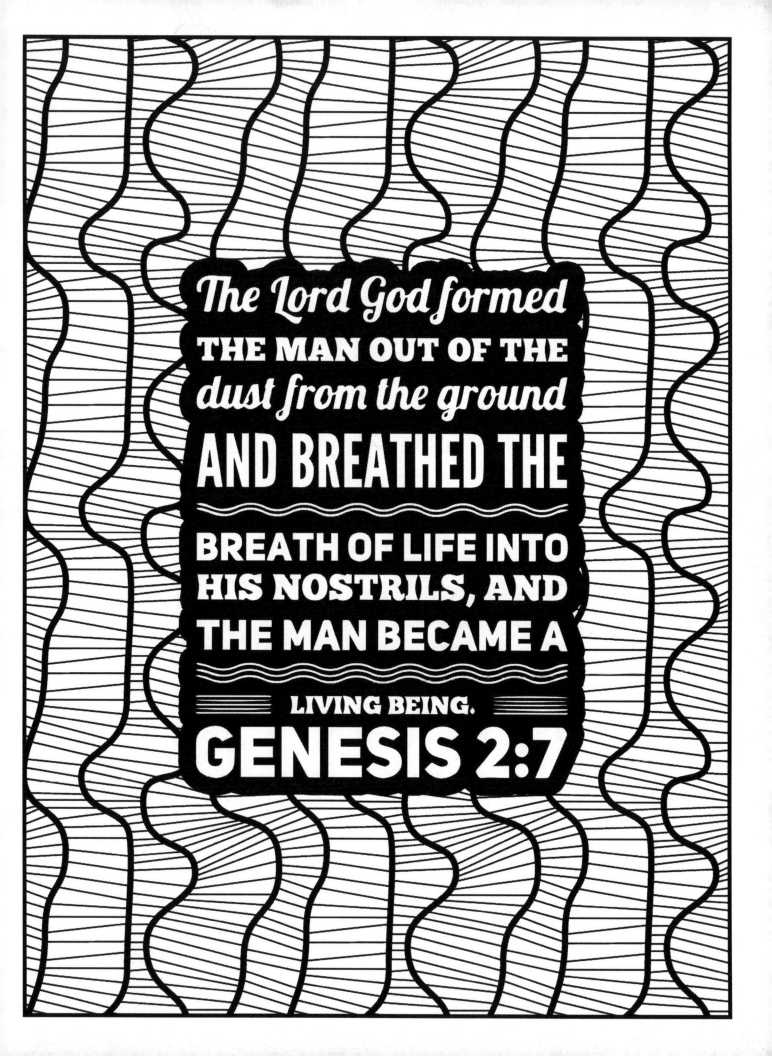

The Lord God formed THE MAN OUT OF THE dust from the ground AND BREATHED THE BREATH OF LIFE INTO HIS NOSTRILS, AND THE MAN BECAME A LIVING BEING. GENESIS 2:7

Then the Lord God formed
the man out of the dust from the ground
and breathed the breath of life into
his nostrils, and the man became
a living being.

Genesis 2:7 (HCSB)

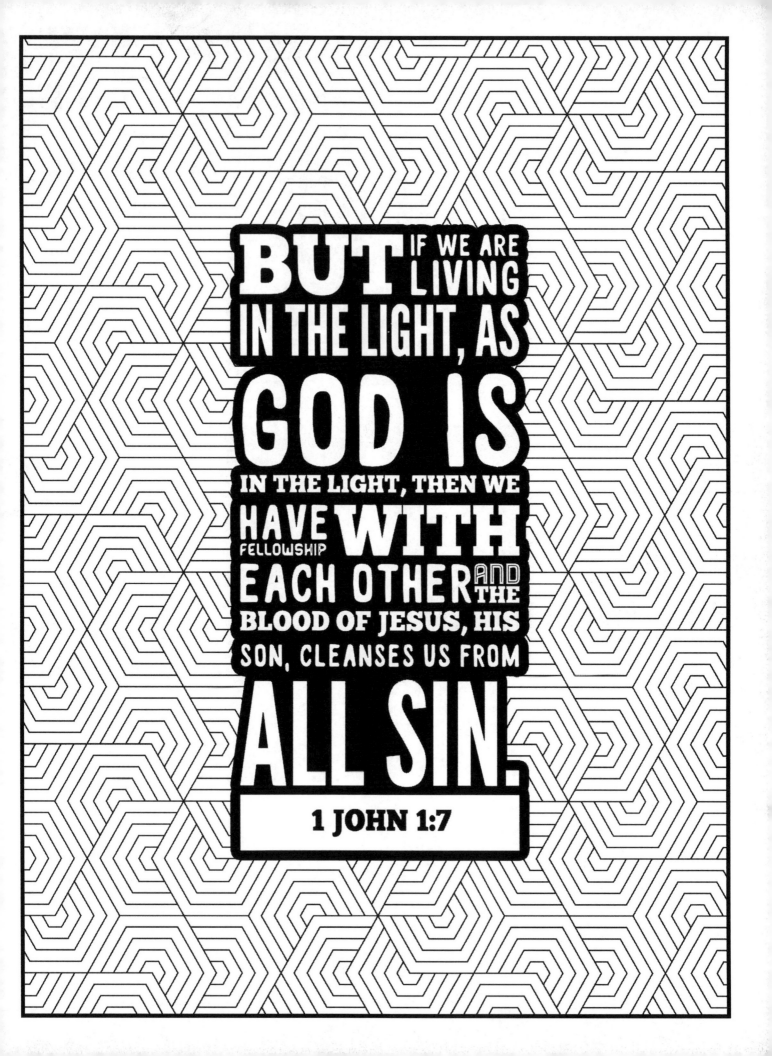

BUT IF WE ARE LIVING IN THE LIGHT, AS GOD IS IN THE LIGHT, THEN WE HAVE FELLOWSHIP WITH EACH OTHER AND THE BLOOD OF JESUS, HIS SON, CLEANSES US FROM ALL SIN.

1 JOHN 1:7

But if we are living in the light,
as God is in the light, then we have
fellowship with each other, and the blood
of Jesus, his Son, cleanses us from all sin.

1 John 1:7 (NLT)

BUT HE WAS PIERCED BECAUSE OF OUR TRANSGRESSIONS, CRUSHED BECAUSE OF OUR INIQUITIES; PUNISHMENT FOR OUR PEACE WAS ON HIM, AND WE ARE HEALED BY HIS WOUNDS.

ISAIAH 53:5

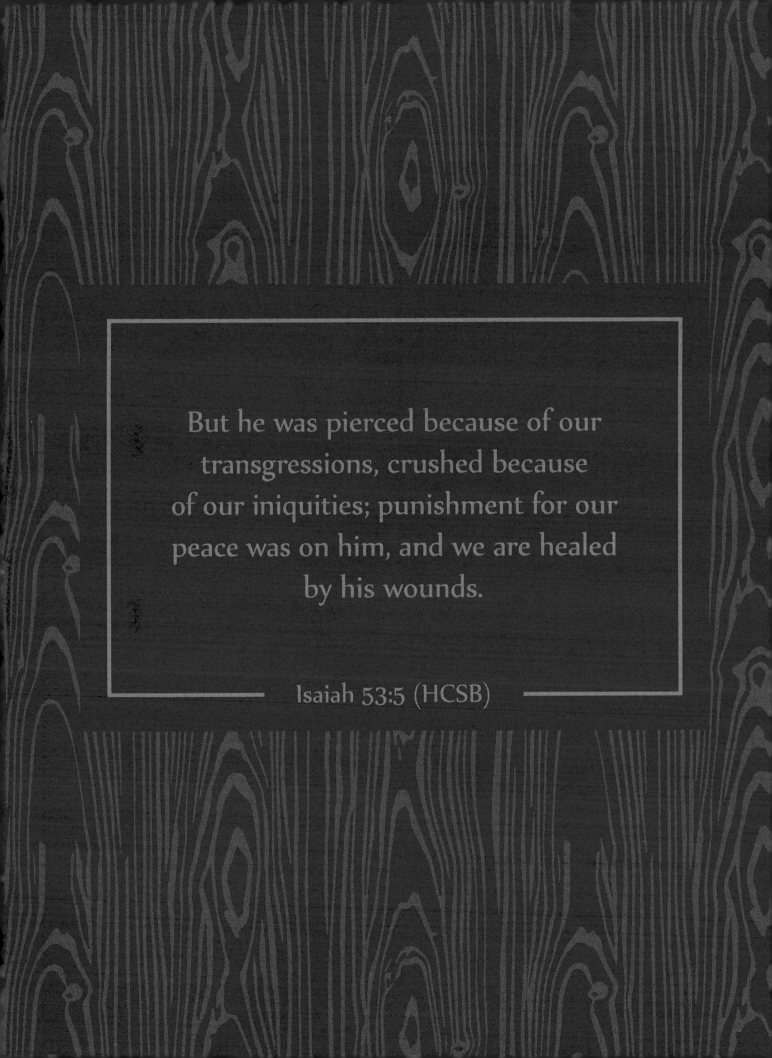

But he was pierced because of our transgressions, crushed because of our iniquities; punishment for our peace was on him, and we are healed by his wounds.

Isaiah 53:5 (HCSB)

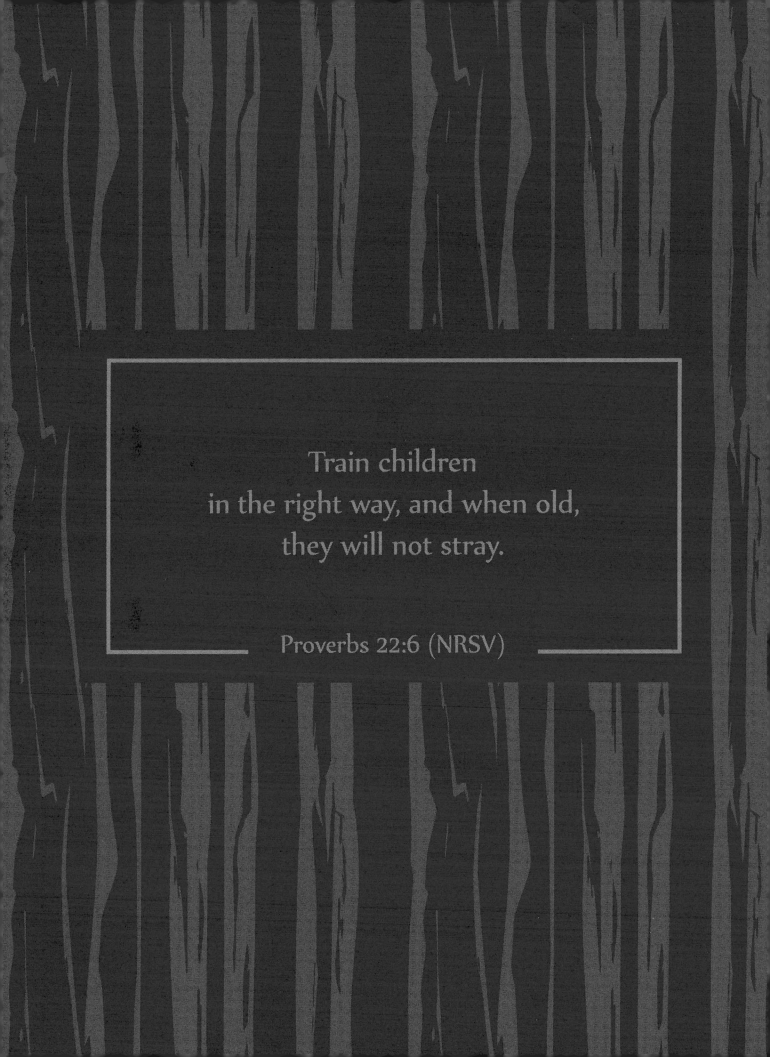

Train children
in the right way, and when old,
they will not stray.

Proverbs 22:6 (NRSV)

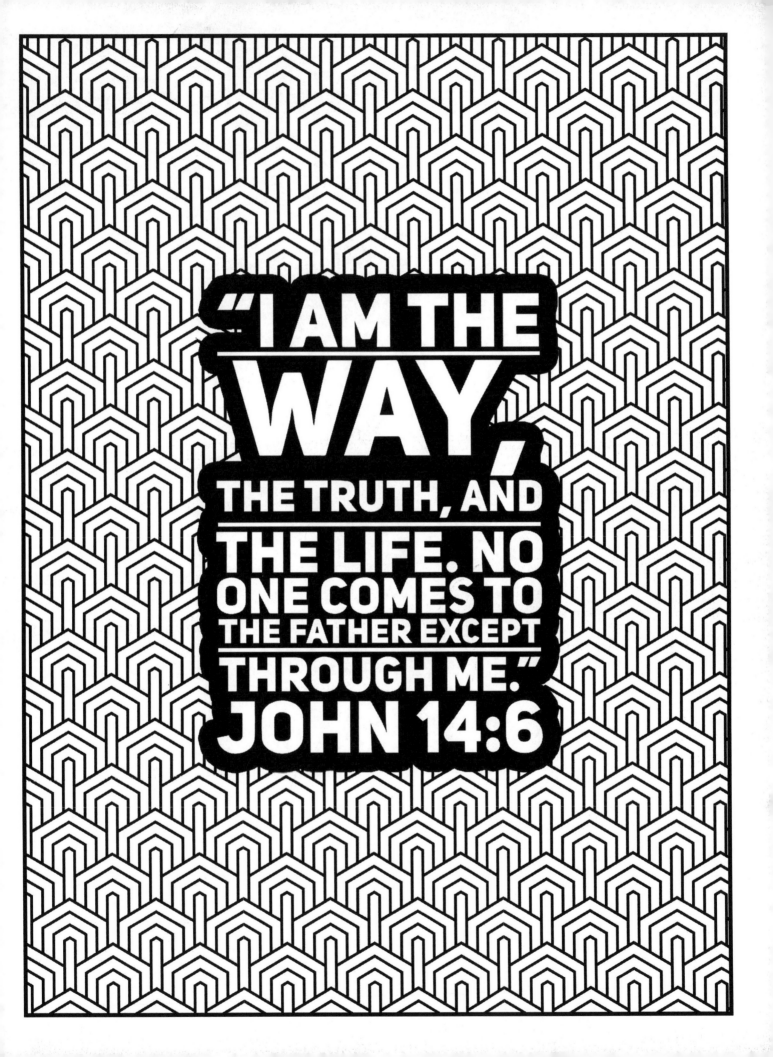

"I AM THE WAY, THE TRUTH, AND THE LIFE. NO ONE COMES TO THE FATHER EXCEPT THROUGH ME." JOHN 14:6

I am the way, the truth, and the life.
No one comes to the Father
except through Me.

John 14:6 (NKJV)

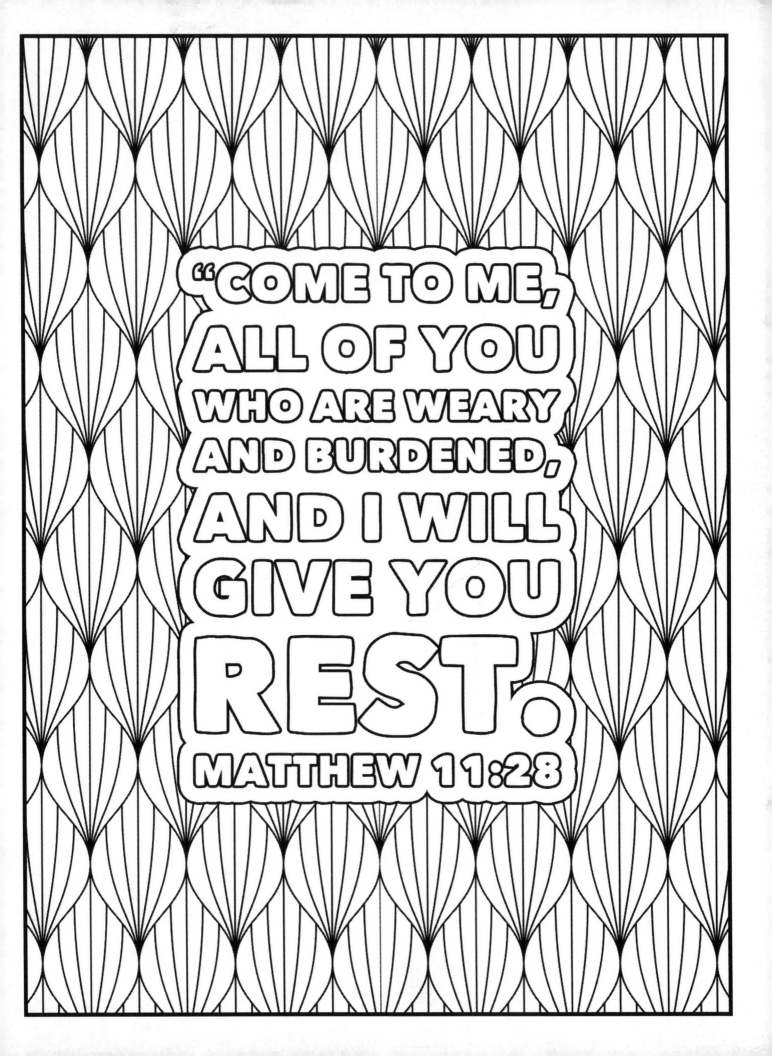

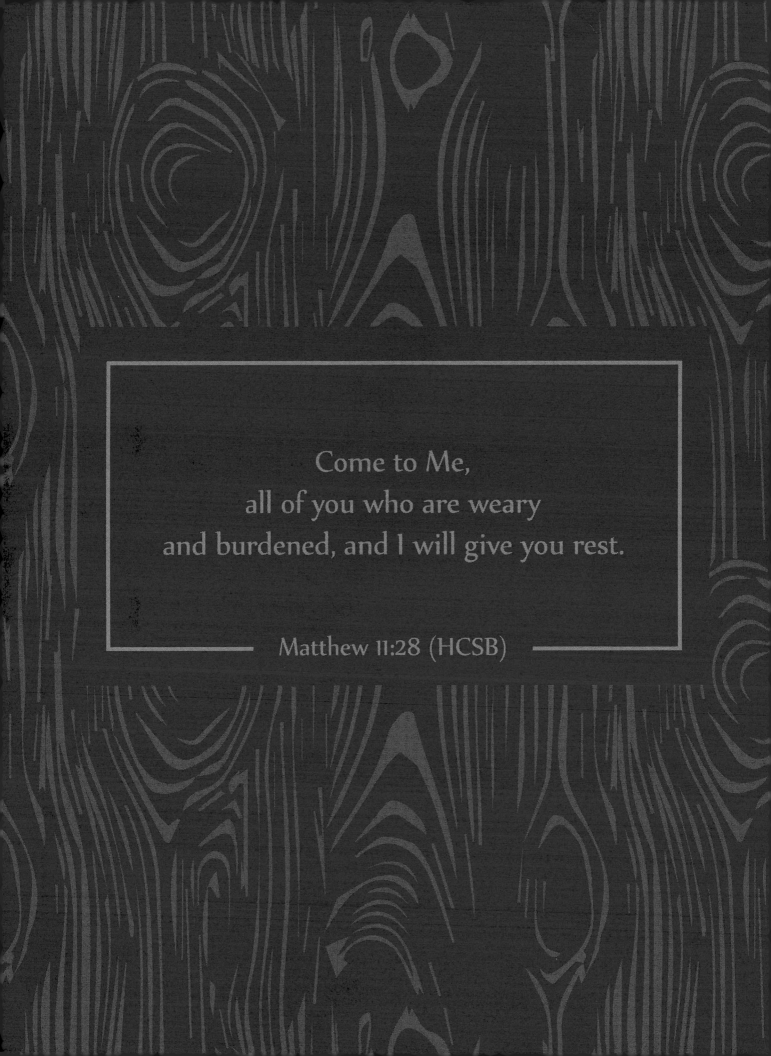

Come to Me,
all of you who are weary
and burdened, and I will give you rest.

Matthew 11:28 (HCSB)

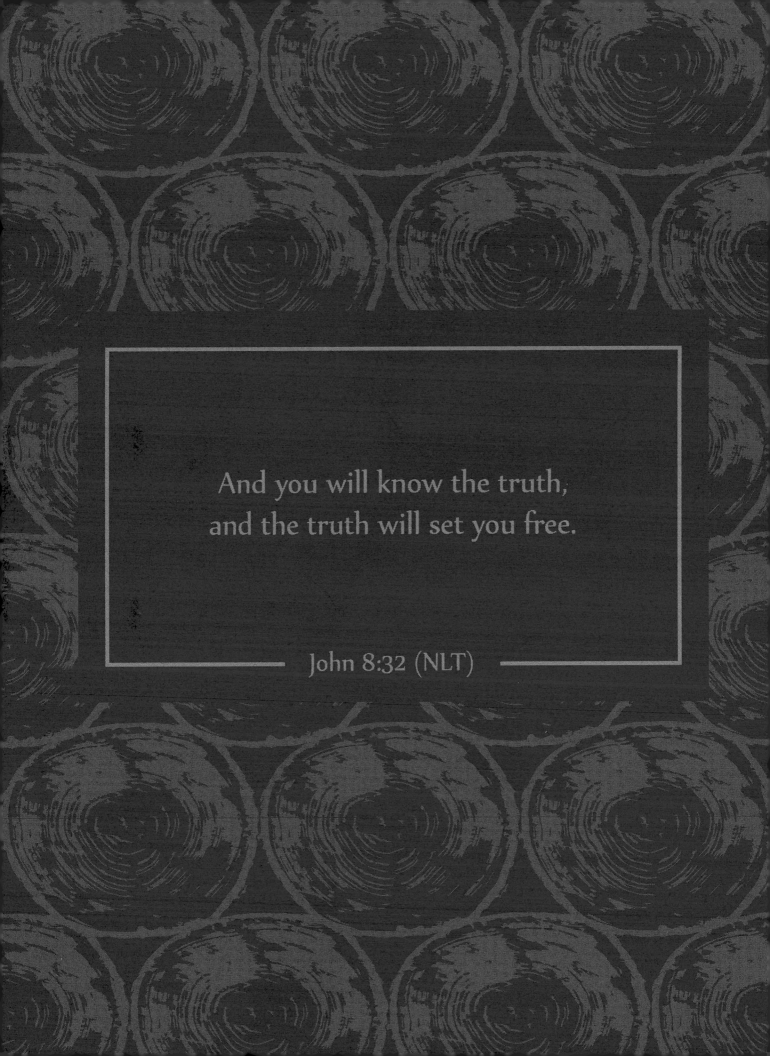

And you will know the truth,
and the truth will set you free.

John 8:32 (NLT)

If any of you is lacking in wisdom,
ask God, who gives to all generously
and ungrudgingly, and it will
be given you.

James 1:5 (NRSV)

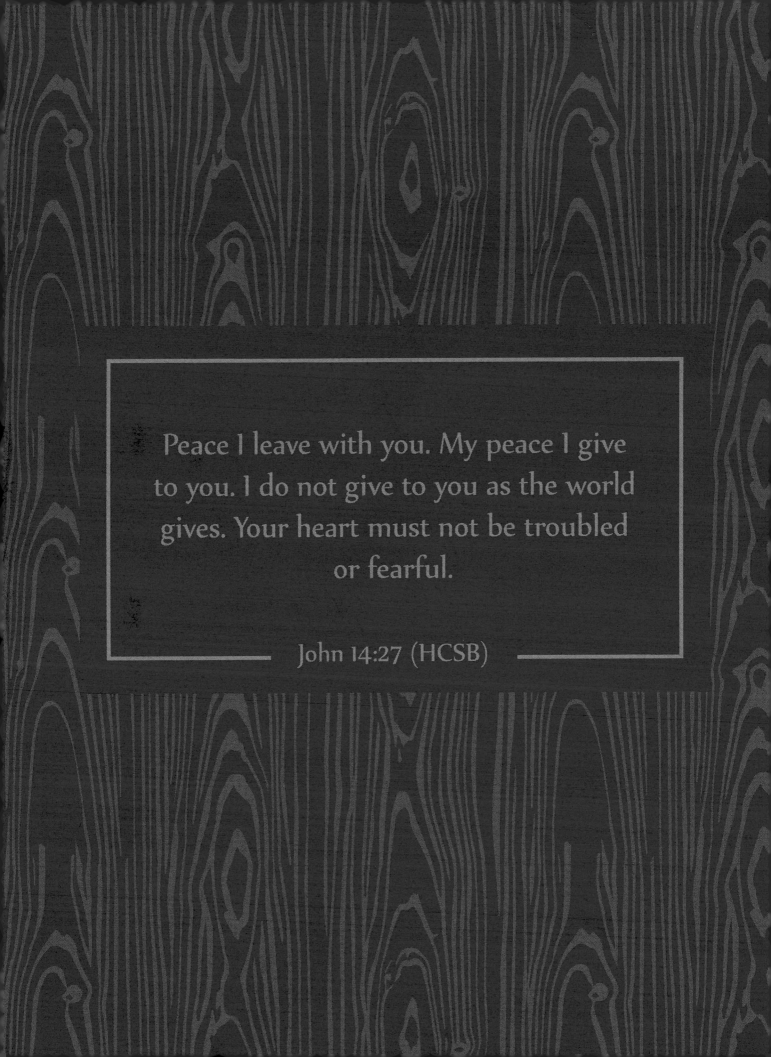

Peace I leave with you. My peace I give to you. I do not give to you as the world gives. Your heart must not be troubled or fearful.

John 14:27 (HCSB)

For the grace of God has appeared,
bringing salvation to all

Titus 2:11 (NRSV)

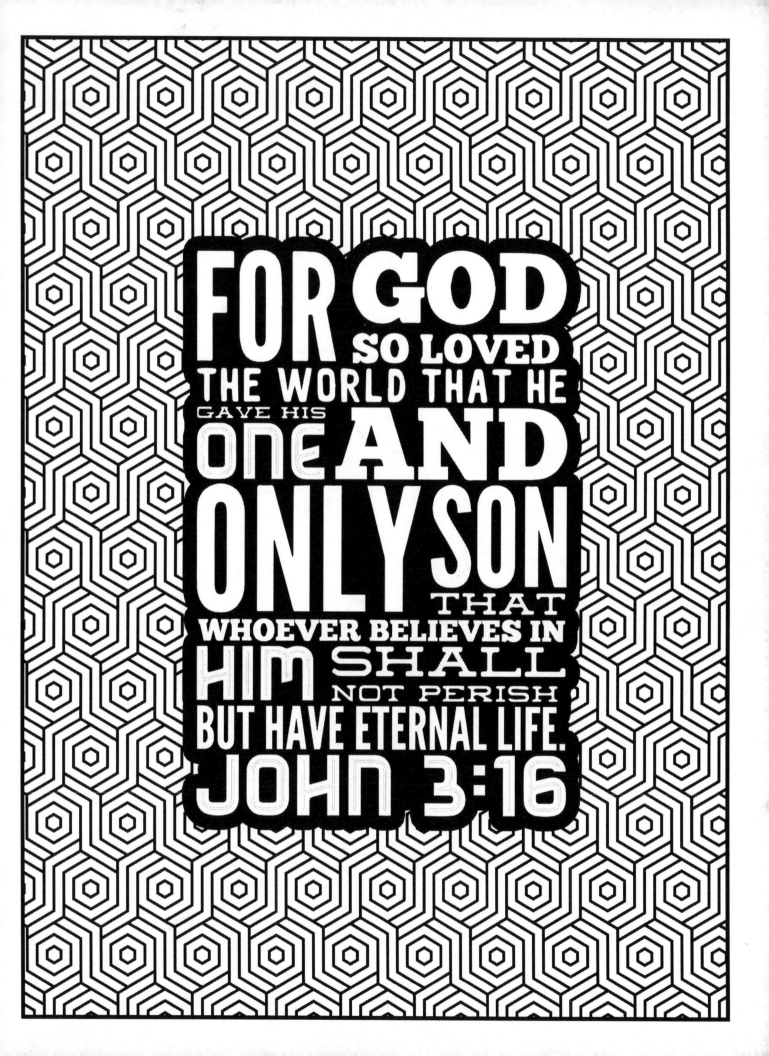

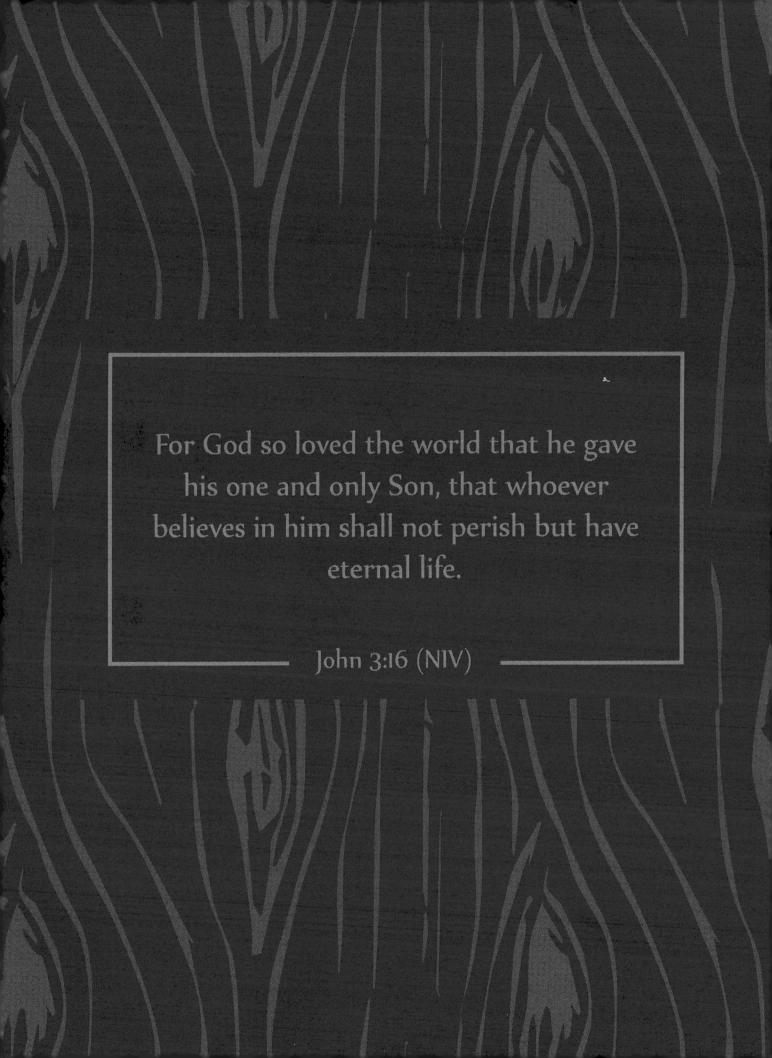

For God so loved the world that he gave his one and only Son, that whoever believes in him shall not perish but have eternal life.

John 3:16 (NIV)

FREE DOWNLOAD LINK
VERSES FOR MEN
WOODGRAIN EDITION
WITH WOODGRAIN FRAME CENTERS

www.inspiredtograce.com/usvfm

DOWNLOAD CODE: VFM1572

 @INSPIREDTOGRACE

INSPIRED TO GRACE

Verses FOR Men

CHRISTIAN COLORING BOOKS